DAWN MACLEOD

A BOOK OF HERBS

DAWN MACLEOD

A Book of Herbs

THE GARDEN BOOK CLUB
121 Charing Cross Road, London, W.C.2

First published 1968
Second impression 1969

Text and shadow photos © 1968 by DAWN MACLEOD

SBN 7156 0406 6

Printed in Great Britain by Butler & Tanner Ltd., Frome and London

To my husband

ALFRED WILSON

with gratitude for his constant interest and help
with classical references

Contents

Acknowledgements

The author is indebted to her friends Margery Fish—who in her Lambrook garden demonstrates the potentialities of many herbs as decorative garden plants—and the late Margaret Brownlow, B.Sc., who so generously shared her botanical knowledge and long experience of herb-growing at Seal.

Thanks are offered to Andrew Young and Alasdair Alpin MacGregor for permission to quote from their poems; to the Hon. Lady Meade-Fetherstonhaugh for demonstrating the restorative effect of Soapwort, and for the quotation from *Uppark and its People*.

The author also acknowledges help obtained from the herbals and garden books of Mrs Grieve, Mrs C. F. Leyel, Mrs C. W. Earle, V. Sackville-West, Margery Fish, Eleanour Sinclair Rohde, D. G. Hewer, B.Sc., Margaret Brownlow, B.Sc., Mary Quelch, Geoffrey Grigson, Juliette de Bairacli Levy, Kathleen Hunter, Joan Ryder, Rosetta Clarkson, Violetta Thurstan and Ethel Mairet; from articles in the handbook *Dye-Plants and Dyeing* edited by Ethel-Jane Schetky, Elizabeth Scholtz and Carol Woodward, issued by the Brooklyn Botanic Garden, New York; and from *Mediaeval Merchant Venturers* by E. M. Carus-Wilson.

Finally, gratitude is due to the Trustees, British Museum (Natural History) for permitting reproduction of pictures, and to the Keeper of Botany and the Librarian of the Botanical Library at South Kensington for their assistance; to the Royal Horticultural Society and Botanical Staff at Wisley for help with plant names; to Patricia MacGregor for productive clues relating to Woad and Soapwort; and to Herbert Rees for a valued introduction.

List of Illustrations

ILLUSTRATIONS

SILHOUETTES

I. Introducing Herbs

What is a herb? *The Shorter Oxford Dictionary* begins by saying that it is a plant of which the stem does not become woody and persistent, but dies down to the ground (or entirely) after flowering. This is the botanist's definition; if we accept it, then many of our best-known 'herbs'—such as Sage, Thyme, Lavender and Rosemary—are not herbs at all. The next definition, coming second in the same dictionary, tells us that 'herb' is applied to plants of which the leaves, or stem and leaves, are used for food or medicine, or for their scent or flavour. This is closer to the generally accepted view (in the herbalist's ors her barist's sense) of what a herb is; but it omits to mention that ome-perennial herb plants, e.g. Elecampane, contain their valuable properties in the root; others, like Caraway, Dill and Anise, concentrate their virtues in the fruit or seed. Then there are such old favourites as the Gillyflower or Clove Carnation, Marigold and Lavender, which are prized for their flowers. By quoting only 'stem and leaves' the dictionary has deprived herb-fanciers of the Elecampane root to cure a cough; the seed-cake made with Caraway; Dill pickles; floral pot-pourri; Lavender sachets, and much else.

That self-styled knight, 'Sir' John Hill, in his eighteenth-century *Family Herbal*, writes 'concerning the methods of collecting and preserving plants and parts of them for use: in some only the leaves are to be used; in others the whole plant cut from the root; in others the flowers only; in others the fruits; in others the seeds; in some the roots; of some trees the barks . . .' He is here dealing solely with herbs for use in home-made remedies. As he words it, 'this work will tend to instruct those charitable ladies who may be desirous of giving this great relief to the afflicted poor in their neighbourhood'.

I

Today our chief practical aim in growing garden herbs is to supply flavourings for the cook. For the rest, we may cultivate the fragrances of Lavender and Bergamot, of Southernwood, Chamomile, Penny-royal and Eau-de-Cologne Mint, purely to please the nose: a delight which we seldom regard as serving any useful purpose. It was not so in earlier centuries, when not only were all these taken internally or applied externally as remedies and salves, but when scents, too, were believed to possess tonic virtues of themselves. Although at first sight this claim may seem to us far-fetched, it is plain that scents, most evocative of reminders, have a powerful influence upon the brain; and so, if the mind can affect the body, may it not be possible after all that some aromas are capable of stimulating courage and strengthening will-power, in accordance with the tenets of our forefathers?

Before the examination of dictionary and herbal has proceeded far, it appears that an herb—pronounced in Britain until the nineteenth century without the aspirate—is very much what the individual likes to make it. The old lady who vowed that the glorious aroma of coffee being made would revive her on her deathbed may well have regarded that bean as a remedial herb. In the seventeenth century those early settlers who took with them to the New World many seeds and roots of medicinal, culinary and fragrant herbs with which they had been familiar in Europe, soon added to these certain indigenous plants whose uses were demonstrated by friendly 'Red' Indians.*

But the colonists' womenfolk required plants for yet another purpose: as vegetable dyestuffs for colouring their handspun thread and handwoven fabrics. So it came about that they took to cultivating dye-plants such as Madder, Weld, Dyer's Greenweed, Safflower, Indigo-fera and Poke-Root, conveniently to hand within the walls or fences of their herb-gardens, and these became known as dye-*herbs*. When in 1964 I helped to make a herb exhibit at the American Museum at Claverton Manor near Bath, we included dye-plants and examples of fleece dyed with these, to correspond with the usage of the early settlers.

The subtle and lovely colours produced in this way created intense interest among visitors to the Museum, and the remembrance of it, still vivid, has prompted me to include some dye-plants in this collection of herbs, together with directions for mordanting and dyeing wool.† Without going quite so far as Kipling:

INTRODUCING HERBS

Anything green that grew out of the mould
Was an excellent herb to our fathers of old,

I have chosen to interpret the word 'herb' in a broad sense, as meaning
a plant which gives service of some kind directly to human beings without the interpolation of elaborate techniques in laboratory or factory—
including the live animals that process herbage into the meat eaten by
man. In this interpretation grass is not a herb, because we cannot
utilize it at first hand, but require livestock to convert it into food
for us.*

The usual range of food-plants found in market gardens and green-
grocers' shops has been omitted, because these are dealt with abun-
dantly in books and magazines devoted to the cultivation and cooking
of common vegetables and fruits. Even so, I was confronted with a
vast array of worthy candidates for inclusion here, and, as the volume
is designed for handy use by the general reader, it was obvious that
an arbitrary selection must be made. This has been done in much the
same way as poems would be gathered for an anthology of verse.
Herbs have been chosen because they were well-known and tried
examples of their kind, and each category—medicinal, culinary,
fragrant and dyestuff—has, I hope, been given a fair share of the pages.
If they prove interesting, it should be borne in mind that there are
hundreds more such plants growing in fields, hedges and woods;
maybe even on one's doorstep, unnoticed. Out of the seventy-five
vegetable substances named as useful in salads by John Evelyn, only
half that number was obtainable before the 1939 war from green-
grocers in Britain, and the choice has now declined still further. Many
of them may yet be found in the wild.

Pictures can be helpful as a means of identifying unfamiliar plants
and, in a book such as this, they should also be aesthetically pleasing
and an asset to those readers who do not wish to track down the
living subjects. In making the selection I have tried to achieve a balance
between precise botanical studies and more spontaneous works of art.

Reviving the once popular pastime of shadow photography† for my
own illustrations, I have adapted the original formula to the extent of

* Grass has been eaten in periods of famine, but few people care to consume it
in normal times.
† See *The Lady*, July 29, 1965.

using freshly gathered plants, whose springy condition made handling more difficult than the arrangement of dry, pressed specimens would be in a photographic frame. Additional liveliness in the result seems to justify this trouble, and may excuse minor defects of design. It is a hobby for all who are interested in wild flowers, supplying as it does an accurate and permanent record of short-lived 'finds' together with an inexpensive, absorbing occupation for wet afternoons.

People often ask what a 'pot-herb' is, and seem apt to associate the term with the *bouquet garni* or pinch of dried herb added to food in stewpan or casserole. This is far too narrow a view. The term is many centuries old and belongs to cookery in its most primitive stage, when every edible substance went into one pot, or cauldron, suspended over a fire. When man discovered that flesh became more digestible and palatable after being cooked, he also found out that nearly every tuberous root might be made wholesome by the same means—even those which had proved dangerous in their raw state.

With a very few exceptions (and what pain and grief must have gone to the precise knowledge of these), thorough cooking does neutralize any harmful elements in plants, and the salts they impart to the gravy or broth are valuable assets to the blood. This ancient and primitive method of cookery had the advantage over multi-saucepan sophistication in that these minerals formed part of the dish and were not thrown out with the water, as is so commonly the case today.

The subject of medicinal herbs holds a mysterious fascination for most people, although they are often able to name only two—Witch Hazel and Wintergreen—as being in common use now. Sharp dividing lines cannot be drawn, but it is generally true that in his healing work the herbalist habitually employs more plants than does the orthodox medical practitioner, many of whose synthetic pills and potions emanate from chemists' laboratories now. Yet it is also true that some of the most dangerous drugs extracted from plants, such as Aconite, Bella Donna, Coniine, Colchicine, Digitalis, Hyoscine and Stramonium, are utilized in orthodox medicine but abjured by the herbalist. It is of interest to recall that tobacco, when first introduced into Europe by the Spaniards in 1552, was regarded as a cure-all herb.

Even when we have firmly ruled out the poisons, it must be emphasized that caution on the part of the untrained person who is essaying to treat ailments is just as essential whether natural plant material or manufactured medicines are being employed. There are certain in-

fusions or decoctions, including Chamomile, Sage, Lemon Balm, Thyme and Rosemary teas, which are perfectly safe to use at home without prescription—safe, that is, to anyone who can stomach the usual cup of Indian or China tea; and some who cannot do so find a herbal tea beneficial. Few of the recipes given in the following pages could cause harm if taken in reasonable quantities, but these are intended for the relief of conditions that are not serious enough to see a doctor about. It is customary in France to take teas or *tisanes* brewed from herbs as a matter of course for insomnia (Lime Flowers), chills (Peppermint and Elderflower), indigestion (Chamomile), and headaches (Rosemary); while certain decoctions, such as Elderberry Rob—juice sweetened with sugar and thickened by heat; Coltsfoot Syrup—sweetened with honey or liquorice; also Thyme-and-Linseed Syrup, are soothing remedies for coughs and colds. It is of course advisable to obtain a professional diagnosis as to the cause of any cough that persists for more than a week or two. Beyond such simple remedies as these, and the employment of Nettle-tops, Dandelion leaves and Watercress as blood-purifiers in the springtime, it is unwise for the amateur to venture far. For the treatment of more serious ills, trained herbalists are available for consultation. Membership of the Society of Herbalists costs little, and names and addresses of qualified practitioners are obtainable from the Society's offices at 21 Bruton Street, Berkeley Square, London W.1.; or from the National Institute of Medical Herbalists Ltd., 169 Norfolk Street, Sheffield, Yorks. The last-named body celebrated the centenary of its foundation in 1964. Those who are interested in herbal medicine may be glad to know that medical certificates issued by registered members of the Institute are accepted under National Health Service regulations (for sickness benefit, etc.) and that it runs The Hospital for Natural Healing at Forest Gate, London E.7.

Herbs are the oldest kind of medicine in the world, and herbalism—defined as the art of healing by the use of non-poisonous herbs—can be traced back through the civilizations of Rome, Greece, Assyria and Babylon to Sumerian times. Sir Ernest Wallis Budge (formerly Keeper of Egyptian and Assyrian antiquities at the British Museum) speaks of a Sumerian Herbal described on a tablet 'which was at one time in the library of Ashurbanipal, King of Assyria at Nineveh, 668–626 B.C. . . . It has a note at the end which says that it was copied from a tablet which had been written in the second year of the reign of Enlil-Bani, King of Isin, about 2201–2177 B.C. And the note refers to a tradition from the time of "the ancient rulers before the Flood". Thus it is clear that the Sumerian Herbal was in existence in the second half of the third millenium B.C.'

If our imagination falters at the attempt to picture five thousand years of herbalism, we are on comparatively familiar ground with the Anglo-Saxon word *dregen*, to dry, which gave us (in the dried medicinal herbs) our first *drugs*. In those days there were the Nine Sacred Herbs, one of them a tree, namely: Mugwort, *Waybread* (Plantain), *Stime* (Watercress), *Maythen* (Chamomile), *Wergulu* (Nettle), Crabapple, Chervil, Fennel and the unidentified *Atterlothe*. There were also six 'amulet herbs': Betony, Vervain, Peony, Yarrow, Plantain, Rose. It is not always realized that the Rose in the Middle Ages had great religious significance, and that the first 'rosaries' were made out of pounded rose petals, moulded into beads and threaded. These gave out delicious fragrance when clasped in a warm hand.

In the Middle Ages, too, herbs were commonly hung over doors to protect human beings and cattle from ill-fortune and witchcraft, and keyholes were sometimes plugged with fennel seed to obstruct access for ghosts. The Saxons used the Peony,* both for flavouring purposes and as a charm against evil. That usage seems to have lasted into modern times, for in the Gloucestershire village of Filkins up to 1912 the local Benefit Society marched through the lanes on Whit Tuesday to the sound of its own band, preceded by stewards carrying staffs decorated with bunches of the old double red Peony. Mr George Swinford, who celebrated his eightieth birthday in 1967, member of a well-known family of Cotswold stonemasons, remembers this custom clearly.

There are also living villagers who recall being told of the custom of 'smoking' sick people with herbs—another ancient practice, which can be traced back to Pliny. A quern stone would be heated for many hours in the fire, then prepared herbs were placed upon it and cold water immediately poured over the whole; in the reeking steam the sufferer was held, 'as hot as he could endure it'.

In the realm of medicines taken internally, men gradually learned how to make bitter herb extracts more palatable by blending them with sweetening matter. The vital principles were used in the form of dried

* Named after *Paeon*, the physician of Olympus.

6

and powdered foliage, macerated leaves and flowers, or distillations, decoctions, and tinctures of some part of the herb. When mixed with honey or conserve a draught might be the Julep, a concoction intended for immediate consumption and not to keep; or the Electuary—which was a very stiff, long-lasting compound made from powdered herbs and honey; the Lohoch was similar but less stiff, and the Syrup of pouring consistency. This type of medicine came into Europe with Mohammedan invaders, being an invention of the Arabs. Their taste for sweetmeats such as Turkish Delight gave us all those sickly and sticky medicines, often brightly coloured, which are so much more attractive to children than spoonfuls of dry and bitter powder. It became customary to keep vehicles ready, to which extra drugs might be added when required. That made from honey alone was known as 'a honey', a mixture of honey, water and vinegar was 'an oxymel', while a 'bolus' was a large pill, often decorated imposingly with gold leaf. Then there were 'penettes' of barley-sugar, and 'theriacs', 'theri-acles', 'triacles' or 'treacles', originally devised as antidotes to bites or stings of poisonous reptiles and containing vipers' flesh. Later on, theriacs were considered valuable against the dreaded Plague, and at one time 'treacle' meant 'heal-all'. Thus the healing waters of holy wells were sometimes called 'treacles'. St Frideswide's at Binsey near Oxford has in recent times been spoken of as a 'treacle well'.* Lewis Carroll may have known of this, for the dormouse mentions a treacle-well at the mad tea-party in *Alice in Wonderland*.

One famous recipe, known as 'Venice Treacle', contained sixty-one ingredients. It was prepared in public with much ritual. The seven-teenth-century diarist John Evelyn saw it being concocted in Venice. 'The making an extraordinary ceremonie whereof I had been extremely curious to observe, for 'tis extremely pompous and worth seeing.' At various times and in different places the art of herbal medicine has gathered to itself both public show and secret rite. According to Geoffrey Grigson† it was in ancient times deemed necessary to gather herbs at night, preferably by moonlight. Collecting plants was re-garded as thieving from the Earth Mother, as well as being an act of ill-nature against the plant, so it had to be done furtively at night, without witnesses and above all unseen by the sun. All the better if his enemy the moon lent a hand. It is easy to understand that witches

* See S. R. Hunt, *Pharmaceutical Journal*, December 23, 1967.
† *A Herbal of All Sorts*. Phoenix Press, 1949.

would want to keep from prying eyes on *this* planet the ingredients gathered for their secret 'flying ointment', believed to contain Belladonna and Aconite. The last causes irregular heart action, the first delirium, and the two combined may well have created the sensation of flying, even upon so mundane a vehicle as a broom.

And what of the Elder, that ubiquitous bush which by tradition played the part of Elder Mother to all herbs, with power to watch over and protect them? Did she sometimes close an eye during the hours of darkness, allowing predatory human beings to steal away her charges without retribution? Or were they obliged to seek the plants they needed in places where her dominion did not extend? By the time that peddling of herbs became a recognized and honourable trade, these and similar dark superstitions had faded to little more than shadows on a blind, except in very isolated communities, mostly of Celtic stock. In towns the 'herbwyfe' openly called her wares, while the itinerant hawkers who travelled from village to village were as a rule men.

Nevertheless, the idea that the art of healing with herbs was women's work had sent down very deep roots, and it lingered in Britain until well into the seventeenth century. In his book *The English Housewife* Gervase Markham puts a knowledge of medicine first on his list of essential womanly skills, with cookery and gardening following on. This book went into eight editions, the last being dated 1688. The rationalistic eighteenth century, with its development of medical science by such men as Jenner, Priestley and Hunter, neglected herbalism as a serious study and allowed it to fall into the hands of many quacks and charlatans, who adulterated the herbs with disgusting ingredients, such as dogs' dung and pounded snails, which they bluffed people into swallowing. Yet who shall say for certain that future generations may not view with equal horror the vaccines obtained from diseased animals and injected into passive patients of the twentieth century?

We have had a brief look at herbs and at herbal medicines. Now the story of botanists, gardeners and herbalists who have experimented and worked with these since the dawn of history, although too long and involved to cover here in detail, must at least be touched upon. The famous Greek doctor Hippocrates (460–377 B.C.), whose name is associated with the oath supposedly administered to our medical students before they are permitted to practise, studied herbs and left a list of four hundred 'simples' known to him and in common use at the time. Mrs Leyel, in her book *The Truth about Herbs* (Culpeper Press, 1954) names more than sixty plants mentioned by Hippocrates which were still in use by herbalists when she wrote the book. Among them are Mugwort, Mint, Verbena, Sage, Thyme, Rosemary and Rue.

Hippocrates is often referred to as 'The Father of Medicine', but another Greek doctor, Dioscorides, who lived in the first century A.D., was almost as famous. He is said to have been physician to Antony (and Cleopatra), and he left behind him a Herbal containing details of six hundred plants and their properties which formed the basis of herbal therapy for centuries. Galen (A.D. 131–201), who was physician to Marcus Aurelius, added to the Greek Herbal, and Pliny the Elder, a Roman of A.D. 23–79, included in his voluminous *Natural History* a large section on plants.

The disruption of the Roman Empire seriously impeded the progress of medicine in the West, and the simple virtues of herbal remedies became bedevilled with accretions of magic and superstition, traces of which still linger to alienate modern minds from the real truths of herbalism. In the Middle Ages the Christian duty of caring for the sick became important and much healing work was promoted by the Church, in hospitals and infirmaries run by religious orders, and by pious ladies of rank and substance. Plants required for this service were grown in monastic herb gardens or enclosures belonging to the great houses. The Emperor Charlemagne (A.D. 742–814) had a herb garden in which he took great interest, and one of the earliest monastic gardens of which records are extant was the Benedictine St Gall near Lake Constance in Switzerland, where ninth-century monks cultivated Lovage, among other herbs.

Our own *Leech Book of Bald*, an Anglo-Saxon Herbal of the time of Alfred the Great (849–899), was compiled by one Bald, who blended the herb-lore of the ancient Britons with prescriptions of eastern origin sent by the Patriarch of Jerusalem to King Alfred, who allowed Bald access to this material. At this early date herbalists in Britain were cognizant of upwards of five hundred healing herbs, although a German Herbal of 1485 contains fewer than four hundred.

The Saxon suffix 'wort' (or 'wyrt') connotes a healing herb, and 'wyrtzerds' were herbyards. It is interesting to come across the term 'yard' in common use today in North America to denote an enclosed garden behind the house. In Britain 'yard' has now a narrower meaning and refers to a paved or cemented court housing dustbins, dog-kennels and washing-lines; while any plot where plants grow, however small, is known as a 'garden'.

In the thirteenth century an Englishman named Bartholomew, who was a professor of theology in Paris, wrote a large work, *De Proprietatibus Rerum*, running into seventeen volumes, of which one dealt with plants. It was originally written in Latin, and translated into English and printed by Wynkyn de Worde in 1493. Following this came Banckes's *Herbal* in 1525 and the *Grete Herbal* of 1526, compiled from many sources. Francis Bacon (1561–1626) in his much-quoted essay 'Of Gardens'—'God Almighty first planted a garden; and, indeed, it is the purest of human pleasures'—was one of the earliest writers to praise the aesthetic delights of gardening, as distinct from the utilitarian aspects of the craft; and in Tudor and Stuart days the pleasaunce with its pleached* alleys, knot gardens of fragrant clipped herbs such as Lavender, Thyme, Hyssop, Savory, Marjoram and Santolina, and mount or mound artificially contrived to give strollers a different viewpoint, became increasingly fashionable.

William Turner, sometime Dean of Wells, produced in the mid-sixteenth century a splendid study of plants and their uses which earned him the title of 'Father of English Botany'. He was a pupil and friend of Ridley, the martyred Bishop of London. During the reign of Mary, Turner was obliged to flee the country, but later returned to end his days happily in a London physic garden; his contemporary, John Gerard, had the first garden of medicinal herbs in that city, his being in Fetter Lane. Born at Nantwich in 1545, he became Master of the Apothecaries' Company, and his *Herbal* of 1597, illustrated with a magnificent set of woodcuts, has been admired for more than three hundred and fifty years.

In 1640 Parkinson completed his *Theatrum Botanicum*; this work was soon overshadowed by *The English Physician and Complete Herbal* of Nicholas Culpeper (1616–1654), which remained for some two hundred years the most popular guide to herbal medicine in these islands. Culpeper, a member of a well-to-do family with properties in Kent and Sussex, had a chequered career. Extravagance and dissipation at Cambridge, and a disastrous, abortive attempt at elopement with a young heiress (on the way to join her lover she was killed when light-

* Arched or fenced with interlaced boughs.

ning struck her coach), led to his refusal to resume his studies at the University or to enter the Church as planned. In consequence of all this he forfeited his inheritance. His widowed mother is said to have died from shock.

At twenty-three the orphaned Nicholas was apprenticed to an apothecary in London, where he gained an excellent knowledge of *materia medica*, and studied astrology also. He met with strong opposition from the College of Physicians for translating the Latin Pharmacopoeia into English,* and during the quarrel his astrology was held up to ridicule. Notwithstanding this, he had his own practice as a doctor in London, where he is said to have treated the poor free of charge. He fought on the side of Cromwell at Edgehill in 1642, and died of tuberculosis at the age of thirty-eight.

In him, two streams of thought coalesced around the art of healing with herbs: astrology and the so-called 'Doctrine of Signatures', neither of which commends itself to Western minds in the twentieth century. The Swiss Paracelsus and the Italian Giambattista della Porta developed in the latter the idea that nature has signposted everything for man's guidance, and that plants show by their outward form what healing virtues they contain. Thus the blotched leaves of *Pulmonaria* (Lungwort) were thought to resemble lungs; in fact, this plant can be of service to sufferers from lung disease, but so can others which are not thus marked. It would seem that the powers of Lungwort were known to the Anglo-Saxons long before the fancied 'signature' was adduced to disclose the plant's purpose.

Some of the resemblances are far-fetched. The convolutions of a walnut suggest a brain, therefore walnut will cure brain troubles; similarly, the little Eyebright was thought to resemble a human eye, therefore it would soothe inflamed and sore eyes. Other suggestions are disconcertingly incomplete. Members of the Natural Order *Cruciferae* are all said to be benign, and the arrangement of petals in the form of a cross is the sign of this beneficence. But what about the many Orders of plants of great worth to mankind which are not so signed? Then the blood-purifiers are seldom red-leaved or red-flowered, and no other hint of their function is given to the eye. If with an open mind the inquirer tries to elucidate this doctrine, he or she comes up against a mass of vagueness and inconsistency which would appear to justify the scepticism of the orthodox medical practitioners from Culpeper's day

* *A Physicall Directory*, 1649.

onwards. The theory has a certain imaginative charm, but one is obliged to admit that it lacks firm guiding principles.

It may be concluded that the accretion of this doctrine and of the arcane language of alchemy and astrology did great disservice to the basic truths of herbalism, and accorded so ill with the advancing medical science of the eighteenth and nineteenth centuries that it was altogether passed by.

In small rural communities genuine herbal remedies continued in vogue, dispensed by people with handed-down knowledge who were personally known to their neighbours and trusted by them; but in mushroom cities created by the industrial revolution herbalism degenerated and went underground into mean little back street shops, sometimes keeping these solvent by the sale of love-potions for the young, and other nostrums to reduce fertility, for which overburdened women would scrape up money in desperate efforts to avoid bearing additional, unwanted, children. Although hints are dropped freely, it is difficult to obtain precise evidence of this. Until very recent times, attempts to limit families to such numbers as could be decently fed and housed by the parents were made in secrecy and fear, some methods being outlawed by the State and all (except sexual abstinence) by the Church.

From this atmosphere of seamy misery and degradation the late Mrs C. F. Leyel (1880–1957) sought to lift up and rehabilitate the ancient art of the herbalist. Early marriage had put a stop to her training as a doctor; but she maintained her interest in orthodox medicine and served as a Life Governor of three London hospitals.* Meanwhile, in her own words, she was

haunted by the thought that herbs, in which my studies of their history had given me a profound faith, were not being used as widely or as effectively in the service of stricken humanity as they deserved to be. Why do we not receive herbal treatment? Is it due to professional prejudice? Considering their own limitations, which the greatest of modern doctors and scientists readily acknowledge, what justifications have they for ignoring and despising herbalism, the accumulated wisdom of so many past centuries? Do they not themselves acknowledge that medicine is partly an empirical science—that is to say, one based on observation and experiment? Observing any cure, by no matter what unorthodox means, are they not therefore bound to test it?

---

* St. Mary's, the West London, and the Royal National Orthopaedic Hospitals.

Her desire to disseminate knowledge of herbs and to revive herbalism in the modern world led to the opening of a bright, attractive herbalist's shop in London's Baker Street in 1927. This was named Culpeper House—for Mrs Leyel was either less critical of Nicholas Culpeper than I, or else had decided that his name, in consequence of the popularity of his *English Physician and Complete Herbal*, would suggest herbalism to the public better than any other. Writing about the establishment of this business, known as The Society of Herbalists, Limited, Mrs Leyel describes her intention as

merely to present the still-room elixirs, distillations, lotions and creams of our ancestors in an agreeable and attractive setting that would immediately convey an impression of modern hygiene . . . I wanted to destroy the idea fixed in many people's minds that a herbalist's shop inevitably meant a small shabby room with dirty windows, dingy walls, and dusty shelves littered with rubbish, all suggestive of mysterious and probably evil practices.

She succeeded so well that the demand for herbal remedies soared beyond all expectation, and in a very short time it became clear that purchasers needed proper advice as to their use.

People suffering from rheumatism, indigestion or headache would come to the shop asking for something which had cured a friend. But herbs are not nostrums. There is not one herb which cures rheumatism, another which cures headache, and a third which cures indigestion. They do not stop pain instantly, but work on its cause . . .

I thus decided that it was impossible to continue the indiscriminate sale of herbal medicines over the counter, and started giving consultations. The medical side of the Society of Herbalists developed in response to the insistent demand of the public. By undertaking this work the Society broke entirely fresh ground. For the first time herbalism was competing with the most up-to-date methods and theories of modern scientists; and this, not in any isolated district in the country, but within a few hundred yards of Harley and Wimpole Streets. Herbal remedies were being offered, not to unsophisticated country folk with a predilection for the nostrums of their grandmothers, but to highly sophisticated modern Londoners. They were not induced to try herbs by any promises or alluring advertisements, for none defaced Culpeper House. Nor were they promised quick results, for herbs, except in some cases and some individuals, work very slowly.

The success of herbs in many cases surprised me as much as it did my patients, for I was experimenting at first with only the traditional knowledge to fall back upon. If my early experiments and experience had not been successful, or if the results had only been negatively successful, I should have abandoned the practice of herbalism. I may claim not to be a fool; my patients were not fools either; and unorthodox and unregistered practitioners have no protection whatsoever from the law if they harm their patients. But I found that herbs did exactly what they have always had the reputation of doing—they healed, sometimes slowly, sometimes remarkably quickly, yet always most effectively.

From the very beginning of my work many doctors were interested in it and most friendly disposed towards me. The late Sir Henry Simpson* was especially kind and helpful. His wife, Miss Lena Ashwell, was one of our first directors, and I am always glad to remember that herbs rewarded her powerful co-operation by curing her of a gastric ulcer when other treatments had failed.

In 1936 a new organization, called the Society of Herbalists but entirely separate from the Limited Company (which was re-named Culpeper House Ltd.), was formed with many members who had derived benefit from herbal medicines, believed in them, and wanted to protect and further their own interests and those of herbalism.

Modern herbal practice is based on the principle that herbs are the natural medicine for human disease; that they can cure diseases which purely animal or mineral medicines, or herbs blended with such medicines, cannot do. They are both a stimulus and a food for tired cells. To the herbalist, the separation of that part of the herb which is purely medicinal from the rest of the plant—which is natural nourishment—is a mad way of using herbs. The doctors and chemists who do this are ignoring the wisdom of nature in providing stimulus and food in harmonious combination.†

These words have been taken from the writing of Mrs Leyel, but are so much curtailed as to be merely a guide to her ideas and not a full summary of them.

Against this conception of the essential 'wholeness' of herbal medicine, doctors and chemists set their argument that herbs contain different amounts of the drug, and this of varying quality according to the soil and climatic conditions in which the plants grew. In their opinion, drugs produced in laboratories are equivalent to the vital

---

* Sir Henry Simpson, K.C.V.O., was Hon. Consulting Surgeon to the Hospital for Women, Soho Square, and Gynaecological Surgeon to the West London Hospital. He was gynaecologist to the Queen Mother and brought Queen Elizabeth II and Princess Margaret into the world.

† *The Truth about Herbs*, Mrs C. F. Leyel. Culpeper Press, 1954.

principles (alkaloids) of herbs, made to known standards so that the dosage can be accurately measured, while any elements which have been omitted from the preparation are so trifling as to be safely disregarded.

For my part I am inclined to scepticism about descriptions of cures effected by 'marvellous' herbs, chiefly because the language has so often seemed too strong and the proofs too weak. But, having seen another kind of cure performed on aged and faded textiles with the herb *Saponaria* (Soapwort),* it now seems credible to me that some herbs may have an equally restorative effect upon human tissues, given suitable circumstances. Soapwort will not carry out its work unless it is used in association with pure spring water. Our chlorinated tap water appears to inhibit or destroy its vital properties; it is possible that medicinal herbs, too, require the right conditions.

Whatever the truth about herbs may be, it will not be helped in the long run by the use of obscure language or complicated ritual. Unfortunately there is in some human beings a primitive desire to be impressed by awesome mumbo-jumbo, and the rites of the witch-doctor are still found profitable at times by those who do not scruple to use some modern equivalents, whether under the cloak of orthodoxy or not. If nonsense has been published about herbalism in the past, today's scientific medicine is not entirely free from absurdities. That very modern drug, penicillin, was derived from the vegetable world of mould fungi: the most prolific source of *Penicillium notatum* having been, according to its discoverer Sir Alexander Fleming, the cantaloup melon in very overripe condition. After Sir Alexander had lectured at Strathpeffer in 1947, the great man showed amusement next day when a certain Scottish newspaper reported that penicillin was a mould 'found on rotting antelopes'.

Leaving the tricky subject of herbalist versus orthodox medical practitioner, we may turn with pleasure to those who have cultivated herbs for their taste, fragrance and beauty of foliage or flower. In the last hundred years the best known of these in Britain have been women, all of them skilled writers as well as gardeners. The great Gertrude Jekyll (1843–1932) became famous in her middle years for pioneer work in the natural, as opposed to the formal, layout of pleasure gardens, a talent that she often displayed in successful

* See pages 135–138.

collaboration with the celebrated architect Sir Edwin Lutyens. She commended numerous herbs for their admirable qualities as garden subjects rather than for any specific uses. Writing in her second book, *Home and Garden* (1900), about the setting of country houses, she suggests keeping the more showy flowers to the main garden, and furnishing entrance courtyards with quieter subjects, many of them herbs: '. . . the use of such restraint involves no penance, for what is more delightful than Bay and Rosemary, and the handsome ground greenery of Lent Hellebore, *Megasea* [now *Bergenia*] and Acanthus?' Her own garden, at Munstead Wood near Godalming in Surrey, survives.

A contemporary and friend of Miss Jekyll's, Mrs C. W. Earle (1836–1925), who also gardened in the county of Surrey, wrote books that were an odd mixture of garden lore, cookery, house-furnishing and general comment on life, under the apt titles of *Pot-Pourri from a Surrey Garden* (1897), *More Pot-Pourri* (1899), *A Third Pot-Pourri* and *Pot-Pourri Mixed by Two* (1914), the last in conjunction with Ethel Case. These were enormously popular, and Miss Case* (then in her lively nineties) told me in 1967 that the publishers, Smith, Elder and Co., were believed to have made £30,000 from them—a handsome sum in those days.

I was not surprised to hear this, for every country house in my childhood and youth had in one or other of its guest-rooms a set of Mrs Earle's *Pot-Pourri* books on bedside shelf or in a bookcase, and it became a regular ritual to seek these in each strange house we stayed at. Mrs Theresa Earle, known as 'Aunt T.' to Ethel Case and others who were not actually her nieces, was both well-connected and well-informed, and she possessed a sharp but not unkind wit. Lady Eve Balfour (a genuine great-niece) told me of an encounter in the Balfour home between Aunt T. and a neighbour, none other than that formidable lady composer Dame Ethel Smyth, who found herself unable to make any impression upon Mrs Earle and rose in a huff to take her leave. 'We do not agree on a single subject, so I may as well go,' she said. But Mrs Earle had the last word. 'I do not accept that. You think yourself a remarkable woman, and so do I. There is *one* point of agreement at least!' Theresa Earle was a vegetarian, and she displayed a particular interest in herbs and their uses. She owned a fine set of old herbals. Some recipes from her books are quoted on pages 171 and 172.

Another prolific writer, also a vegetarian, who specialized in herb

* Ethel Case died at Sidmouth in June 1968.

lore was Eleanour Sinclair Rohde (1881–1950). She came of a Danish family which had settled in England early in the eighteenth century. A pupil of the well-known Ladies' College at Cheltenham and later a history student of St Hilda's Hall, Oxford, she, too, gardened in Surrey, having for most of her adult life a herb garden at Reigate. Of the score of books she produced, two—*The Old English Herbals* (1922) and *The Story of the Garden* (1932)—seem likely to become classics in their genre.

She also wrote several books dealing in detail with herbs, and, judging by the price they maintain on the second-hand market, these are still in demand: *A Garden of Herbs* (1920), *The Scented Garden* (1931) and *Herbs and Herb Gardening* (1936).

Mrs Grieve, author of that standard work of reference, *A Modern Herbal* (1931), raised herbs at her home at Chalfont St Giles in Buckinghamshire, and her friend and editor, Hilda Leyel (Mrs C. F. Leyel), founder of the Society of Herbalists, lived and gardened at Shripney Manor in Sussex. The latter wrote a whole series of books under the umbrella title of *The Culpeper Herbals*, published by Faber in the nineteen-thirties.

All in all, the years between the two World Wars can now be seen as a particularly flourishing period for the herb-grower and herbalist. That word is another controversial subject, for it is used in Britain to denote one who studies the subject of herbal therapy, and we have no specific name for a herb-grower; whereas in America anyone who practises the arts of herb-growing and herb usage, not confined to medicine, is known as a herbarist. (It is still customary in the United States and Canada to eliminate the aspirate, as was done in Britain prior to the nineteenth century, from 'herb'.)

One Englishwoman who merited the description 'herbarist'—the late Miss Dorothy Hewer, B.Sc.—started in 1926 the Herb Farm at Seal in Kent, an enterprise still flourishing after forty years, and until the spring of 1968 under the direction of Margaret Brownlow (1917–1968), also a B.Sc. and a dedicated herb-lover. Her books, lectures and designs for herb gardens, including scented gardens for the blind, are deservedly well known, and her nursery has supplied herb plants to gardens great and small in many parts of the United Kingdom and beyond. In the same county 'Vita' Sackville-West (1892–1962), famous as poet, novelist, travel writer and garden columnist of *The Observer*, made a particularly lovely herb garden at her home, Sissinghurst

Castle. In a secluded corner of this estate, where scents and the hum of bees refresh and restore even the most jaded spirits, weary travellers may rest on a seat of *Mentha requienii* and sink into the peace of past ages.

A different kind of herbarist is Lady Meade-Fetherstonhaugh of the great house of Uppark in Sussex, where many fragrant herbs ramble in the Repton-haunted demesne, but one herb—the pink-flowered Soapwort—is given pride of place. With this saponaceous plant and the purest of spring water, marvellous results have been obtained over the last thirty years in the restoration of faded and decrepit tapestries, damasks and banners. At the late Mrs Leyel's request, Lady Meade-Fetherstonhaugh became President of the Society of Herbalists in 1958. She has lectured on her work with *Saponaria* in the United States, where the Herb Society of America knits together all who are interested in growing herbs, using them, or simply enlarging their knowledge of herb lore. And there is still plenty for us all to learn.

One favourite plant has been omitted from this collection—the Rose. It is of such importance, and the subject of its origin and development so complex, its history so rich, and its appeal to poets so great, that it seemed impossible to contain it in the requisite number of pages. The rose rightly demands a whole book to itself. Anyone who wishes to grow such old favourites as the Damask Rose (traditionally brought to Europe from Damascus by the Crusaders); or *Rosa gallica officinalis*, the red Apothecary's Rose used for medicinal purposes in the Middle Ages and then cultivated extensively at the French town of Provins;* or *Rosa centifolia*, the Cabbage Rose grown by Gerard in Holborn in 1597; or the pink-and-white striped York and Lancaster Rose mentioned by Shakespeare, will find all these and countless others in the Portland Nurseries at Shrewsbury. Miss Hilda Murrell, a granddaughter of Edwin Murrell, the founder of this business, rebuilt the nurseries after World War II, and has developed the Shrub Rose and Old Rose sections to a very high standard.

Mrs Margery Fish, who gardens at Lambrook Manor in Somerset, is one of the best-known plantswomen in Britain today. Not only are her various books best-sellers and her lectures popular all over the country, but she also runs a nursery where unusual plants may be had, many of them old favourite cottage-garden subjects which she has rescued from near-extinction; while in her own demesne she demon-

* Hence often called 'the Provins Rose'.

strates on a homely scale just how to use such plants to the greatest advantage. Here may be seen in profusion Angelica, Bugle, a number of different Artemisias, Fennels, Helichrysums, Hellebores, Lungworts, Mallows, Periwinkles, Sages, Santolinas and very handsome Spurges— to name but a fraction of her herbal treasure. It is a far cry from the ancient, unlettered crone creeping about on her secret business of herb-gathering by moonlight, to the glare of television upon Margery Fish as she introduces viewers in a million homes to the silvery elegance of *Artemisia ludoviciana*;* but such comparison serves to demonstrate the unbroken thread of human interest in the subject of herbs from the remotest glimmer of civilization to the present day.

* See page 29.

II. Selected Herbs

Page references at each title are to illustrations.

ACONITE   *Aconitum napellus*   [*p.* 135

Known today as Monkshood, and in the past under other such descriptive names as Wolf's Bane, Friar's Cap, Blue Rocket and in Shakespeare's England as Helmet-flower (the Scots preferred to call it Auld Wife's Huid), this attractive-looking plant contains a deadly poison which, according to tradition, was used to bait traps for wolves when these wild beasts were a menace to people living in the British Isles. It is not a truly native species of Aconitum, but must have been introduced from Europe at a very early stage in our history; it appears in plant vocabularies dating from before the Norman conquest and is found in early English medical recipes. The Anglo-Saxons understood its nature and properties, for they labelled it *Thung*—a word which was applicable to any highly poisonous plant.

The botanical name Aconitum is possibly derived from the Greek *akon*, a dart, because primitive peoples used it to make their poison arrows, and the specific name, *napellus*, meaning 'a little turnip', describes the appearance of the root. There are several varieties, but the old-fashioned garden plant with deeply cut foliage and purplish-blue hood fitting down close upon the underparts of the flower is considered to be the best for medicinal purposes. Aconite, which comes under Part I of the Poisons List, is extracted from the whole plant, although the chief supply is stored in the roots. It is used as an anodyne, diuretic and diaphoretic and externally in liniments for the relief of rheumatism and neuralgia, sometimes mixed with chloroform or belladonna. According to that well-known herbalist Mrs C. F. Leyel, the medicinal uses of Monkshood include the relief of cold in the head, inflamed gums, and over-sensitive hearing and smell, particularly when those conditions have been induced by fright.

As a garden subject it was very commonly grown in the years before World War II, and I can remember as a child looking up at those tall stems crowned with quaint, blue, hooded flowers in many a herbaceous border. Nobody ever warned me of its perils, and it seems remarkable that accidental poisoning by this plant was, apparently, unheard of—seeing that professional growers of drug plants take the precaution of wearing gloves when they handle it. The poison is very swift in action, and if it enters the system (either by the mouth or through a cut in the skin) prompt measures are essential. Like the buttercup, of the same Order of *Ranunculaceae*, this Aconite may be dangerous to cattle when green, but appears to be rendered harmless by drying. At times of famine the field-mouse will gnaw at almost any plant, but leaves Monkshood severely alone. *Aconitum napellus* grows wild in places, as a garden escape, and its indigenous relative, *Aconitum anglicum* (also called Monkshood) which resembles it in appearance but flowers earlier, in the months of May and June, is found by shady streams in S.W. England and in Wales.

In the ancient world *Aconitum napellus* belonged to Hecate, the moon-goddess of the witches. The mysterious 'flying ointment' concocted by witches in Britain is believed to have contained Aconite and Belladonna. The first causes irregular action of the heart, the second delirium, so the combined symptoms could well have produced a sensation of flying. Aconite is traditionally thought to be the poison used by Medea to prepare her fatal cup for Theseus; presumably such abuses were not uncommon in the time of the Roman Emperor Trajan, who made the growing of Aconite an offence punishable by death.

The cultivated Monkshood may be raised from seed or propagated by root division, and if planted in good rich loam in a moist place it will grow to a height of five or six feet. When raised from seed it takes several years to come into flower. Although it is a perennial, each root lasts for one year only, and new 'daughter' roots surrounding the parent carry on the plant's life. Monkshood should not be confused with the small yellow Winter Aconite, *Eranthis hyemalis*.

AGRIMONY *Agrimonia eupatoria*

In many old herbals this was spelt Argemoney, ascribed by Eleanour Sinclair Rohde to the Greek *argemon*, a white speck on the eye, which this plant was supposed to cure. The tall, slender spikes of yellow flowers, with their delicate scent resembling apricots, are a familiar feature of British hedgerows from June to September. The blossoms are succeeded by stiff, hairy little burrs which gave rise to the country name of Cocklebur, although some authorities maintain that this was reserved for the Burweed, *Xanthium spinosum*. The truth is that vernacular descriptions vary in different localities, and plants often exchange names from county to county and also from one country to another, as witness Wintergreen (see page 158).

Another English name for Agrimony, Church Steeples, well depicts the tapering spires of this plant. The Saxons knew it as Garclive, and Chaucer as Egremoine, while later on Liverwort was adopted to describe its medicinal properties. The plant was also used at one time to flavour beer. French peasants, who still believe in its health-giving virtues, drink a tea made by pouring a pint of boiling water on a handful of freshly gathered leaves, flowers and stems. The beverage is left to stand until cold, then strained off and drunk. For use during the rest of the year, whole plants of Agrimony are gathered, bunched, and hung up to dry in a current of air. When dry enough to rub down, the herb is powdered and stored in airtight jars. The whole plant yields a good yellow dye.

AGRIMONY, HEMP *Eupatorium cannabinum*

This tall, rather coarse-leaved plant is sometimes known as St John's Herb or Holy Rope. In Britain it grows wild in large masses, usually in moist soil on river banks. The flower heads, in dense terminal trusses, are a dull pinkish mauve, and often appear in late summer beside the sharper magenta Loosestrife. In my part of Wiltshire, near the Somerset border, these two plants often combine with patches of golden flowered Tansy to give a rather gaudy trimming to the banks of the Bristol Avon in the holiday months of August and September.

Hemp Agrimony has no connection with the hemp plant and is not used in rope-making, nor does it produce the narcotic drug cannabis, hashish or bhang which a variety of Indian hemp (*Cannabis indica*) provides. A fancied resemblance between its hairy leaves and the fibrous giant, *Cannabis sativa*, led to the somewhat confusing name of Hemp Agrimony. It is occasionally cultivated in gardens, although the American species, *Eupatorium purpureum*, known as Joe Pye Weed, is more colourful. According to the Herb Society of America's Kitchawan Field Station, Joe Pye was a medicine man of importance among the 'Red' Indians. Another American plant in this family, *Eupatorium perfoliatum*, which has white, fluffy flower heads, is known as Boneset, and was said to cure 'break-bone fevers' and to relieve aching bones. It was greatly esteemed by the 'Red' Indians.

The name Eupatorium is said by Mrs Leyel to have come from Mithridates Eupator, a king of Pontus famed for his herbal remedies. In Britain herbalists use Hemp Agrimony in the treatment of fevers and jaundice, but it is no longer listed in the official pharmacopoeia.

ALECOST *Chrysanthemum balsamita*

A pleasantly scented herb whose long, narrow green leaves have a bluish bloom on them. The broader lower leaves were often used as book-markers in church, hence the vernacular name of Bible Leaf. This plant is also known as Costmary. The roots run near the surface of the soil, and spread rapidly, and when top growth reaches a height of three or more feet in July and August, little yellow button flowers appear to crown the spikes. These are insignificant on so tall a plant, and I prefer to remove them. By lowering the stem, further growth of young foliage is encouraged, and this gives a pleasant minty tang to salads, stuffings and soups. According to Eleanour Sinclair Rohde, mention in old recipes of 'A blade of Mace' refers to Alecost, although the true mace is a spicy powder prepared from the dried outer covering (aril) of the nutmeg.

Alecost was introduced into England from the Orient in the sixteenth century and was much used in Elizabethan houses as a strewing-herb to sweeten floors, shelves and closets. In medicine an infusion of the leaves was given to alleviate catarrh. A *tisane* is made by infusing a small bunch of fresh leaves in three-quarters of a pint of boiling water; or the herb may first be dried. It is spread on a screen or a clean tray in a dark, airy room for a week or more. When brittle, leaves are stripped from their stalks and stored in airtight containers. A teaspoonful of the dried and powdered herb takes the place of fresh leaves in the recipe.

In a herb garden this plant must be given a warm and sunny place, well drained, to ensure the best flavour and scent. Roots should be divided and replanted every three years.

'Sir' John Hill in his *Family Herbal* of the eighteenth century describes Costmary as 'a garden plant kept more for its virtues than its beauty . . . It was once greatly esteemed for strengthening the stomach, and curing head-achs [*sic*], and for opening obstructions of the liver and the spleen, but more seems to have been said of it than it deserved.'

Alecost is one of the many herbs used to flavour beer before the hop was cultivated in Britain. The bruised leaves are soothing when rubbed on bee-stings.

ALEXANDERS *Smyrnium olusatrum*

This is a native British herb, sometimes misnamed Black Lovage or Black Angelica. It was also known in the past as Black Potherb, Monk's Salad and Stanmarch. It is a perennial plant, three to four feet high, with glossy dark green leaves and yellow flowers in solid, rounded umbels—the only British umbellifer to combine dark glossy green foliage with yellow flowers. It is common in hedgerows and waste ground near the sea and uncommon inland, except in the vicinity of old monasteries, where it was formerly cultivated as a vegetable but now runs wild. The fruit when ripe is almost black.

The plant derives its name from Smyrna in Macedonia, country of Alexander the Great. It is aromatic, and the scent was thought to resemble myrrh—a corruption of 'Smyrna', whence myrrh was imported, and on this tenuous connection the generic name was formed. Alexanders grows profusely in parts of Scotland, but I cannot discover evidence that the thrifty Scottish people have gathered and consumed it within living memory. The leaves were used in salads and not usually dried for storing. When growing in a large clump this herb gives off a scent very like that of sweet peas.

ALKANET, GREEN
Pentaglottis sempervirens (syn. *Anchusa sempervirens*) [*p.* 150

This perennial herb, growing to a height of two feet, is found naturalized and growing wild on waste ground, frequently near the habitations of man or places that were inhabited in the past. It has small clusters of flat, white-eyed flowers of brilliant blue, like a large Forget-me-not or Speedwell, and harsh, hairy foliage. It flowers from May to August and is a dye-plant, giving a red colour from the root which was used by fabric dyers, and by cabinet makers as a wood stain. It belongs to the family *Boraginaceae* and has sometimes been mistaken for Borage.

A close relation, *Anchusa officinalis*, is often known as 'Common' Alkanet. It was used in herbal medicines as an expectorant, aperient and to induce perspiration. This Anchusa has rough, hairy foliage similar to the first one, and grows to the same height, but the flower differs from that of Green Alkanet in having at first a rosy tinge which later turns to blue. Seed of both species germinates easily, and propagation may also be made by means of root division in October. Anchusas thrive best in a sunny position on well-drained soil.

The tall (5–6 ft) Anchusa commonly seen in herbaceous borders, *Anchusa italica*, also yields a red dye, which was used in ancient Egypt as a face-paint. Another relative, *Anchusa tinctoria* (syn. *Alkanna tinctoria*) has purplish flowers and its root gives a reddish-brown dye. Mr William Robertson grows it in his garden of dye-plants at Dundee. Violetta Thurstan, in her handbook *The Use of Vegetable Dyes*, does not rate Alkanet very highly, but no reason is given for this. Possibly it is said to be 'impracticable' because of its scarcity in the wild. It certainly goes back to Pliny's day as a dyestuff for textiles.

ALLSPICE   *Calycanthus floridus* and *C. macrophyllus*

These aromatic shrubs are related to the better-known Winter Sweet (*Chimonanthus fragrans*, syn. *Calycanthus praecox*), which bears fragrant ivory and purple blossom on leafless boughs in January and February and comes to us from China and Japan. *Calycanthus floridus*, the 'Carolina Allspice' from the southern United States of America, flowers in August, its blossom being of a brownish-purple colour, and the allspice scent which gives it a name exudes chiefly from the foliage and wood. It is deciduous, and moderately hardy if given some winter protection from other shrubs or a wall. Full sun, and light soil with peat added, will suit this plant and its Californian relative, *C. macrophyllus*, which has red flowers in August and grows to nine feet. This foliage has an even more powerful scent, which reminds some people of roast beef. Both may be propagated by layering shoots in July and August.

This is not, however, the Allspice (or Pimento) of commerce, a flavouring made from the dried, unripe but fully-grown berries of *Pimenta officinalis*, a West Indian evergreen tree of the Order *Myrtaceae*, which grows to a height of twenty to forty feet. It will not thrive outdoors in Britain.

ANGELICA
Angelica archangelica (syn. *Archangelica officinalis*)   [*p.* 55

This stately herb is said to flower on St Michael's Day, May 8th,* and so it is specifically named for the archangel. Its therapeutic value was revealed to a monk by an angelic messenger during a terrible epidemic of the plague, which gave rise to the generic name. With such a doubling of angelic titles we should expect it to be the most virtuous of plants.

Certainly the great umbels of cream-coloured flowers look heavenly when placed at focal points in a garden design, and the handsome shining green foliage is also worthy of a place outside the seclusion of kitchen or herb garden. The snag is that if allowed to bloom the plant is only biennial and must be re-sown (or allowed to self-sow) every year to ensure continuity. Otherwise, if flowering stalks are removed at once, before any seed has set, it will probably survive as a perennial. Such treatment will deprive the bees, who are greatly attracted to Angelica blossom. It is also alluring to queen wasps, and some cunning gardeners lie in wait to catch and destroy these in May, thus saving themselves and their fruit from wasp damage later in the year.

The only vernacular name I have been able to trace for this plant, Root of the Holy Ghost, did not deter village boys from making whistles out of the hollow stems. They used mostly the wild Angelica (*Angelica sylvestris*) which is common in wet woods, fens and damp grassy places, also found sometimes on cliffs. It is a little smaller— from three to five feet in height—and flowers later than the garden species; it should not be confused with the larger and coarser Hogweed which, unlike Angelica, is a hairy plant.

A complete list of the uses of Angelica would fill a page. Most people know the toothsome stalk, which may be eaten raw but is usually candied for cakes and confectionery. Some cooks put the fresh stalk into a stewed fruit dish, either by itself or with rhubarb to reduce the tartness. It is also made into jam, preferably with green tomatoes and ginger.

Industrial techniques with this plant are less familiar. They include the production of oil from the seeds, which is used in perfumes and wines and sometimes as a substitute for Juniper berries in gin. Angelica

* The Apparition of St Michael; not to be confused with St Michael and All Angels, September 29th.

26

was also an ingredient of the old French *Eau d'arquebusade*, and in Lapland poets were traditionally crowned with wreaths of the plant 'for inspiration of its scent'.

Medicinal uses include a tonic tea made by infusing the leaf in boiling water, and poultices for chest complaints. Leaves steeped in hot water were applied to reduce inflammation, and to 'bite and chaw' a root of Angelica was recommended as a specific against the Great Plague of 1665. From earliest times it was reputed to have mighty powers against the dreaded witchcraft, as might be expected from the Root of the Holy Ghost.

Cultivation is easy. The plant will grow in almost any soil, given some moisture and preferably a little shade; but for culinary purposes quickly grown tender leaf-stalks are best, and these will be produced in rich, damp soil. Angelica self-sows readily, but as it does not always choose a convenient site gardeners often put seed (which must be fresh) under glass in March and April or outdoors in early May. The little plants should be moved to their permanent home when small, and left undisturbed. This seed soon loses its power of germination.

Some recipes are given on page 172.

ANISE *Pimpinella anisum*

This half-hardy annual has as ancient a history as any plant in the collection: it appeared in an Egyptian herbal written in 1500 B.C. It is a fine-leaved umbelliferous herb, two feet in height, and in Britain is raised from fresh seed sown outside in April. Seedlings may be thinned out, but owing to the fragile roots should not be transplanted. Provided that a sufficiently warm season ensues, the round, aromatic seeds —'Aniseed'—may be gathered in late summer. These are used in cakes, liqueurs and cough medicines. The whole plant should be reaped at ground level directly the first umbels of seed are ripe, and spread out on paper in a warm place to dry off. It is best grown on dry, light soil—not very rich—and in a warm sunny place.

The Romans put aniseed in their spiced cake, to which our modern wedding-cake may be traced. The Anise plant was grown in British herb gardens as early as the fifteenth century, having been imported from its native Egypt. It was taken to America by the first settlers and has been popular in American herb gardens ever since. Mention of Anise may be found in St Matthew's Gospel xxiii. 23: 'for ye pay tithe of mint and anise and cummin . . .' (It now appears that 'anise' is a mis-translation here—see DILL.)

ARNICA   *Arnica montana*

This plant, sometimes known as Mountain Tobacco, is a hardy herbaceous perennial found in woods and high pastures in central Europe. (Other species are native to N. America.) A flower stem about two feet high rises from a rosette of leaves, and bears one or more orange-yellow daisies. These flowers, picked whole and dried, are used in medicine, also the rhizomes, which are harvested and dried in autumn. Tincture of Arnica is used in a paint for unbroken chilblains, and applied to sprains and bruises. It must not be taken internally.

ARTEMISIA

This genus provides many useful and interesting plants for the herb garden; some of them are welcome too in ornamental borders for their fragrance and their finely cut grey foliage, which is equally valuable to set off brightly hued growing flowers and in floral arrangements within doors.

The Latin generic name may have been derived from Artemisia, Queen of Caria, whose statue is in the British Museum; although Pliny attributes it to the goddess Artemis, who 'discovered its virtues and gave them to mankind'. Garlands were traditionally made from this plant and thrown on the Midsummer Eve fire as a sacrifice to keep the thrower safe from ill fortune for a year.

Three important members of this family are described elsewhere: *Artemisia abrotanum* under SOUTHERNWOOD, *A. absinthium* under WORMWOOD, and *A. dracunculus* under TARRAGON.

Of the rest, *A. borealis* and *A. chamaemelifolia*, known respectively as Old Lady and Lady's Maid, possess delicate foliage, the first grey and aromatic, the second green, and grow to a height of eighteen inches. *A. lanata pedemontana* is a rock garden version, not more than six inches high, silvery and fragrant, while *A. rupestris* is a similar plant with green foliage. The green species are less fragrant than the grey-leaved kinds. *A. canescens* makes a low, rounded clump like a silver hedgehog with distorted quills.

Two tall, silvery Artemisias now becoming popular with gardeners

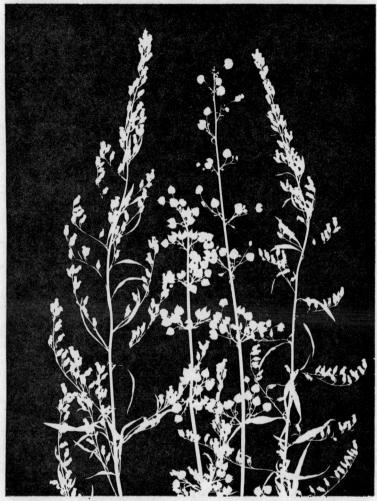

MUGWORT (left and right)   WATER FIGWORT (centre)

and flower-arrangers in Britain are the three-foot American *A. ludoviciana* ('Western Mugwort') and the five-foot Chinese *A. lactiflora* ('White Mugwort'). Both plants are beautifully grown in the garden of Mrs Margery Fish at East Lambrook in Somerset, and roots may be obtained from her nursery.

Our native Artemisias are Wormwood and Common Mugwort; the latter, *A. vulgaris*, superficially resembles Wormwood but its foliage has silver down on the underside of the leaves only; they are a dark green on top, and grow on purplish stems. With its rather dirty looking greyish flowers in summer, this plant is commonly seen at roadsides and in waste places, a slightly aromatic perennial two to four feet high.

Mugwort was at one time used to flavour beer, and in Cornwall it was a popular substitute for tea. Mugwort tea is made by infusing one ounce of flowering tops in a pint of boiling water. The whole herb, including the root, was used medicinally in the treatment of epilepsy and for expelling tapeworm. This plant was known on the continent of Europe as the herb of St John the Baptist, and Italian peasants used to put it secretly beneath the pillow of a sick person. If he fell asleep it was a sure sign that he would recover.

The Artemisias are not difficult to cultivate, although *A. lanata pedemontana* dislikes severe winters. The species with silver foliage keep their colour best in light, rather poor soil, and they need sun. Propagation is by cuttings or, for the herbaceous types, by division in October. Creeping offsets of the miniatures may be taken in spring or autumn.

BALM, LEMON   *Melissa officinalis*   [*p.* 134

A native of southern Europe, this plant has in some localities become naturalized as a wild herb in Britain. It is often confused with the more richly scented Lemon Verbena, which is slightly tender and needs to be cherished, and sometimes with Lemon Thyme. Lemon Balm is the commonest of the three, and will thrive almost anywhere, increasing with great vigour. It is a hardy perennial, three to four feet high, with foliage of a fresh, light green, somewhat nettle-shaped leaves, and insignificant two-lipped whitish flowers. The leaves retain their lemon scent and flavour well when dried, and this herb (fresh or dried) has many uses in the kitchen, notably in soups, stuffings, cooked with fish and put fresh-picked into salads and cider-cups. It is refreshing as a herb tea, made by pouring a pint of boiling water on an ounce of the tips, or some people prefer a few leaves added to a pot of ordinary Indian or China tea. This plant is used industrially in perfumes and liqueurs.

Lemon Balm is a favourite bee-plant (the generic name *Melissa* is from the Greek for 'a bee'), and it was an old country custom to rub fresh leaves on the hives to induce the owner's bees to return and bring others with them. At one time herbalists regarded it as excellent medicine for the brain. The Arabs have a saying: 'Balm makes the heart merry and joyful', but it is not certain to which plant this refers. In Elizabethan England it was used as a strewing-herb and the dried leaves were put into sweet-bags.

Plants may be raised from seed sown outdoors in March, or propagated by root division after flowering. Light, warm soil suits it best. For drying and storing, the shoots must be gathered directly the first flowers appear. In early autumn the whole plant is cut down to the ground. For use in the flower garden the rarer gold-variegated variety is more attractive, and it serves the same culinary purposes.

Recipe for Lemint vinegar, page 180.

BALM OF GILEAD *Cedronella triphylla*

This herb is not the true Balsam of Gilead, but it is an attractive plant for the garden, with three-lobed aromatic foliage and pink two-lipped flowers in August and September. It is tender, and should be treated as a half-hardy perennial, planted out when frosts have ceased and wintered under glass, with cuttings taken in early autumn.

BALSAM or BALM

Those who detest botanist's Latin (sometimes referred to by the scholarly as 'Dogrose' Latin) might do well to consider the confusion that would occur if vernacular names were the only ones available. Balsam is a perfect example. We have seen that Cedronella is commonly known as Balm of Gilead—which it is not. The true Balsam of Gilead, yielding the balm mentioned in the book of the prophet Jeremiah, is a small tree, *Commiphora opobalsamum*, which is found growing on both sides of the Red Sea and produces a much-prized resinous sap.

But there are other trees to which western nations have given the name of Balsam. The 'Balsam' Poplar, *Populus balsamifera*, known too as Cottonwood in its native land of America, bears fragrant young foliage which wafts a balsamic odour down many a town street in the United States and in Britain also. Another poplar, *P. candicans*, even more aromatic than the last when in bud, is invariably referred to as

Balm of Gilead by Americans. The resinous coating of the buds is (or used to be) soaked off in boiling water, and the tincture used for alleviating chest complaints. In America there is also a fir tree, *Abies balsamea*, which is called the Balsam Fir.

We have not yet finished with 'Balsams'. There are several common plants in the Order *Balsaminaceae* of the *Impatiens* genus, known to herb-fanciers as Jewel-weed; the cottager's favourite house-plant, 'Busy Lizzie', is one of these. A more imposing species, *I. roylei*, a hardy perennial from the Himalayas, has escaped from English gardens and travelled from Cumberland to Devonshire in comparatively recent years, covering the banks of many a river with its six-foot-high red stems bearing toothed leaves and mauve-pink blossoms with triggered seeds.

The dwarfer European *I. noli-me-tangere*, with golden flowers, is about the only example of fun in botanical names. 'Touch-me-not' denotes the explosive manner in which *Impatiens* plants fire their ripened seeds around when the slightest vibration sets off the delicate mechanism. Another handsome member of the family seen growing wild in some parts of Britain, *I. fulva* (syn. *I. capensis*), has orange-red flowers which certainly deserve the name of Jewel-weed. It, too, inhabits river banks.

The Touch-me-not and a small, unimposing species, *I. parviflora*, have both been used in medicine for external application to cure warts and corns; but the old herbals are full of warnings about using these plants internally, because of irritant effects produced by their acrid juice.

Finally there is the pretty annual Balsam, *I. balsamina*, whose flowers of rose, scarlet and white used to adorn many a country garden, although it is less commonly seen now than when I was a child.

BASIL, COMMON or SWEET   *Ocimum basilicum*   [*p.* 55

Sweet Basil is well named, and of all culinary herbs has the most generally pleasing warm flavour, adaptable to many varieties of dish. It is a native of India, about twelve inches high, and may be regarded as a half-hardy annual in Britain. It should be sown under glass in March, then pricked out, and finally planted in a sheltered, sunny place in June. It succeeds, too, if sown outside in May, provided that the weather does not turn wintry again.

The aromatic foliage may be harvested twice in the season if a small quantity is cut before any flower buds open, leaving the rest of the plant to grow on for a second crop before the first sharp frost kills it. Indoors it will grow in pots, although the Bush Basil, *Ocimum minimum*, which is only six inches high, is a neater subject for pot culture. Both species have cream two-lipped flowers, and were introduced into Britain early in the sixteenth century. Other kinds, *O. basilicum* var. 'Crispum', the Italian or Curly Basil, and *O. gratissimum*, with pale mauve flowers, are grown in the same way. All require well-drained soil and a sunny position, and should be watered freely in dry weather.

The many culinary uses of Basil include the flavouring of soups, egg and tomato dishes, fish, cream cheese, green peas, potatoes and salads. It was employed by herbalists to treat mild nervous diseases; by housewives to banish flies from indoors; and (in a fine powder) was formerly taken as snuff. The whole plant in earlier times was gathered for use as a 'strewing-herb'. It is beloved by bees.

Fresh, tender leaves may be used for flavouring as soon as they are big enough to pick. To produce dried Basil for winter needs, the plants are cut down to six or eight inches once or twice during the season, and the harvested tops spread out on a clean, dry tray to parch in a warm and preferably shady spot. The dried leaves are a brownish-green colour, and should be stripped from the stems and packed in opaque, airtight jars.

In the East this is a herb with sacred associations, and the Hindus in India grow *Tulasi* (Basil) near temples and dwellings to give protection from misfortune and guide the way to heaven. There is no salvation in this world or the next for anyone who dares to molest this plant. But the mysterious Basil has an altogether different reputation in some parts of Europe. In Crete it is thought to be under the domination of the Devil, and the ancient Greeks believed that it would grow only if planted with rough treatment and words of abuse. From this stems the French expression '*Semer le Basilic*'—i.e. slandering.

Yet many people of western Europe had faith in the power of Basil to protect them from the evils of witchcraft, and in Italy a sprig of Basil is an emblem of love and fidelity still worn by courting peasants in remote districts. There is an old English country tradition that Rue and Basil will not thrive together, but in my garden they seem reconciled.

Some recipes are given on pages 172–178.

BAY, SWEET *Laurus nobilis*

This hardy evergreen, grown as a shrub or small tree, was introduced into Britain from southern Europe in the middle of the sixteenth century. Known by the self-explanatory names of 'Victor's Laurel' and 'Poet's Laurel', it has figured in the literature of Mediterranean countries since classical times. It has also a long history of medicinal uses. The Greek physician Dioscorides recommended that leaves of Bay be laid on with barley flour and bread to assuage inflammations. The aromatic leaves are currently used, either fresh or dried, in the culinary *bouquet garni* for flavouring soups, stews and soused herring, and a small leaf is sometimes added to rice pudding, custard and cornflour mould. The flavour is very potent.

Sweet Bay is not easy to propagate, although the tips may be layered in July or August, and young cuttings taken in summer can be rooted if given close conditions and bottom heat. Viable seed is difficult to obtain. Frost damage is a risk in the early years of life; a position sheltered from cold winds should be selected, and the plant given a bucket of good compost and a well-drained site. A healthy tree will reach a height of twelve feet after about twenty years.

This tree must not be confused with the 'Portugal Laurel' (*Prunus lusitanica*) which bears spikes of white flowers, or with the Laurel commonly used for hedging, *Prunus laurocerus*. The vernacular names of these plants cause much trouble, for the Bay is a tree Laurel, with small yellow flowers in May followed (in warm summers) by purple berries, although it is never referred to as 'Laurel'; the so-called 'Portugal Laurel' is really a Prunus, and so is the hedging 'Laurel'. As for the popular shrub Laurustinus, with its pinkish flowers, this is a Viburnum, although many people think that it is a kind of Laurel.

In America there is a plant commonly seen growing wild from Nova Scotia to Florida, known as Bayberry (*Myrica cerifera*), whose dark green deciduous leaves are often used for cooking instead of true Bay. The decorative waxy berries were used for making Bayberry candles, and in earlier times the dried and powdered root bark was used medicinally as an astringent. In *A Modern Herbal* Mrs Grieve describes this plant as 'the only member of a useful family (*Myrica*) that is regarded as official'—in pharmacopoeias.

BELLADONNA (DEADLY NIGHTSHADE)
Atropa belladonna [*p.* 71

This poisonous plant (which comes into Part I of the chemist's Poisons List) is found widely distributed in central and southern Europe, south-west Asia and Algeria. It has been cultivated for centuries in England, France and north America. It grows wild on chalk and limestone in England but is comparatively rare in Scotland. The Latin *Atropa* derives from the Greek *atropos* and refers to the Fate who held the shears ready to cut human life-lines—an allusion, of course, to the poisonous nature of the plant. *Bella donna*, more light-heartedly, indicates that ladies in Italy were accustomed to dilate the pupils of their eyes with an extract of this plant, in pursuit of glamour.

Oculists have made use of this herb's power of dilation for the examination and treatment of eye diseases for a very long time, and still do today. Before the Reformation it was cultivated in monastic herb gardens and used by the infirmarians as a narcotic in various treatments, by reason of its action on the nervous system, heart and muscles. The alkaloid present, atropine, can cause symptoms of poisoning when only one-tenth of a grain has been swallowed. At the present time various preparations of belladonna are in use; some are locally applied as lotions, liniments or plasters to relieve the pains of neuralgia, gout, sciatica and rheumatism. As a drug it is used to check excessive secretions and allay inflammation, and as an anti-spasmodic in intestinal colic and asthma, also to relieve whooping-cough and false croup in children. It acts rapidly on the circulation and is beneficial in the collapse of pneumonia and typhoid.

Vernacular names include Devil's Cherries, Great Morel and Dwayberry; in Chaucer's day Dwale—possibly from the Scandinavian *dool*, meaning delay or sleep. It is a large shrubby plant, some two to four feet high, with thick leaves of a dark green, dingy purple bell-shaped flowers and black berries. When crushed it exudes a vile smell. As every part of the plant is poisonous it should be handled with great care. Although man is susceptible to this poison, most farm animals seem to be immune, but not dogs and cats.

Belladonna is traditionally supposed to be the poison that killed Marcus Antonius's soldiers during the Parthian Wars, as told by Plutarch; and in sixteenth-century Scotland it was said that Macbeth's men plied an invading army of Danes with liquor containing Dwale, after which they murdered the drugged men without resistance.

Apart from those who cultivate it professionally for medicinal purposes, this plant is not of interest to the gardener. It is normally raised from seed, sown under glass in early March and planted out in May. It is very slow to germinate. Crops of top growth are harvested in June and September, and roots, which become huge by the third year, are also lifted and dried for extraction of the drug.

Another poisonous plant, the Mandrake (*Mandragora officinarum*), was used in Pliny's day as an anaesthetic for operations. The Woody Nightshade or Bittersweet (*Solanum dulcamara*), which commonly climbs in English hedgerows, has bright mauve 'Turk's cap' flowers followed by yellow and red berries. It contains the alkaloid solanine, a narcotic, but is far less deadly than Belladonna.

BERGAMOT, SCARLET *Monarda didyma*   [*p.* 70

This American herb, a perennial which attains a height of two to three feet, is also known in its land of origin as 'Oswego Tea' and 'Bee Balm'. It is an aromatic swamp plant, and an infusion of its young leaves used to be a common beverage in many parts of the U.S.A. It yields an oil similar in composition to the Thymol derived from its relative, *Monarda punctata* (American Horsemint), although the secretion is less strong in *M. didyma*.

As an ornamental garden subject it is valuable, preferring a moist, light soil in semi-shade. It may very easily be propagated by division of the creeping root-stocks in spring, or by cuttings taken in May and rooted in a shady corner, like other mints. There are also various named modern hybrids in rose, lavender, purple, white and deep crimson, and another, taller, American variety, *M. fistulosa*, known as Wild Bergamot in north America. This has purple flowers.

The oil of Bergamot used in Eau-de-Cologne is not derived from the Monardas but from the Bergamot Orange.

BETONY, WOOD
Betonica officinalis (syn. *Stachys betonica*)   [*p.* 54

With the possible exception of Vervain, no herb was more valued in olden times than Betony. The Saxons believed that it cured every ill, including nightmares. But it was efficacious only if gathered and prepared without the use of iron implements. In dried and powdered form this herb was for centuries a nostrum for headaches, and it served also to prevent the access of evil spirits or witches to the user's dwelling. From belief in such miraculous powers the Italian peasant evolved the proverb 'Sell your coat and buy Betony'. The ancient Greeks also extolled its virtues, and it was prized in Spain.

According to Pliny the name Betony was at first *Bettonica*, from the *Bettones*—a people of Spain. Later authors tried to discredit this theory and ascribe the name to the primitive Celtic form of *bew* (head) and *ton* (good), because the herb was specially valued as a cure for headaches. Erasmus wrote that amulets made of Betony sanctified those who wore them, being an efficacious means of 'driving away devils and despair'.

This plant comes up year after year from a thick, woody root. The slender stems are square and furrowed, bearing at wide intervals a few pairs of oblong leaves without stalks. Lower leaves spring from the root and are heart-shaped on long stalks, but as Betony commonly grows wild in the hedgerows these leaves are often unnoticed in the other herbage. Betony grows to about eighteen inches high, and has crimson-mauve two-lipped flowers in July and August. These are mostly borne at the summit of the stem, arranged in whorls to form a short spike. Then there is a break, with a piece of stem bearing only one or two pairs of leaves, and below them more flowers. This interrupted spike differentiates Wood Betony from all other labiate plants.

Herb-fanciers today often brew a pleasant tea from Betony by pouring one pint of boiling water on one ounce of the dried and powdered herb. An older method consists of simmering two ounces of flowers and leaves in two quarts of water until the liquid has been reduced to one and a half pints. We are told that Betony Tea has somewhat the taste of Indian tea, and all the good qualities of that beverage without the bad. But one of the old writers gave warning that if fresh, not dried, Betony were used it would have an intoxicating effect. At one time a yellow dye was obtained from this plant. It was formerly cultivated in monastic herb gardens and in the physic gardens of apothecaries, and a common vernacular name was Bishopswort.

Some gardeners are now taking an interest in our native Betony, as an ornamental plant; other species cultivated are *S. coccinea*, a scarlet-flowered plant from Mexico; *S. corsica*, pink and cream; *S. lanata*, the grey woolly 'Lamb's Ear', and *S. sieboldii*, the pink-flowered 'Chinese Artichoke' which has white edible roots.

BISTORT   *Polygonum bistorta*

The Latin name of this species of Polygonum, *bis*, twice, *torta*,

BISTORT

38

twisted, refers to the twice-twisted (or S-shaped) character of the root stock. An old country name is Twice-Writhen. Other vernacular names are Osterick, Snake Weed, Adderwort and Easter Mangiant. The last word, a corruption of *mangeant*, relates to the traditional Easter pudding made in Lancashire and Cumberland from the young leaves of Bistort and Nettle, chopped up with barley and oatmeal and boiled in a bag; eggs and butter were beaten in before the pudding came to the table.

A native of northern Europe and Siberia, Japan, and western Asia up to the Himalayas, Bistort was formerly cultivated in Britain as a wound-herb and as a green vegetable. It was sometimes served as a dish called Patience Dock or Passions, although no aphrodisiac qualities have been ascribed to the plant.

The curiously twisted root, externally black with a red core, contains tannic and gallic acids in considerable amounts, making it one of the strongest vegetable astringents known. It is prized for medicinal use and for tanning leather. The root also contains much starch, and in times of famine it was dried and ground up for use as flour. Some writers say that starving people found it particularly beneficial because its astringent properties shrank the intestines, so reducing the quantity of food required.

Bistort may easily be propagated by root division in early autumn or spring. With its large oval leaves, bluish green above and grey below, and its tall, erect, pink flower-spike, this is a good ornamental plant for the moist part of a rockery or a shady border, provided that it is kept within bounds. The roots creep, and in low-lying agricultural land the plant can become a pest.

BORAGE   *Borago officinalis*

Borage has at various times and in different places been known as Ox-tongue, Cool Tankard, Bee-Bread and Llanwenlys (Herb of Gladness). According to Dioscorides and Pliny, Borage was the famed Nepenthe of Homer; wine in which it had been steeped brought absolute forgetfulness to those who drank of it. Presumably the quantity used was important, for John Evelyn, writing in the seventeenth century, said that sprigs of Borage 'would revive the hypochondriac and cheer the hard student'. No student would find absolute forgetfulness cheering, unless he had first failed his examinations. The Latin tag

Ego Borago gaudia semper ago—I, Borage, bring always courage—has been quoted for over a thousand years. Flowers of this brave herb were traditionally floated in the wine of stirrup-cups given to Crusaders before their departure.

The whole plant is rough, with stiff white hairs; it has succulent hollow stems, much branched, and large oval alternate leaves. The flowers are brilliant blue stars with black cone-shaped anthers. Many of the finest English embroideries have depicted the Borage flower with its distinctive black 'beauty spot', and it may be seen in the flowery background of the famous French mediaeval woven tapestry, *The Lady with a Unicorn*.

This is an annual—or maybe biennial—plant, growing at times to three feet in height. It self-sows copiously, and will often form a strong rosette in autumn which over-winters to put forth flower stems early in the following summer. It is seen to the best advantage when placed on a wall, for its flowers hang their heads and their charm can only be appreciated to the full from below.

The fresh young leaves have a subtle flavour of cucumber, and are delicious in salads. The flowers were at one time candied for use in confectionery, and added to claret and similar 'cups'. In France a *tisane* made by pouring a pint of boiling water on one ounce of fresh leaves is used for alleviation of fevers and pulmonary complaints.

Borage is an excellent bee-plant. An uncommon white form of it may be seen in the Oxford Botanic Gardens. There is also a perennial species, *B. laxiflora*, a blue-flowered native of Corsica, about twelve inches high.

CALAMINT   *Calamintha officinalis* (syn. *C. ascendens*)

This native herb belongs to a genus closely related to the Thymes and to Catnep (Catmint) and Ground Ivy. It is an erect bushy perennial, nine to twelve inches high, with square stems, downy, and inconspicuous mauve labiate flowers in late summer. It is sometimes found growing wild on chalk downs and along waysides. The foliage has a sweet, camphoraceous smell. A cordial tea, made by infusing one ounce of dried leaves and tops in a pint of boiling water, was formerly in vogue as a remedy for flatulence.

The lesser Calamint (*C. nepeta*) has a stronger odour of mint, resembling that of Pennyroyal. It has smaller and greyer leaves and is found wild in U.K. in East Anglia. Both species were used alike in herbal medicine, under the generic name of Calamint. Vernacular names for these plants include Mountain Balm, Basil Thyme and Mountain Mint; but the true Basil Thyme (*Acinos arvensis*) is a prostrate annual plant.

The common Calamint is a pleasing subject for odd corners in paved or herb gardens, unremarkable in appearance but pleasantly aromatic and tolerant of passing feet. If kept cut down it will persevere in throwing flower stems, and by late September or October the delicate spotted mauve flower spikes are welcome when much else has faded. It self-sows freely, or may be easily propagated by root division. Some gardeners prefer to raise the more showy *C. grandiflora*.

CAMPHOR PLANT *Balsamita vulgaris*

The true Camphor is a white crystalline substance obtained from the Asian tree *Cinnamomum camphora*, but the so-called Camphor plant, a hardy herbaceous perenial three to four feet in height, has a pungent camphoraceous odour and its dried leaves serve to deter moths in clothing and blankets. The tall stems with greyish foliage and white 'daisy' flowers supply valuable height at the back of a herb border. It is very easily propagated by division of the root-stock in autumn or spring.

CAPER SPURGE see SPURGE

CARAWAY *Carum carvi*

A feathery biennial plant, somewhat like a small Fennel, two feet high when in flower, a native of central Europe, Asia and north Africa. This plant is best grown from seed sown outside in light, warm soil in April, spaced nine inches apart when the seedlings are large enough to thin. These will flower in the following May and ripen their fruits in July, given good weather. The umbels do not all ripen simultaneously, so it is wise to cut off the stems at ground level directly ripening begins, and hang them up in a warm, ventilated place with sheets of paper or polythene spread to catch the seeds as they fall.

Caraway has long been esteemed for its medicinal (carminative) properties, but today is largely cultivated for flavouring confectionery, liqueurs and cakes. Culinary uses are believed to have originated in Arabia; the fruits have for centuries been known to the Arabs as *Karawya*. The Greek physician Dioscorides recommended oil of Caraway for anaemic girls, and in Shakespeare's day Caraway was a favourite 'relish' to be put in baked fruits, bread, cakes and comfits.

In *Henry IV* Squire Shallow invites Falstaff to 'a pippin with a dish of caraways'. The custom of serving roasted apples with an accompanying dish of Caraways was maintained at Trinity College, Cambridge and at some of the London Livery Companies' dinners until the last war. The liqueur known as Kummel is flavoured with Caraway.

To many people over fifty in Britain this flavour is a vivid reminder of Victorian and Edwardian tea-tables, with their fine china, plates of thin bread-and-butter, and 'Seed-cake'. As a child I detested the flavour but because the Highland grandmother who made and offered me this delicacy was greatly loved, I did not disclose my aversion. Caraway is now nostalgically prized for the memories it evokes, although its taste remains unpalatable to me.

There used to be a curious folk-belief about the plant, which was supposed to prevent the theft of any article that contained its fruits, and even to have the power of holding captive any would-be thief until the rightful owner arrived. In like manner it retained love, prevented fickleness, and was an essential ingredient of love-potions. Country people also used Caraway to prevent their domestic fowls and pigeons from straying; some say that to this day pigeon-fanciers who put Caraway dough in their lofts never lose a bird.

Housewives who dislike the smell of cooking cabbage would do well to put a teaspoonful of Caraway into a muslin bag and boil it with the vegetable. It improves the flavour, and aids digestion, too.

CARNATION, CLOVE *Dianthus caryophyllus*

The Clove Gilly-flower was beloved in Chaucer's day (he called it *Gilofre*), and in the sixteenth and seventeenth centuries it vied with the rose for first place in the hearts of men and women. Although not indigenous like the Cheddar Pink (*D. gratianopolitanus*, syn. *D. caesius*), or the Maiden Pink (*D. deltoides*), or Cottage Pink (*D. plumarius*), it was so much planted everywhere in these islands that it ran wild from the reign of Edward III until the Civil War, when it seems to have suffered an eclipse. Afterwards the cultivation of carnations passed into Dutch hands, and thence the plant returned later to Britain —although, it is thought, in a less hardy form.

The name 'Carnation' is supposed to derive from 'coronation', because this was the flower traditionally used to make floral wreaths for great festivals. Queen Henrietta Maria was particularly fond of the Clove Carnation, and nearly fifty varieties were listed as being in cultivation during the reign of Charles I.

A famous grower of carnations in the days of Elizabeth I was Master Ralph Tuggie of Westminster, described by Parkinson as 'the most industrious preserver of nature's beauties'. Among the varieties propagated by Tuggie were the enchantingly named 'Ruffling Robin', 'Fair Maid of Kent', 'Lustie Gallant' and 'Master Tuggie's Princesse'; also one lengthily called 'John Witte, his great tawny Gillow Flower'.

In the seventeenth century another great gardener, William Lawson the Yorkshireman, wrote about his 'July Flowers, commonly called Gilly-flowers or Clove July-flowers', that they 'have the name of cloves of their scent. . . . I have of them nine or ten severall colours, and divers of them as bigge as Roses: of all flowres (save the Damask Rose) they are the most pleasant to sight and smell.'

The petals of Clove Gilly-flowers were used, in Tudor and Stuart days, in even more ways than were rose petals. Wine was flavoured with them; from this habit sprang the popular name 'Sops-in-wine'. Clove Gilly-flowers were also candied, pickled, made into conserves, and served up in a sauce to eat with mutton.

This plant was employed by the physicians, too. William Coles, writing in 1657, said that a conserve made from these flowers and sugar was

exceeding cordiall, and wonderfully above measure doth comfort the heart, being eaten now and then, which is very good also against the plague or any kind of venome. It is likewise good not only for the falling sickness, palsy, giddiness and cramp, but for the pestilence . . . The syrup of the said flowers strengthens the heart, refresheth the vital spirits and is a good cordiall in feavers, expelling the poyson and fury of the disease, and greatly comforting those that are sick of any disease where the heart hath need of relief. Moreover, the leaves of the flowers put into a glasse of vinegar, and set in the sunne for certain dayes, do make a pleasant vinegar and very good to revive one of a swoon, the nostrils and temples being washed therewith.

In her book *The Scented Garden*, the late Eleanour Sinclair Rohde, describing the contents of her great-aunt Lucilla's store-cupboard, gives details of how both rose and carnation petals were preserved by

coating them on both sides with white of egg well beaten. It was a fascinating process, done with a tiny brush like a paint brush. Then the petals were spread out on very large dishes, and castor sugar carefully and evenly shaken over them. Then they were turned over, and the other side sugared. My great-aunt invariably dried these petals in the sun, and perhaps that is why they were so sweet. When dry they were beautifully crisp, and put away in layers with paper between each layer in airtight boxes. And such syrups! Elder syrup, which was very pungent and luscious, mint syrup (quince juice strongly flavoured with mint), and clove carnation syrup, the best of all. [Recipe on page 173.]

What a picture of horticultural opulence these quotations conjure up! Who, in these days, has enough clove carnations to spare the blooms in sufficient quantity to make *syrup*? Some of the old herbal recipes are floral counterparts of Mrs Beeton's cookery instructions. Instead of 'Take a quart of cream and two dozen eggs', we are told to 'Take a thousand Damask Roses'.

A modern version of the old-fashioned dark red clove carnation has been brought into cultivation by herb-growers, although it is unlikely that those we see today have the full strength and savour of the originals. Even so, they are to me the greatest glory of the summer herb garden. Perhaps this is in part due to a romantic association with my seventeenth year, when I discovered that poetry was capable of meaning more to me than the endless mulling over *Lycidas* and *The Ancient Mariner* at school, with examinations in mind, had suggested. Two slim volumes entitled *Poems of To-Day*, issued by Sidgwick and Jackson for the English Association, were bought in the mid-twenties—on a sudden impulse—with money intended for another purpose. They did me a great service.

A feeling for plants, nurtured since early childhood by a green-fingered grandmother of the MacLeod clan, ensured that my first choice of a poem to be learnt by heart—for love and not marks—was one called *The Deserted Garden*. It had been composed in 1917 by a very young man, Alasdair Alpin MacGregor, on the Western Front during a lull before the third battle of Ypres. In a recent book he has described how his poem came to be written.* It pictures the peaceful garden where his beloved used to linger:

> Each summer brings the drowsy bees that doze
> Among the lazy flowers till you return:
> Around your arbour the clematis grows,
> And red carnations burn.

Those carnations burned themselves into my imagination; their home became *my* garden, to which I constantly repaired, with tremulous hopes of meeting there the young soldier who had so sweetly written of it in the midst of hideous carnage. Alas, I never did. In any case he had doubtless changed with the passing years. Yet the magic of his lines persisted:

> The jessamine that twinkles in the light,
> Still watches idly through the window-pane:
> While scented stocks do weave their spell each night,
> In case you come again.

Years later I discovered that the author of my 'special' poem had become well known as a writer of books and articles, largely about his native Scotland. They were about my lamented grandmother's Scotland, too—for her Western Isle he knew well. The borrowed, the begged and the bought volumes were all loved by me, and mingled their essences with *The Deserted Garden*.

Recently, after forty years of faithful readership, I came into personal contact with my poet: an oddly slanted meeting, for was not he counted among my oldest friends, yet I to him a total stranger? But the unexpected happened. Instead of casting on me the *cold eye* of Yeats's horseman, he very soon remarked in surprise to his wife, Patricia, that he seemed to have known me all his life. Not only was he unaware of my youthful attachment, but, as a man of striking honesty, he seemed incapable of uttering false or careless words in order to be pleasant. Had those carnations, in some mysterious fashion known only to themselves, initiated a mutual kinship between two characters, one of whom was not consciously aware of the other until forty years afterwards? The clove carnations in my garden are now regarded with even greater respect than of old—and with considerable awe.

As a tailpiece to my little anecdote it may be worth recording that

* *The Golden Lamp* by Alasdair Alpin MacGregor. Michael Joseph, 1964.

the authorities are at variance in regard to the 'meaning' of this genus in the old Language of Flowers. Some say that the Dianthus symbolizes 'the heart's pure affection'; others, 'faithfulness'; the red carnation is singled out by one as 'an emblem of talent'.

CATMINT   *Nepeta cataria*

Catmint (or Catnep) is a native British plant belonging to the family *Labiatae*, a relative of the Mints, Dead-nettles and Ground Ivy. The true native Catnep, unlike the usual garden Catmints, will grow up to three feet in height and has square stems, heart-shaped toothed leaves, pale pinky-white flowers with red spots, borne in dense whorls and forming spikes. The whole plant is covered in downy hairs which give it a grey look. It is aromatic when crushed, and the odour has a powerful attraction for cats, who will roll on and destroy any plant which has been bruised sufficiently to release the scent. It is detested by rats.

Before the introduction of tea from China and India, country people in Britain infused a tea from dried flowering tops of Catmint. This was made in America too, for in that old children's classic *The Wide Wide World* by Elizabeth Wetherall, little Ellen Montgomery brewed some Catmint tea for Miss Fortune. The root when chewed has the alarming effect of making gentle natures quarrelsome. There is a legend that a certain executioner could never bring himself to hang a man until he had eaten Catnep root.

Cultivation is easy, for this plant will thrive in almost any soil and it is not thirsty like other Mints. It may be raised from seed, sown where the plants are to grow, or propagated by root division in spring. The species preferred by gardeners are *Nepeta mussinii*, nine to twelve inches high, and *N. grandiflora*, with flowers of deeper mauve. There are also hybrids with such names as 'Six-Hills Giant'. All the 'garden' varieties have flowers of lavender or mauve colour.

In the fifteenth century Catmint was used as a culinary herb. Fresh leaves were used for rubbing meats before cooking, and also sprinkled in mixed green salads. It is an excellent bee-plant.

CHAMOMILE
Chamaemelum nobile (syn. *Anthemis nobilis*)

The name of Chamomile is applied to several different plants, sometimes with the prefix Roman (*C. nobile*), Wild (*Matricaria recutita*), or Scotch, which is a single form of *C. nobile*. Then there is Yellow Chamomile (*A. tinctoria*), which used to be employed as a hair-dye, and was known as Dyer's or Ox-eye Chamomile. A less attractive plant, *A. cotula*, is known as Stinking Chamomile.

The annual German Chamomile has single white 'daisy' flowers, lacy foliage and the best apple scent, but it grows to three feet in height and is unsuitable for making a Chamomile lawn. The common perennial species, *C. nobile*, is of a short, spreading habit and, as it improves with a reasonable amount of treading down it makes a good lawn. This plant has double cream-coloured 'daisies', but these should be kept sheared if a good turfy sward is required. It gives out the true Chamomile fragrance, described by Margaret Brownlow as 'a mixture of apples and bananas'.

The Greeks named it Ground-apple—*chamai*, on the ground, and *melon*, apple. Today the Spaniards call it Manzanilla, signifying Little Apple, and their sherry of that name is flavoured with this herb. It has been valued throughout recorded history. The Egyptians reverenced it, and the old European herbals agree that it is too well known to need description. An ancient Saxon document contains these lines: *Have a mind thou Maythen, What thou accomplishedst At Alderford. That never for flying ill Fatally fell man Since we to him Maythen For medicine mixed up.* Maythen was the Saxon name for Chamomile. This was one of the Nine Sacred Herbs.

Medicinal virtues are centred in the flower heads, and although both single and double forms of *C. nobile* were used, the British Pharmacopoeia directed that 'official' dried Chamomile flowers should be those of the cultivated double variety, and these were variously prepared as a decoction, an infusion, an extract and an oil. The infusion, Chamomile tea, made by pouring one pint of boiling water on an ounce of the flowers, is an old remedy for hysteria. The effect is sedative but quite harmless. Bags of Chamomile flowers, steeped in boiling water, were formerly used as fomentations, and considered particularly good for facial swellings caused by abscesses.

In the Middle Ages this plant was commonly used as a strewing-herb. Its flowers are put into hair shampoo to improve the colour of blonde tresses. A strange old belief states that Chamomile is a 'herb doctor', with power to revive any sickly plant near which it is set.

Propagation is by seed or by small plantlets detached from the mother plant; this may be done in the autumn in sheltered places, but elsewhere it is better left until spring. To make a lawn, levelling and firming is carried out as for a grass one, and the plantlets are set 6 in. apart in each direction. Good compost dibbled in the holes is advised. Within two months the plants should have joined up, and a first shearing is indicated. The mower must not be used until the roots are firmly established. A lawn of Chamomile should not be allowed to flower.

The Treneague Chamomile Farm in Cornwall has produced what is described as 'a new flower-less Chamomile ground-cover', but I have not as yet tried this plant.

CHERVIL *Anthriscus cerefolium*

This lacy herb is a half-hardy annual, about fifteen inches high, called *Cerfeuil* in France where it is very popular as a culinary herb. It is a native of south-east Europe and western Asia. It bears umbels of small white flowers (if allowed) and has the flavour of a mild, subtle Parsley. It is used as a flavouring and a garnish, is more liked when fresh than when dried, and the French include it in their favourite blend of *fines herbes* (p. 176).

Seeds will germinate readily; but the seedlings are very difficult to transplant. Chervil grows best in medium rich soil where some moisture is retained in hot weather, and it does well in light shade.

It is believed to have been introduced into Britain by the Romans, and is certainly a very old inhabitant of the British herb garden. There is also a bulbous-rooted relative, known as turnip-rooted Chervil (*Chaerophyllum bulbosum*), which John Evelyn recommended 'for aged persons'. The roots, washed but not scraped, were boiled for several hours and allowed to get cold before being eaten.

CHICORY *Cichorium intybus*

This plant is a native of Britain, commonly called Wild Chicory or Succory. It may easily be identified by twiggy stems, two to three feet high, along which are laid in the axils of the leaves many bright blue flowers about the size and shape of Dandelions. The Chicory blossoms look as though they have been 'stuck on' to the stems, which are so exceedingly tough that most children who run to pick the attractive flowers find it an impossible task for unaided fingers. By early afternoon the temptation has departed, for every bloom closes—however sunny the day. Linnaeus used Chicory in his floral clock at Upsala because of its regularity in opening at 5 a.m. and closing at 10 a.m. in that latitude. In Britain it wakes between 6 a.m. and 7 a.m. and sleeps soon after noon.

The specific name, *intybus*, is a modification of an Eastern word for this plant, *Hendibeh*. The Endive, which is related to Chicory, derives its name from the same word. Succory may have been derived from the Latin *succurrere* (to run under), because of the depth to which the plant's roots penetrate. The Romans ate Succory as a vegetable and in fresh green salads, and its uses are mentioned by Horace, Virgil, Ovid and Pliny.

On the continent of Europe Chicory is cultivated as a vegetable and salad herb and also for animal fodder, while the root is roasted and ground for blending with coffee. In France and Belgium the foliage is forced and blanched for use as a winter salad under the name of *Barbe de Capucin*. A fine strain for that purpose, known as Witloof, is cultivated in Belgium; for coffee-blending the Magdeburg or Brunswick types are preferred.

Chicory is a hardy perennial and will thrive in most soils. Plants from seed sown in April or May are thinned to 6 or 8 in. apart in June or July, and for blanching they are lifted in October. After exposure to the air for a week or two they are planted in deep pots or boxes of sand, covered to exclude light, and put in a warm place. The new leaves grow elongated and tender, almost white in colour. This forced foliage is well-nigh free from the bitter taste found in open-air plants.

A decoction made with one ounce of root to one pint of boiling water has been found effective in jaundice, gout and rheumatic afflictions. Tusser in 1573 considered Succory and Endive to be useful remedies for the ague. The flowers, together with violets, were employed to make a confection called Violet Plates in the time of Charles II; and the leaves were at one time gathered for use as a blue dye.

The plant known as Swine's Chicory or Lamb's Succory (*Arnoseris pusilla*) is a weed of the cornfields with small yellow flowers.

CHIVES   *Allium schoenoprasum*   [*p.* 54

This hardy perennial bulbous plant, with a delicate suggestion of
onion in taste and smell, was formerly known as Chibbole or Chibbal.
The name Rocambole is sometimes given to this Allium, but more
properly belongs to *A. scorodoprasum.*

CHIVES AND CHAMOMILE

The Chive has a silvery-pink flower rather like that of Thrift, and grass-like foliage, six to ten inches long or more, which grows quickly and may be cut all through the summer to provide a relish for salads, omelettes, herb cheeses and the like. Some nurseries supply a plant described as 'Giant Chives', fifteen to eighteen inches high, with mauve flowers. Chefs often rub steaks with chives before grilling.

This plant makes a good edging for a herb border. It may be propagated by seed, but is usually increased by division of the clumps of little bulbs in spring or autumn, or in late June after flowering. For culinary purposes it is best to remove all the flower buds, but as the blossom provides an attractive addition to the garden a compromise is often made: alternate plants are kept free of buds for use in the kitchen, and their neighbours are left to bloom, being trimmed before seeding. Chives will do quite well in pots, boxes and tubs. Some recipes will be found on pages 173 and 176.

CINQUEFOIL *Potentilla reptans*

This herb, known also as Five Fingers, Sunk Field and Synkefoyle, is a creeping plant with yellow flowers, and is sometimes confused with Silverweed. The palmate leaves of the Cinquefoil are usually divided into five 'fingers' (occasionally six or even seven), and are not silvery on the underside. The Silverweed has pinnate leaves, with leaflets alternately large and small, and is silver on the underside or on both sides. The Potentillas were known to Dioscorides, and named by Theophrastus for their potent value in curing fevers. Today herbalists use the herb (mostly in dried form) for its astringent properties, in gargles, mouthwashes, and to arrest haemorrhages from the nose and other organs of the body.

Of old this plant had a reputation as a love-divining herb, and was used in the casting of spells; witches put it into their secret ointment and fishermen used it in bait. This consisted of corn boiled in Thyme and Marjoram water, mixed with nettles, Cinquefoil and the juice of the Houseleek. When placed in the nets it was thought to ensure heavier catches.

The outer bark of the root, taken up in April and dried, has been used as a remedy for diarrhoea and haemorrhages. A decoction made by boiling 1½ ounces of root in a quart of water until the liquid is reduced to one pint, or an infusion of one ounce of the dried leafy

tops, steeped for ten or fifteen minutes in a pint of water, are both
suggested in old herbals.

CLOVE-TREE
Syzygium aromaticum (syn. *Eugenia aromatica*)

A native of the Southern Philippines and Molucca Island, this is a
small evergreen tree whose trunk soon divides into large branches
covered with smooth grey bark. The leaves are long, lanceolate and
bright green. The flowers grow in bunches at the ends of branches,
and it is the embryo seeds which are beaten from the tree and dried to
form the most valuable spice of commerce. The various species of
Eugenia are known as 'fruiting Myrtles'.

Cloves were introduced into Europe many centuries ago. The finest
come from Molucca, but quantities are now exported from the East
and West Indies, Mauritius and Brazil. In the Peradeniya Botanic
Gardens at Kandy in Ceylon I have seen the Clove or 'Kara-bu-Neti'
growing as tall as thirty feet.

Medicinally, the volatile oil of this tree is the most stimulating of all
aromatics. It is prescribed in powder form for infusion for nausea,
flatulence, indigestion and dyspepsia, chiefly to assist the action of
other medicines.

In cookery, the Clove has for ages been used in apple-pie and
roasted apples, and the ground spice still goes into many a spiced cake
and gingerbread. Recipes for making Clove Oranges and Pomanders
are given on pages 166–7.

COLTSFOOT   *Tussilago farfara*   [*p.* 151

Through the ages this common plant of our countryside, which throws
its yellow flowers in March before any leaves appear, has been valued
as a remedy for coughs and all respiratory troubles. The botanic name
Tussilago is derived from the Latin *tussis*, a cough. The bright golden
flowers are sometimes mistaken for those of the Dandelion, and the
silky fluff which follows after petals fall is occasionally confused with
the 'clocks' produced by *Taraxacum*. Andrew Young describes it:

> When Coltsfoot withers and begins to wear
> Long silver locks instead of golden hair, . . .

This fine silky material was at one time collected by Highland women for stuffing mattresses and pillows, a practice long since relinquished by mankind, although goldfinches continue to line their nests with Coltsfoot down.

The leaves are fairly large, up to four inches in diameter, and hoof-shaped. Their appearance obviously gave rise to many a vernacular name, including Hallfoot, Horsehoof, Ass's Foot, Foalswort, Field-hove, Bullsfoot and Donnhove.* Another popular name of ancient origin, *Filius-ante-patrem*, The-son-before-the-father, refers to this plant's habit of flowering before producing foliage.

Medicinally, both flower-stalk and leaf were most commonly used, although the small white roots have also some value. All parts of the plant contain mucilage, a little tannin, and traces of a bitter amorphous glucoside. The flowers contain also Phytosterol and Faradial. The action of this herb is demulcent, expectorant and tonic; hence its reputation as a cough cure. Pliny advocated the inhaling of smoke from dried Coltsfoot leaves to relieve a cough, with a sip of wine between each inhalation. A herbal tobacco made in Britain is composed largely of Coltsfoot leaves, together with some Betony, Rosemary, Thyme, Chamomile, Lavender, Eyebright and Buckbean. As a smoking mixture this relieved asthma and other troubles, without the harmful effects of tobacco.

A decoction of Coltsfoot leaves—one ounce in a quart of water, boiled down to make one pint of liquid, then sweetened with honey or liquorice—is taken in doses of a wineglassful to ameliorate stubborn coughs and asthma. Coltsfoot tea, made by infusing one ounce of leaves in a pint of boiling water, is also helpful, and a manufactured product known as Coltsfoot Rock was popular at one time. The British Pharmacopoeia for many years listed Syrup of Coltsfoot, made from the flowering stalks, for use in chronic bronchitis. In Paris the flower of this plant was traditionally painted as a trade sign upon the doorpost of pharmacies.

Close relations of the Coltsfoot—Butterbur and Winter Helio-trope—are also used in herbal medicines. The large leaves of the Butterbur were much used by dairymaids for wrapping up pats of butter before the days of greaseproof paper or polythene, and this practice helped to provide the country name for a very prolific and common wild plant.

* Derived from *Donn*, an old word for horse—hence donkey, a little horse.

COMFREY *Symphytum officinale*

This tall, rough, perennial plant with its one-sided clusters of creamy yellow or purplish flowers, which blooms on river banks and in many other fairly damp places throughout the English summer, was for centuries a favourite wound-herb. Its vernacular names, Knitbone, Knitback, Consound, Bruisewort and Boneset, indicate some of the uses to which our forefathers put it. Comfrey is a member of the Borage and Forget-me-not tribe (*Boraginaceae*).

In her book *A Modern Herbal* Mrs Grieve quotes a Wiltshire correspondent as saying that the valleys around Salisbury contain Comfrey with rosy-pink flowers, and I have seen in the Martock–Lambrook district of Somerset some Comfrey with rich cherry-coloured blossom. It would seem to be a variable plant in this respect.

Another species, *S. tuberosum*, which is smaller and less branching, with creamy flowers always, is commoner in northern England and Scotland. A tall variety with flowers mostly blue, *S. asperrimum* (syn. *S. asperum*), often called Prickly Comfrey, was introduced into the United Kingdom in the nineteenth century as a fodder plant, and has naturalized in places. A hybrid, *S. peregrinum*, and the so-called 'Blue' Comfrey, *S. caucasicum*, are also grown in Britain and are sometimes seen in the wild as garden escapes. There is a country belief that the blue-flowered Comfreys helped to prevent foot-and-mouth disease, as well as acting as a cure for it before wholesale slaughter was enforced by law.

The European *S. grandiflora*—a low-growing spreader—is now gaining favour as a ground-cover plant. It has large clusters of creamy flowers, coral-red in bud, and I have found it naturalized in a Cotswold hedgerow. It may be seen in the famous Gloucestershire garden, Hidcote.

Country people used to cultivate Comfrey (*S. officinale*) in every cottage garden because of its enormous reputation as a wound healer. In the days of sword and spear, of scythe, sickle and ploughing on foot, many must have been the ugly wounds suffered by the flesh of man from metal blade and ploughshare, and most people had to doctor themselves. They cured ulcers with this herb, too, and used it to assist the mending of fractures.

The botanical name *Symphytum* is derived from the Greek *symphyo*, I grow together; and Comfrey is a corruption of *confirma*, an allusion

HYSSOP   LIQUORICE   FLAX

CHIVES   GARDEN SORREL   WOOD BETONY

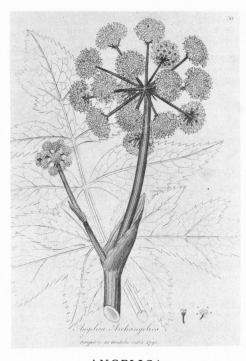

ANGELICA

GREAT MULLEIN

COW PARSLEY

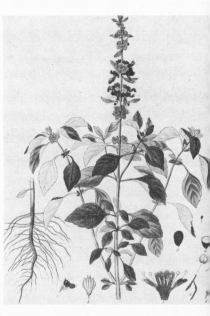

BASIL

to the uniting of broken bones which the herb expedites. The Greek physician Dioscorides is said to have named this plant nearly two thousand years ago. Herb lore gained all kinds of accretions, and one of these in the Middle Ages was to the effect that cream-flowered plants should be used in the treatment of women and purple ones for men, but the rosy ones are not mentioned. Leaving aside such quaint fancies, it is certain that the Comfreys possess valuable medicinal and nutritive properties.

Both the root and leaves are used medicinally. The root contains an abundance of mucilage, some allantoin, a little tannic acid and starch. It has been prescribed, like Marshmallow, for intestinal troubles—a gentle remedy for diarrhoea and dysentery. A decoction, made by boiling half an ounce or an ounce of crushed root in a quart of water may be taken in wineglassful doses frequently. This appears to be a very safe herb for the amateur to employ.

Externally, Comfrey leaves were applied as fomentations for sprains, swellings and bruises, and as a poultice for severe cuts, boils, abscesses and gangrenous ulcers. By reduction of swelling in the vicinity of fractures this herb is believed to foster union: hence the name Knitbone. Allantoin, which it contains, is said in orthodox pharmacopoeias to promote the formation of epithelial tissues. The plant is rich in vitamin C. For everyday use the leaves were traditionally infused, one ounce to a pint of boiling water, to make a 'tea'. This is more palatable with lemon added. In a modern liquefier the fresh leaves are quickly turned into valuable juice—which must be used when newly made.

Comfrey thrives in almost any soil, but it likes moisture and some shade. The brittle roots are very difficult to dig up entire, and the smallest segment will take hold and grow, so that if the gardener wishes to eradicate any species of this plant he is advised to use sodium chlorate weedkiller.

In a world of expanding populations, with food shortage already a grim reality in some continents, the long-term research being undertaken by the Henry Doubleday Research Association in Essex into the use of Comfrey as a crop for fodder, human food, medicinal and other purposes—described by the Director, Lawrence D. Hills, as 'a vegetable jet engine at Group-Captain Whittle stage'—may have far-reaching consequences for mankind.

CORIANDER *Coriandrum sativum*

This umbelliferous annual, one to three feet high, is a native of southern Europe. It may be found growing wild in some parts of England, having escaped from cultivation. It is one of the many herbs brought to Britain by the Romans, and has been cultivated and used by mankind since very ancient times. Hippocrates and other Greek physicians believed in its medicinal virtues.

The name *Coriandrum*, given to the plant by Pliny, is derived from *Koris*, a bug, in reference to the foetid smell of the foliage. This grows particularly strong just before the seeds ripen in August, and is succeeded by a pleasant aroma when the herb is ready to harvest. The chief uses for Coriander 'seed'—botanically it is a fruit—in Britain are as a flavouring for gin and other alcoholic beverages, and in medicine to disguise the taste of active purgatives and to correct their griping tendencies. In the East, Coriander is an important ingredient of curry, and in northern Europe it is used in bread-making.

The Coriander fruit contains about 1 per cent of volatile oil, which is the active ingredient, and it yields also malic acid, tannin and some fatty matter. The powdered fruit, fluid extract and oil are all put to medicinal use. At one time Coriander water was popular as a carminative for windy colic. If used to excess the seeds may act as a narcotic.

In Pliny's day the best Coriander came from Egypt, and the plant grows best in a warm, light, dry soil. It is usually sown in mild April or May weather, in shallow drills about half an inch deep and nine inches apart. Germination is slow. When the disagreeable odour becomes pleasantly aromatic the plants are harvested and dried, after which the fruit is threshed out. It is light brown in colour, finely ribbed and globular. In some countries the parsley-like leaves are put into soup. According to an ancient Chinese belief this plant confers immortality on those who consume it. At various times and in widely separated places it has been used to cure erysipelas and to tone down over-florid complexions. Many eastern recipes advocate it as a complexion bleach. It is also regarded as an aphrodisiac.

A recipe for curry powder containing Coriander will be found on page 173.

COW PARSLEY *Anthriscus sylvestris* [*p.* 55

In Europe this is not generally regarded as a herb at all, but it produces a brilliant yellow dye and I am adopting the American custom and including such plants as 'dye-herbs'. The practice of cultivating dye-plants in herb gardens seems to have grown up among the early settlers in New England, and when I was asked by the American Museum in Britain to prepare a herb shop and exhibit alongside a 'colonial' herb garden, it seemed clear that a collection of dye-plants and of samples of vegetable-dyed wool must be included. In addition to the plants commonly used in Britain, the early Americans employed for home-dyeing the Pokeberry or Poke Root (*Phytolacca americana*), Bloodroot (*Sanguinaria canadensis*), Safflower (*Carthamus tinctorius*), Broomsedge (*Andropogon virginicus*), Bayberry (*Myrica cerifera*, syn. *M. pensylvanica*) and Butternut (*Juglans cinerea*).

In 1954 the Garden Club of America prepared an early colonist's 'keeping room', where culinary, medicinal and dye-herbs were shown, as part of the New York Flower Show. Material for producing more than fifty different colours were present. In such a room the mistress of the house would cook, churn, wash, iron, pound herbs, dye yarn, spin and weave, make candles and soap, and very often take meals with her family as well. Her British counterpart at that time had many similar duties, but as a rule dye-plants were grown and prepared by commercial groups and the dyeing was done professionally also, except in the Celtic lands of Wales, Cornwall and the Highlands of Scotland, where wild plants such as heather, bracken, Bog Myrtle and the lichen Crotal were used.

The flowering tops and foliage of Cow Parsley yield a brilliant yellow dye, and, as this plant fills so many hedgerows with its creamy froth of small flowers in late spring, it may be picked in quantity without doing harm to the countryside. The freshly gathered flowers and foliage are tied up in a muslin bag—not too tightly packed—and the bag is plunged into cold water in the dye-bath, together with a little ammonia to extract the colour. When wool, previously mordanted with alum, is boiled in this for half an hour or so, a fine yellow colour is obtained. With longer boiling the shade will become a dull green. Experiments of this sort never fail to interest children, and the necessary wool may be obtained in many rural districts by plucking wisps of fleece from the fences and hedges.

Cow Parsley is generally the commonest white-flowered umbelli-ferous plant seen growing wild in England in late springtime. It makes a lacy trimming at a height of three or four feet in many fields and hedgerows, so that it, rather than the smaller primrose, violet, cowslip and bluebell, is to my mind the most universal and striking floral feature of the English spring scene. The fresh green parsley-like foliage may appear as early as New Year's Day in some localities, but the plant should not be used for dyeing until in full flower.

Directions for mordanting wool with alum and other materials are given on pages 181–183.

COTTON LAVENDER *Santolina chamaecyparissus*

This aromatic herb, which is known also by the name of French Lavender, makes a shrubby plant of up to two feet in height. It is now chiefly of use as a garden subject chosen for its attractive foliage and pleasant scent. At one time the flower was used in medicine, both as a cure for ringworm and as a general vermifuge. The leafy stem, dried, acts as a moth preventative.

The varieties most commonly seen are *Santolina incana*, which has grey foliage and golden disc flowers in July and August; *S. neapoli-tanica* with looser, more finely cut foliage and pale lemon flowers; *S. viridis* with green foliage and flowers either white or yellow. There is also a slightly less robust variety, only twelve inches high, with grey-green foliage and creamy flowers. This is called Lemon Queen.

The Santolinas may be clipped to form small, dense hedges, and well-pruned clumps were used in knot gardens in Tudor times; Parkinson mentions this in his famous book about gardens, *Paradisi in Sole*. Clipping may be done in March, as soon as growth starts, and again—if foliage rather than flower is wanted—in July. Santolinas are easily propagated by cuttings taken in late spring or autumn, rooted in frames or pans under glass.

CROCUS, SAFFRON *Crocus sativus*

Known to most of us as Saffron, this eastern plant is the *Karcom* of the Hebrews (see Song of Solomon iv. 14). The Greeks and Romans were also familiar with the plant. Homer referred to the Saffron Crocus in a description of the nuptial couch of Jupiter:

> And sudden hyacinths the turf bestow
> And flowering crocus made the mountain glow.

Virgil wrote: 'Let there be a garden to tempt your bees with the fragrance of its saffron flowers . . . they feed on arbutus, and cassia, and crocus glowing red.'

In *A Winter's Tale* the clown calls for 'Saffron to colour the warden pies'. The gaily coloured orange-red stigmas of this plant have a delightful scent which has ensured popularity for Saffron in medicine and confectionery, as well as in literature and legend, down the ages.

The yellow colouring matter, with its warm flavour, has for long been especially dear to the people of the English West Country—Devon and Cornwall—and I remember as a child being pressed to consume quantities of Saffron rice pudding, Saffron custard, Saffron cake, Saffron buns and biscuits, in a Devonshire farmhouse where summer holidays were spent in the nineteen-twenties.

The plant is small, with grass-like leaves and large lily-shaped flowers of purple, lilac or white which appear in the autumn. Commercial growers plant the corms six inches apart in well-worked medium rich soil in July, and the flowers are reaped in September. The orange stigmas and part of the style are then picked out and dried between layers of paper under pressure in a kiln. When finished, the product is in the form of cakes. One acre of Saffron will produce only a few pounds during the first season; yield increases to about twenty pounds in the second and third years, and then the corms must be lifted, divided and replanted. It is said that more than 4,000 flowers are required to make an ounce of Saffron. The country around the town of Saffron Walden in Essex was for two hundred years the centre of cultivation of this valuable crop.

The name Saffron is derived from the Arabic word *Zaffer*, and it was the Arab invaders who took the Saffron Crocus to Spain. To the Greeks it was known as *krokos*, and to the Romans as *Karkom*. In classical times this plant was used to dye garments a rich yellow, and the scent as well as the colour and flavour was greatly prized. Saffron water was sprinkled on theatre benches, floors of banqueting halls were strewn with leaves of Saffron and pillows were stuffed with them.

That scholarly gardener the late Canon Ellacombe believed that the Saffron came to Britain before the period usually assigned to it—the reign of Edward III. In his opinion it was first brought here by the Romans, and in the Middle Ages it was cultivated in monastic gardens and used for the illumination of missals before the practice of applying gold was introduced.

Medicinally, the plant, in powder form or tincture, is carminative, diaphoretic and emmenagogic. Prepared as a syrup, it was formerly used to treat impaired vision, particularly when caused by broken blood-vessels behind the eyes. Some people used it as a remedy for cold hands and feet.

CROCUS, AUTUMN   *Colchicum autumnale*

This plant, known also as Meadow Saffron, or Naked Ladies, is not in fact a crocus, but a lily. It bears in autumn after the broad, lanceolate green leaves have died, rosy-mauve flowers on weak, long, whitish stalks. These flowers differ from those of the Saffron Crocus in having less prominent orange stigmas, and the leaves of the Saffron are much narrower and more grass-like. The Autumn Crocus is a poisonous plant, and it seems a pity to call it Meadow Saffron, which suggests that it is edible too. The corms contain an alkaline substance, colchicine, which is used in a preparation for the relief of gout and acute rheumatism—needless to say, in very small doses. This poison is acrid and sedative and acts upon all the secreting organs, particularly the bowels and kidneys. It appears in Part I of the British Poisons List.

That celebrated botanist Dr John Lindley,* after whom the Royal Horticultural Society's library in Westminster is named, once reported that a woman in Covent Garden Market found some sprouting corms of Autumn Crocus which had been discarded by a herbalist, and ate them in mistake for onions. The sign of a herbalist is still legible above an old shop-front opposite the Henrietta Street offices of Messrs Duckworth, who publish this book: 'Jas. Butler Herbalist and Seedsman Lavender Water etc.' Could it have been he who inadvertently allowed those fatal corms to be thrown out? The poor woman died of colchicine poisoning.

* His fine collection of books was purchased by the R.H.S. in 1866 for £600.

CROTAL (CROTTLE) *Parmelia saxatilis*

This brownish crusty lichen grows on rocks, and the kind to give the richest dye (for it is a kind of dye-herb) is found established on or near sea-shores, or beside the sea-lochs of Scotland. No doubt the salt spray has some effect on the colouring matter contained in the Crotal. In the Hebridean island of Harris this is traditionally used to provide the well-known browns, tans and buffs of the handwoven Harris tweed.

The lichen is best scraped off and harvested on windless days in autumn or winter after rain, for when it is dry and brittle much may be broken and lost in the gathering, particularly if a wind is blowing. Unless it is to be used immediately it should be spread out and carefully dried before being stored in bags in a dry place, when it will keep almost indefinitely. In Britain this lichen is found in Devon, Cornwall, the Pennines and Lake District, in Wales and in Scotland. As all lichens take a long time to grow it is a mistake to gather more than is actually needed.

We are told that lichens were among the first plants seen on earth; by breaking up the rock surfaces they help to produce soil in which other vegetation can grow. They are composed of two plants, one a fungus, the other an algae, living together in symbiotic harmony. They need light and pure air, and will not thrive in the polluted atmosphere of our cities. Crotal contains altranorine and salicinic acids, which are the source of the colouring matter. Formation of these acids depends on the amount of light the lichen obtains, so it is easy to understand why the best dye comes from Crotal grown in a sunny position, after a fine summer.

Unlike most other vegetable dyes, the Crotal is not as a rule tied up in a muslin bag before being plunged into the dye-bath. The Hebridean crofter-weaver, using about one pound of dry Crotal to a pound of wool, puts alternate layers of the lichen (well crushed and bruised) and wool into a large pan and fills it up with soft, acid water from the burn. This is gradually brought to the boil, and the depth of colour required will dictate the length of time given to the boiling, which is done over the gentle, steady heat of a peat fire. It sometimes takes as much as twenty-four hours.

The dye-bath is allowed to go cold before the wool is taken out, washed in clear water, and shaken to remove the lichen. It is not advisable to wash Crotal before using it, as dye may be lost in the process. Insects, twigs and other foreign bodies are often put into the dye-bath along with the intended material, but it all shakes out when the wool is dry. When dyeing wool with lichen no mordant is needed; for this reason Crotal is known as a 'substantive' dye. The colour produced is very fast indeed, and well suited to the hardwearing nature of Harris tweed. Because in the old days Harris weavers used stale urine to fix and clear the colour of their wool after dyeing, people elsewhere believed that the unmistakable smell of Harris tweed was due to this practice. In fact the aroma comes from the Crotal itself, and this may be detected in the material dyed with it so long as a shred of wool remains.

The Crotal is known in some parts of Scotland as Staney-raw, and in the Shetland Isles as Scrottyie.

CUMIN *Cuminum cyminum*

Cumin is a small annual plant, a native of upper Egypt, cultivated in Mediterranean lands for many centuries. It has finely cut leaves like Fennel, and umbels of white or pink flowers. The fruit is used for flavouring, and in taste resembles that of Caraway. According to Pliny, students used to smoke Cumin fruit (so-called 'seeds') to acquire a studious pallor, hence the expression of Horace, *exsangue cuminum*. Although tobacco (and pipes) were then unknown, Pliny has a reference to inhaling smoke through hollow reeds.

From ancient times down to the Middle Ages this was one of the most prized spices in common use. It is mentioned in the Bible (Isaiah xxviii. 25, 27, and Matthew xxiii. 23) and in the writings of Hippocrates and Dioscorides. Among the Greeks it seems to have had some connection with avarice, for misers were said to have 'eaten Cumin'.

At one time employed medicinally as a stimulant, carminative and anti-spasmodic, it has now been superseded by Caraway. Cumin is still used in veterinary medicine, and a mixture of Bay-salt and Cumin seed is a well-tried remedy for certain diseases of pigeons.

CURRY PLANT *Helichrysum angustifolium*

This plant has nothing to do with the preparation of curry, but in hot sun it exhales a powerful, warm, spicy aroma which to many people resembles that of a dish of curry. It is a good 'silver' plant for the border, or as an inmate of the herb garden, and is popular with flower-arrangers. A species, *H. siculum*, is even brighter in colour and retains its silvery gleam untarnished throughout the winter. Both are propagated by Mrs Margery Fish at Lambrook.

DANDELION *Taraxacum officinale*

The generic name of the Dandelion, *Taraxacum*, is probably derived from the Greek *taraxis*, disorder, and *akos*, remedy, for it is a medicinal herb. It is also used in green salads, and for that reason some authorities prefer to think that the name is a corruption of an Arabic word meaning edible. The earliest known record of this plant in medicine occurs in a treatise by tenth-century Arabian physicians, who refer to it as *Tarakhshagun*. Avicenna, in the eleventh century, called it *Taraxacon*. The leaves, which are coarsely serrated like jagged saws, are supposed to resemble the canine teeth of a lion, from whence comes the French name *Dent-de-Lion*, and our own Dandelion. An earlier Latin specific name, *Dens Leonis*, and the Greek name for the genus to which Linnaeus ascribed the plant, *Leontodon*, both came from the same fancied likeness.

There are hosts of vernacular names for this ubiquitous and showy flower, including Blowball, Gowans, Dashelflower, Swine's Snout, Time-table, Wiggers and Priest's Crown. The golden flower was of old likened to a young student in his prime, the hoary seedheads to his later years in holy orders, and the empty receptacle, after all the seed has been scattered, to the priest's shorn head—a familiar sight in the Middle Ages—hence the name of Priest's Crown.

I do not know why the French peasants call it *Pissenlit* unless they habitually drink too much Dandelion coffee at night before going to bed. To prepare this beverage they lift the roots in autumn, clean and dry them, then roast them slightly until they are the tint of coffee all through, and grind them to powder. Dandelion coffee is a natural, unadultered drink without any of the injurious properties of tea and coffee, and it is now obtainable from most Health Food stores.

The chief constituents of Dandelion root—the part most used in medicine—are Taraxacin, Taraxasterol and Inulin. The root does not contain starch, but early in the year produces uncrystallizable sugar and Laevulin, which diminishes in quantity during the summer and becomes Inulin in the autumn. In former days Dandelion Juice was a favourite preparation, both in official and in domestic medicine. It is diuretic, tonic and slightly aperient. It is a general stimulant to the system, but particularly to the urinary organs, and is chiefly of use in kidney and liver disorders.

According to Mrs Grieve (*A Modern Herbal*) Dandelion affords marked relief in the 'hepatic complaints of persons long resident in warm climates'. She recommends a broth made of sliced Dandelion roots, stewed in water with Sorrel leaves. With the yolk of an egg added, this broth, taken every day for months, is said to have cured intractable cases of chronic liver congestion.

Gipsies are addicted to Dandelion Tea as a spring tonic. They drink half a cupful while fasting on three successive mornings; then, after a four-day pause, resume the dose for another three days. This treatment clears the skin and eyes. They also use the milky juice of the plant to remove warts, squeezing on two or three applications at intervals until the wart withers away. The employment of Dandelion root as a dyestuff may or may not be of gipsy origin, but it gives a magenta hue of the sort gipsies love.

Dandelion Tea is made by infusing one ounce of the flowers and leaves in a pint of boiling water for ten minutes. For a sluggish liver, two ounces of freshly-sliced root are boiled in two pints of water until reduced to one pint. An ounce of compound tincture of Horseradish is added, and the mixture taken in doses of two ounces at a time. To relieve biliousness and dizziness, one ounce of Dandelion root, the same of Black Horehound herb, half an ounce of Sweet Flag and a quarter-ounce of Mountain Flax may be simmered together in three pints of water until reduced to one and a half pints. This liquid is strained and taken in doses of a wineglassful after meals.

Most of us as children played at Dandelion 'clocks', breaking up the seed-heads with a vague assumption (one cannot call it *thought*) that these had been created solely for our pleasure. Later on, as know-ledge of the plant's marvellous construction and many uses increases, so develops a certain measure of apprehension about some amusements of adult humanity: trees heedlessly thrown down, insects and birds poisoned, wild and domestic animals exploited . . . Shall we, if a higher state of being is achieved, perceive in these actions an ignorance sur-passing that of our infant selves with a Dandelion?

DATURA

DATURA see THORNAPPLE

DILL *Anethum graveolens*   [*p.* 150

Dill is a pretty annual plant, a native of the Mediterranean regions
and southern Russia, growing up to about two feet in height with
feathery blue-green foliage and umbels of small yellow flowers. It
grows wild in cornfields in Spain and Portugal and along parts of the
Italian coast. It has been confused, both in appearance and taste, with
the perennial herb Fennel, but the latter, although so much taller and
stronger in habit, has a less pungent flavour.

The name Dill seems to have come from the Saxon *Dillan*, to lull,
because a decoction made from the seeds has for long been used to
dispel windy colics and soothe babies to sleep. This useful and harmless sedative, Dill Water, is still obtainable. According to Dioscorides,
'Dill stayeth the hickets' (hiccough). The fruits were known to the
early settlers in America as 'Meeting-house seeds', being taken to
Sunday worship by the faithful and munched during over-long
sermons. The plant was prized in the Middle Ages as a charm against
witchcraft, and was traditionally a herb of power used by magicians in
their spells.

Although the word 'Anise' is given in the Authorized Version of
St. Matthew xxiii. 23, this is now considered to be a mis-translation
of the Greek word *anethon*, which has been rendered as 'Anise'
from Wyclif onwards. *Anethon* was in fact Dill. This herb occurs
also in a tenth-century vocabulary used by Alfric, Archbishop of
Canterbury.

In cookery, users of Dill are concerned chiefly with the fruits, or
'seeds', although in Scandinavia the foliage is often boiled with
potatoes and peas, much as we in Britain today use Mint. Leaves are
occasionally added to soups and sauces, and the seeds are valued for
flavouring Dill vinegar and that popular German dish, pickled
cucumber.

The herb's medicinal value lies in its aromatic, stimulant, carminative and stomachic properties. Oil of Dill is also used for perfuming
soaps. Dill vinegar is made by soaking a quarter ounce of seed in a
pint of vinegar for a few days before straining off the liquor for use.
John Evelyn, in his *Acetaria, a Book about Sallets* (1680) gives a recipe
for 'Dill and Collyflower Pickle'.

Dill seed is sown in March or April in drills out of doors, nine inches apart, and should be thinned to about the same distance between plants in the rows. Harvesting is carried out directly the first seeds ripen, and the stalks are hung up in a warm place to dry and ripen fully before the fruits are threshed. Commercial growers expect to produce about seven hundredweight of 'seed' to the acre. This product is extremely light, about 25,000 seeds to the ounce.

ELDER   *Sambucus nigra*

This native tree, one of the commonest in Britain, is found in hedgerows and on waste ground nearly everywhere. The current vernacular name, Elder, is derived from the Saxon *Eller*—meaning 'kindler', because the branches, with pith removed, formed useful hollow tubes for blowing alive a newly kindled fire. The generic name, *Sambucus*, causes confusion in many books of reference. Some authorities say that it is derived from the Roman *Sambuca* (Sackbut), an early form of trombone made originally from Elder wood. Others say that the name developed from *Sambuke*. But the *sambuke* was not a wind instrument at all. It was an ancient four-stringed lyre, and it seems unlikely that the hollow branches of the Elder would have entered into its manufacture.

According to *Grove's Dictionary of Music*, there is no authority for supposing that the sackbut was known to the Romans; the first trombone is thought to have been developed from the trumpet early in the fourteenth century, and the name probably derived from the Spanish *sacabuche*, draw-tube; from *sacar*, to draw, and *bucha*, a pipe, originally of boxwood. At the start of the fifteenth century the French had a *saqueboute*, and by the close of that century we in Britain enjoyed music from a *shakbusshe*, later called *saykebud*, *sagbut* or *sackbut*. All this leaves the name *Sambucus* very much in the air, where it is likely to remain. At all events the tree's hollow branches, after the pith has been removed, have since time immemorial had air blown through them to make musical sounds. (This is reflected in the names Bore Tree and Pipe Tree.)

The Elder has played a conspicuous part in mythology. In Scandinavian lore it is dedicated to *Hulde*, the goddess of love, and to *Thor*, the god of thunder. In its branches was supposed to live a dryad, *Hylde-moer*, the Elder-tree Mother, who lived in the tree and watched over it.

She never failed to avenge an injury done to the tree, and belief in this could be traced among country people in England down to fairly recent times, for there was a widespread aversion from cutting down the Elder, and fear of using the wood, when it had been cut, for kindling fires.

Of particular interest to herb gardeners is the tradition that the Elder Mother has power to protect all herb plants and cause them to thrive in her care. An old country custom, now discontinued, was for farm workers to take into the fields green boughs of Elder, with which they whipped growing crops to deter insect pests. The offensive smell of the bruised leaves was supposed to be repellent to aphids and the like. Gardeners used a decoction of the leaves to sprinkle on plants for the same purpose, and as late as 1923 *The Chemist and Druggist* printed a recipe for spraying fruit trees with a liquid containing Elder extract.

The Elder tree provides food, drink and medicine, and the same properties are found in every part of it. The flowers, made into fritters when they are just opening, are delicious. Country people used to make a pickle from the blossoms, and another kind from tender young Elder shoots, and the berries went into ketchup and chutney. Excellent wines were made both from Elderberries and from the flowers. William Cobbett wrote that a cup of mulled Elder wine, served with nutmegs and sippets of toast just before going to bed on a cold winter night, was 'a thing to be run for'.

For centuries a toilet-water made from Elder has been a valued item on the dressing-tables of women, and in 1659 Sir Hugh Platt wrote that water distilled in May from Elder leaves, applied to a freckled face with a sponge 'at the wane of the moon', would remove the freckles. Elder flowers placed in water used for washing the hands and face will both whiten and soften the skin, and a muslin bag of these flowers makes an excellent sachet for the bath at no cost to the user. A good ointment for dressing burns may be made from Elder flowers and lard. Handling the flowers when picking them over for wine-making is sufficient to soften and whiten the skin.

A strong infusion of Elder blossoms, dried, and Peppermint—made by putting a handful of each into a jug, pouring on one and a half pints of boiling water, infusing for half an hour—will speedily cure influenza if taken very hot in bed last thing at night. The drink may be sweetened with honey.

In the opinion of Mrs Grieve (*A Modern Herbal*), the Elder is valuable medicine for colds, catarrh, croup, chest complaints, inflammation of the mouth and throat, for relief of piles, fevers, skin eruptions and to purify the blood. According to an analysis by Kramer, the active principle of the bark is a soft resin, and viburnic acid, which is said to be identical with valeric acid. There are also volatile oil, albumen, resin, fat, wax, chlorophyll, tannic acid, grape sugar, gum, starch, pectin and various salts. The leaves contain an alkaloid, Sambucine, and the glucoside Sambunigrin. From ancient times a 'Rob'—that is, a juice thickened by heat—has been made from Elderberries, simmered and stiffened with sugar, and used as a cordial for colds and coughs. The viburnic acid contained in this preparation is considered to be useful in cases of bronchitis and similar troubles, because it induces perspiration. To make Elderberry Rob, five pounds of fresh, ripe, crushed berries are simmered with one pound of loaf sugar and the juice evaporated to the thickness of honey. It is cordial, aperient and diuretic. One or two tablespoonfuls in a tumbler of hot water, taken at night, promotes perspiration and is soothing to the chest.

Elder Flower Water, known as *Eau de Sureau* in France, is a mild astringent and stimulant. It is employed chiefly in eye and skin lotions. To make it at home, fill a large jar with Elder blossoms, having removed the stalks, and pack them down tightly. Pour on two quarts of boiling water. When cool, add $1\frac{1}{2}$ ounces of rectified spirits. Cover the jar with a cloth and stand it in a warm place for a day, then allow to get cold. Strain the lotion off, bottle and cork tightly.

It is also possible to make a good lotion from the dried flowers, which is cooling and soothing. Infuse in one quart of boiling water $2\frac{1}{2}$ drachms of dried flowers. Leave for an hour and then strain. This is useful for tumours, skin eruptions, headaches and helps to ward off midges and other insects.

An ointment known as *Unguentum Sambuci Viride*, Green Elder Ointment, was formerly popular as a household remedy for chilblains, sprains, bruises and the like. It was made from three parts of fresh Elder leaves, four parts of lard and two parts of suet. These ingredients were heated until all the colour was extracted, then strained under pressure through a cloth and allowed to cool. In 1655 Sir Thomas Browne wrote: 'The common people keep as a good secret in curing wounds the leaves of the Elder, which they have gathered on the last day of April.' These were boiled until soft in a little linseed oil and used as a healing application to haemorrhoids and other painful swellings. Another old remedy is described as follows: 'There be nothing more excellent to ease the pains of haemorrhoids than a fomentation made of the Flowers of the Elder and *Verbusie* or Honeysuckle in water or milk for a short time. It easeth the greatest pain.'

It was usual to employ fresh Elder flowers for the distillation of Elder Flower Water in pharmacies, but as the flowering season is so short the chemist often salted down a supply for later use. The flowers were also dried, for making Elder Flower Tea. Flowers for drying are collected when just in full bloom and piled in heaps. After a few hours the corollas are loosened and may be sifted out. The flowers are not easy to dry with a good colour; if left too long in the sun before being picked, they will be brown when dried. If left too long in the heaps, the whole mass will turn black. If the inflorescence is but partly open when gathered, the flowers must be sifted more than once, for they do not open all together. They must be dried quickly—in a heated copper pan or in a cool oven with the door open, being moved about for a few minutes until drying is complete. In country districts the herbalists used to sell Elder Flowers in dried bunches as well as the sifted product. Elder Flower Tea, good for soothing the nerves and alleviating headaches, is made by putting a handful of fresh flowers or about one ounce of the dried product into a jug and covering with boiling water. When cold this liquid is strained off and may be used cold or re-heated. A pinch of the fresh or dried flowers will add a subtle flavour to an ordinary pot of Indian tea.

Recipes for making Elderberry Wine and Elder Flower Pancakes, together with jam, jelly, chutney, ketchup, syrup and vinegar, will be found on pages 173–175. Various dyes have been obtained from Elder: blues and mauves from the berries, green from the leaves, black from the root. Alum was the mordant used, plus salt with the berries to obtain a mauve colour. Black obtained from Elder was popular among the Highlanders of Scotland, who wore always black clothes on the Sabbath and other important days. The Romans used Elderberry juice as a hair-dye: I could not find their recipe, but an old English one says that 'the hair of the head washed with berries boiled in wine is made black'.

Legends about the Elder are many and varied. In *Love's Labour's Lost* Shakespeare mentions the mediaeval idea that Judas was hanged on an Elder, and in Langland's *Vision of Piers Plowman* we find the same story:

> Judas he japed with Jewen silver
> And sithen Eller hanged hymselve.

Sir John Mandeville, in an account of his travels written about the same time, says that he saw by the Pool of Siloam the *Tree of Eldre that Judas henge himself upon*. Later it was assumed that the Judas-tree (*Cercis siliquastrum*) was in fact the one Judas chose. It is certainly a much stouter tree to bear the weight of a hanging man. Another grim old tradition says that the Cross of Calvary was made from Elder wood. In consequence of these beliefs the Elder became an emblem of sorrow and death.

A happier legend, imported into these islands from Denmark, says that if you stand under an Elder tree at midnight on Midsummer Eve you will see the King of the Elves ride past, attended by all his courtiers and servants. Another piece of folk-lore relates to the pith. Small flat pieces were cut from Elder branches, dipped in oil, and floated upon water in a glass. These were thought to direct their light towards any witches or sorcerers who happened to be lurking in the vicinity.

In that delightful book *Home and Garden*, published in 1900, Miss Gertrude Jekyll wrote of her Elder trees:

Any one who is in close sympathy with flower and tree and shrub, and has a general acquaintance with Nature's moods, could tell the time of year to within a few days without reference to a calendar; but of all dates it seems to me that Midsummer Day is the one most clearly labelled, by the full and perfect flowering of the Elder. It may be different in more northern latitudes, but in mine, which is about half way between London and the South Coast, the Festival of St John and the flowering of the Elder always come together.

Some attractive varieties for the flower garden are *Sambucus nigra aurea* (golden), *S. aurea marginata* (gold-edged), and *S. pulverenta* (variegated white). Mrs Margery Fish grows all three at Lambrook.

ELECAMPANE *Inula helenium*

Elecampane, known also as Scabwort, Elf Dock and Horseheal, is a strikingly handsome perennial plant, related to the Daisy, which grows to a height of seven feet when well established in good, moist soil. The stout stem is furrowed and, near the top, branched. It produces a

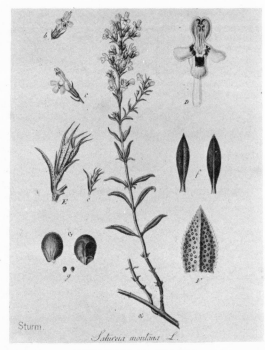

FRENCH SORREL

WINTER SAVORY

SCARLET BERGAMOT

POKE-WEED

TARRAGON

BELLADONNA

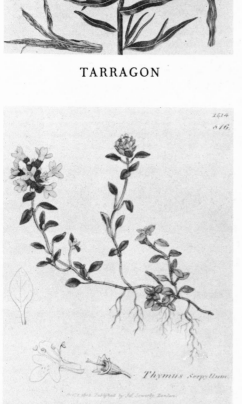

WILD THYME

WOAD

radical rosette of huge ovate leaves which may be as much as eighteen inches long, velvety underneath, borne on long stalks. Higher up the leaves are smaller, and they clasp the stem. The plant is in flower from June to August, and has shaggy yellow blossoms resembling double sunflowers but much smaller in relation to the size of the plant. I have been amused to hear bystanders, while they peered over a wall at my huge plant of Elecampane, making derogatory remarks about the poorness of my 'sunflowers'. As a foliage plant it is most valuable, and the seedheads are interesting in shape and of a velvety dark brown colour.

In ancient times the plant was named *Enula campana*, because, it is said, it grew on the Roman *Campagna*; the words *Enula*, *helenium* and Elecampane are all attributed to Helen, wife of Menelaus, who traditionally held a bunch of this herb when carried away by Paris. The virtues of Elecampane were extolled by Dioscorides; by Galen, who said it was 'good for passions of the hucklebone called sciatica'; and by Pliny, who wrote, 'Julia Augusta, let no day pass without eating some of the roots of *Enula*, considered to help the digestion and cause mirth.' It is mentioned in Anglo-Saxon herbals written before William the Norman came to Britain, and it is an ingredient of the medicine called 'Marchalan' by the famed thirteenth-century Welsh physicians of Myddfai.

This plant used to be cultivated in monastic enclosures and in private herb gardens too. It is probably native to the south of England, but specimens now found in the wild further north seem likely to be descendants of garden escapes. The root, containing Inulin, was chiefly used in cough medicines, but at one time it was candied and eaten as a sweetmeat. This candy, in flat, circular cakes coloured pink with cochineal, was sucked to ease asthmatical troubles; and by people who had to travel by river the active principle of Elecampane was thought to be a specific against poisonous fumes and bad air. In those days sewage ran straight into rivers and there was plenty of foul air.

The medicinal action and uses of Elecampane are listed by Mrs Grieve as diuretic, tonic, diaphoretic, expectorant, alterative, antiseptic, astringent and gently stimulant. The root was employed by the ancients in treatment of dropsy, phthisis, skin affections and certain diseases of women. The name of Scabwort relates to its power of healing sheep-scab.

This herb has been used in some countries, notably Switzerland and France, in the preparation of Absinthe; and a cordial made by infusing Elecampane roots with sugar and currants in white port was popular in Britain a century or two ago. A tonic may be prepared by simmering half an ounce of root in one quart of water until the whole is reduced to one pint. A wineglassful is taken three times a day.

The plant is propagated by seed, sown under glass in spring, or by root division.

A related herb, *Inula conyza*, known by the lovely vernacular name of Ploughman's Spikenard, also contains Inulin. It was regarded as a good wound-herb and a decoction was administered to cure ruptures, bruises, wounds, pains in the side and difficulty in breathing. It was an ingredient of the famous Greek ointment, *Baccharis*.

The plant is a biennial with stiff upright stems, about eighteen inches high, purplish and downy, branched, bearing many small inconspicuous flowers of dingy yellow tinged with purple. The leaves are narrow and of a dull green. It is faintly aromatic, and this gave rise to the name Cinnamon Root. The flowers are succeeded by little black seeds, each one crowned by a feathery plume. Ground into a powder, this herb was at one time much used to repel and destroy insects in the home.

EUCALYPTUS   *Eucalyptus globulus*

A native of Australia and Tasmania, this genus of tree includes at least three hundred species, some of which have now been established in America, Africa, India and southern Europe. It is such a feature of the Australian scene that many people think of it as Australia's national tree. It is known there as 'Gum' or 'Blue Gum'. Few tree-lovers realize that certain species of 'Gum' can reach the gigantic size of four hundred feet or even more—a height to out-top the famous Californian Redwood, *Sequoia sempervirens*.

Many Blue Gums yield essential oils, but these oils differ in character and it is inexact to speak of 'Eucalyptus oil' without stating the species from which the oil has been produced. That obtained commercially for medicinal purposes comes chiefly from *E. globulus*, but oils from other species are also extracted in large quantities for industrial use.

The tree contains a volatile oil, chlorophyll, Eucalyptol, resin and tannin. It is employed as a febrifuge, tonic, restorative, as an antimalarial agent and anti-periodic. For medicinal purposes the fresh leaves are more active than dried, and the narrow-shaped foliage found on full-grown trees is more potent than the juvenile foliage.

The anti-periodic properties of Eucalyptus make the oil derived from its foliage of value in the treatment of malaria, typhoid, phthisis, catarrh and other infections. *E. globulus* is sometimes known as the Fever Tree, having been planted in swampy places because of the powerful drying action of its roots in the soil. In temperate regions this tree has been introduced for its ability to drain marshy places, such as the Roman Campagna and parts of Sicily. When swamps are drained the malarial mosquito is unable to breed.

As children we all knew the strong, warm scent of Eucalyptus, which was sprinkled on handkerchiefs when someone had a cold in the head. People still have just as many colds, but this pungent smell is seldom met with today. The leaves of this tree, which contain oil glands, are aromatic and I think very much pleasanter than the bottled oil sold by chemists. Good ornamental Gums for gardens in Britain are *E. perriniana*, *E. glaucescens*, *E. vilmoriana*, *E. gunnii* and *E. parviflora*. These may be kept within bounds in a small space by cutting them down and growing on as bushes. The juvenile foliage will then be produced constantly, and this is the most attractive and useful to flower-arrangers.

In the well-known gardens at Inverewe in Wester Ross, in the north of Scotland (where I worked with the late owner, Mairi Sawyer), Douglas Fir, Californian Redwood and *Eucalyptus coccifera* stand in one group, all about a hundred years old and a hundred feet in height. Other species of Gum grown in this famous garden (now the property of The National Trust for Scotland) include *E. cordata*, *E. gunnii*, *E. pauciflora* and *E. salicifolia*. Some of them used to drop their bark in pieces about nine inches long and four or five inches wide, which rolled up to look like cigars for giants. These rolls, collected in the late summer and autumn, made kindling for log and peat fires which gave off a delicious fragrance.

FENNEL   *Foeniculum vulgare* (syn. *F. officinale*)

This fine upstanding plant grows to a height of five or six feet, and bears above its feathery maze of foliage large flat umbels of golden flowers in July and August. That is, if the gardener allows it to flower

FENNEL

at all. The myriad little blossoms soon turn to showers of fine seed, and if these are allowed to scatter the whole garden may become a forest of tiny plumed Fennel trees in the following year. To obtain a constant supply of fresh leaf for culinary purposes, and to prevent the formation of a Fennel forest, it is advisable to cut the stalks down several times during a season. This brutal treatment forces the plant to throw up more and more stems furnished with a plentiful supply of 'grass' for the cook, and everyone is happy—except the flower-arranger and those who like to use dried seedheads of the plant for winter decorations.

I have worked out a system of compromise, in which some of my Fennel plants (they are perennial) are constantly springing up anew from ground level, others are in a bowery state of fresh leafage, and the rest, leaner and drier, have reached their full status and wear golden crowns. A few of the latter are permitted to seed, so that a supply of seedlings is always available for friends and casual callers. The common green Fennel is quite attractive, but nobody who is acquainted with the bronze variety—its rufous young shoots like fox-brushes stuck into the soil, its blue-grey shining stems and bronzy-green adult foliage—could fail to think it superior as a garden subject. If you can bear to consume anything so elegant, it is just as good for cooking as the green kind. It is sometimes referred to as 'Black' Fennel, but there is nothing black about it.

Propagation of this plant is by seed, sown outside in a sunny bed in April or May; or roots may be divided in spring or autumn. Fennel is a Mediterranean herb, now naturalized in many parts of Britain. When growing wild it is usually found in chalky districts, particularly on chalk cliffs near the sea. The generic name *Foeniculum* comes from the Latin *foenum*, hay.

For many centuries it has been esteemed both as a culinary herb and as a medicinal one, with especial virtues for treatment of the eyes. In the kitchen it is chiefly used for adding piquancy to fish and shell fish; leaves may be laid on cutlet, fillet or rissole, or chopped into a white sauce in a similar manner to Parsley. At one time the consumption of leaves, seeds and root of the plant was believed to assist people who wished to reduce their weight. As William Coles put it: 'Both the seeds, leaves and root of our Garden Fennel are much used in drinks and broths for those that are grown fat, to abate their unwieldiness. . .' The Greeks must have had the same idea, for their name for Fennel, *marathron*, is derived from *maraino*, to grow thin. Their athletes used it as a food when competing in the Olympic games, because it strength-ened them without making them fat. Wreaths of Fennel were worn by the victors, too.

Fennel tea is made by pouring half a pint of boiling water on a teaspoonful of bruised Fennel seed. This used to be employed as a carminative. The fruit, commonly called 'seed', of the plant is chiefly used in medicine to reduce the griping-tendencies of purgatives.

In ancient times there were the Nine Sacred Herbs, namely Mugwort, *Waybread* (Plantain), *Stime* (Watercress), *Maythen* (Chamomile), *Wergulu* (Nettle), Crab-apple, Chervil, Fennel and the unidentified *Atterlothe*. When Fennel was administered the incantations used were many; one, which includes Thyme also, runs as follows:

> Thyme and Fennel, two exceeding mighty ones,
> These herbs the wise Lord made
> Holy in the Heavens; He let them down,
> Placed them, and sent them into the seven worlds
> As a cure for all, the poor and the rich.

The Fennel commonly used as a vegetable in Italy is another variety, *F. vulgare* var. *dulce*. This is an annual, about a foot high, with whitish stalks a little like Celery. The heart, which is blanched and forms a solid head, is very sweet and delicious when cooked with a cheese sauce. It is called *Finocchio* by the Italians.

Fennels were grown in the earliest monastic gardens in Europe, and they have now spread to most parts of the world. In times of greater superstition it was customary to hang up bunches of Fennel in the home as a protection against evil spirits, and those who were afraid of ghosts used to stuff the keyholes of their doors with Fennel seed.

Recipes using Fennel will be found on pages 175–176.

FLAX *Linum usitatissimum* [p. 54

Common Flax, a slender blue-flowered annual about eighteen inches high, with narrow lanceolate leaves, has been cultivated since very early times for its seed and fibre. Flax seeds, together with cloth woven from linen thread, have been found in Egyptian tombs. The plant has appeared in so many places that its country of origin cannot now be exactly determined, for it escapes from cultivation and is found growing wild wherever it has been introduced.

The biblical 'fine linen' was undoubtedly made from Flax, and there are references to the product of this plant in Genesis, Exodus, Joshua and Isaiah in the Old Testament, while in the New it is said to have formed the clothing of Jesus when he was laid in the tomb. It was used for cord and for sail-cloth; the 'white sails' described in Homer's Odyssey were linen ones.

The five-celled capsules of this plant's seed-vessels are referred to in the Bible as 'bolls', and when the Flax is said to be 'bolled' it is ready to be pulled, tied in bundles, and 'retted' or soaked in water. Thomas Tusser in *Five Hundred Points of Good Husbandry* (1557) describes the manifold duties of the country housewife in his day. Among other things she had to sow, pull, ret, clean and dry all the Flax needed in the home. Her work also involved the breaking, beating, heckling and spinning of Flax fibres required for the weaving of linen. In Tusser's time English farmers were compelled by law to sow one rood in every sixty acres of arable land with either Flax or Hemp. The very exhausting nature of this crop made it unpopular with farmers in Britain. Impoverishment of land resulting from cultivation of the Flax plant was well known to the ancients. Pliny referred to 'scorching' of the ground.

The fruit is a spherical capsule like a small pea, and contains mucilage, a light yellow oil, and proteins, together with wax, resin, sugar, phosphates and a small amount of the glycoside Linamarin. The oil is obtained by expression with little or no heat, and the cake which remains is fed to cattle under the name of oil-cake. When ground up this is known as Linseed meal, and employed in making poultices. The oil of linseed is largely used by painters (tradesmen and artists alike) for its properties as a drying oil.

In medicine, the Flax plant is emollient, demulcent and pectoral. The crushed seed or linseed meal may be used as a poultice alone or mixed with mustard. Linseed is often added to cough mixtures, and linseed tea with honey and lemon juice is a good homely remedy for coughs and colds. The tea is made by infusing one ounce of whole seeds in a pint of boiling water. Linseed oil is much used in veterinary work, and the seed is often given as food to small birds.

Annual Linums, the common blue variety and the red and rosy-pink kinds, may be sown outside in spring and thinned but not transplanted. There are also perennial kinds and a shrubby yellow-flowered species from Crete, *Linum arboreum*.

As might be expected of a plant which has been closely associated with mankind throughout recorded history, many legends and traditions have grown up around Flax. In the Middle Ages Flax flowers were believed to give good protection against sorcery, and in Central Europe there was a charming custom which sent young children to dance between the rows of growing Flax plants in order to be made beautiful. Flax was supposed to be under the protection of the Teutonic goddess *Hulde*, who first showed mankind how to cultivate it and thereafter taught women to spin the thread and weave linen cloth with that.

FLAX, MOUNTAIN *Linum catharticum*

This little herb, known also as Fairy Flax, Dwarf Flax and Purging Flax, is an annual with white flowers. At first sight it could easily be mistaken for Chickweed. It grows in hilly pastures, and the whole herb is gathered for medicinal use. It is a brisk purgative, and is most satisfactory when combined with a carminative such as Peppermint. Dried, it is made into a tea (one ounce infused in a pint of boiling water), and taken in doses of a wineglassful for rheumatism, catarrh, liver complaints and jaundice.

FOXGLOVE *Digitalis purpurea*   [*p.* 134

Only one country name for this well-loved wild plant—Throatwort— shows any sign of the important place achieved and maintained by the drug Digitalis in medicine. Folk's Glove, Fairy Thimbles, Gloves of Our Lady, Dog's Lugs, Thimble Flowers, Dead Men's Bells, King's Elwand, Butchers' Gloves, Bloody Fingers and Snoxums are a few of the other inventions. The generic name *Digitalis*—a finger, i.e. glove or thimble—is supposed to have been first bestowed on the plant by Leonard Fuchs in his *Herbal* of 1542. The earliest known version of Foxglove is the Anglo-Saxon *Foxes glofa*, and another spelling, Folk's Glove (glove of the 'good folk' or fairies), is found in a plant list made in the reign of Edward III. In Scandinavia, fox and 'good folk' are united in a legend that fairies gave the blossoms to a fox for use as moccasins, to soften his tread when robbing hen-roosts.

The name King's Elwand may relate to the belief that the leaves of Digitalis, bruised, or made into an ointment, would cure the King's evil—scrofula. The distinctive mottled patterns on the flowers were of old thought to be a warning, placed there to draw man's attention to harmful juices secreted by this plant, which caused the Irish peasants to call it Dead Man's Thimbles. It is curious that the Greeks and Romans omitted to name this plant, and Shakespeare makes no mention of it. In Scotland it is the badge of Clan Farquharson; a little unfortunate, because in the Language of Flowers it symbolizes insincerity. It appears in a thirteenth-century manuscript describing herbs used by Welsh physicians of that time, and in 1554 Dodoens prescribed it, boiled in wine, as an expectorant—a custom perpetuated in the name Throatwort.

The normal life of a Foxglove plant extends over two seasons, but sometimes the roots persist, and throw flower stalks for three or more years. In the first year a rosette of leaves develops, and in the second season this produces a stem, three or four feet in height, crowned with a long spike of drooping bell-like blossoms from June to July and August. The true wild Foxglove used in medicine has magenta-pink flowers, and the most valuable extracts are made from plants that have grown in a sunny position. Leaves from two-year-old plants are selected, and must be picked just prior to the formation of seed.

The Foxglove yields several glycosides which are in use as heart stimulants. That named digitoxin is an extremely poisonous and cumulative drug. Two others, less cumulative, are called digitalin and digitonin. A mixture of glycosides prepared from the seeds is known as digitalin. The leaves also contain oil, fatty matter, starch, gum, sugar, etc. Many early herbalists and physicians seem to have used this potent herb in a manner which modern practitioners would consider to be dangerous, while the really valuable properties of digitalis were neglected. In present-day medicine it is most valued in the treatment of heart cases. The drug comes into Part I of the British Poisons List.

GARLIC   *Allium sativum*

This pungent bulb, related to the onion, has a history of service to mankind as ancient as that of any plant in my collection. It has spread from south-west Siberia all over Europe, and is now found naturalized as far south as Sicily. It is particularly well liked by people in the Mediterranean countries, but earlier in this century and in Victorian days it was frowned upon by polite circles in Britain. Since the advent of cheap air travel and package tours abroad for everybody, the prejudice has dwindled—as have also the polite circles.

Garlic was consumed in large quantities in ancient Greece and Rome, as mentioned by Virgil in his *Eclogues*; but Horace detested the stuff, which even then he, together with a small section of his countrymen, regarded as vulgar—an opinion later shared by Shakespeare in England. The vernacular name, Poor Man's Treacle (meaning Theriac, or Heal-All), suggests that the less refined members of society have always put the plant to good use. It is popularly supposed to be an aphrodisiac.

This plant is included in many old English horticultural writings from the tenth to the fifteenth centuries, and it is mentioned in most of the Herbals issued in the sixteenth century. From Coles's *Art of Simpling* we learn that cocks which had been fed on Garlic were 'most stout to fight', and that if a garden is infested by moles, Garlic will make them 'leap out of the ground'. The name Garlic is Anglo-Saxon, derived from *gar*, a spear, and *leac*, a plant (or leek).

In cultivation, the ground is first prepared as for the onion—that is, well dug and trodden firm. The bulbs are divided up into cloves and each dibbled in, in February or March, about two inches deep, six inches apart, with a foot space between the rows. A dressing of soot is useful. This plant thrives best in full sun, and it must be kept free from weeds. In a good summer the Garlic bulbs should be ready for lifting in August, when the leaves begin to wither, but in poor seasons this may not occur until September.

The active properties of Garlic lie in an essential oil, a sulphide of Allyl, rich in sulphur, and present in all members of the onion family. The intense smell of Garlic is so penetrating that it is said to be exhaled in the breath of anyone who has even had a clove of it applied to the soles of his feet. Medicinally it is diaphoretic, diuretic, expectorant and stimulant. Miraculous powers of healing have been attributed to it. In war it has been recognized as a valuable antiseptic and employed to control the suppuration of wounds. In World War I the juice of Garlic was applied to wounds on swabs of sterilized sphagnum moss.

Garlic was an important ingredient in the legendary 'Vinegar of the Four Thieves', which they used to make themselves immune from the plague, and so dare to rob the bodies of those who had succumbed to the disease. In cookery it is supposed to aid digestion and to assist in keeping healthy the lining of the stomach. Farm animals and fowls like it, but although beneficial to their health it is apt to spoil the flavour of eggs and milk. It is said that gorillas frequently found their colonies where Garlic flourishes, so presumably they too know of its good effect on their health.

The broad-leaved Garlic known as Ramsons (*A. ursinum*) is sometimes mistaken by townsfolk for wild Lily-of-the-Valley, until they smell it. It grows in profusion in damp woods and on shady banks, and because cattle like it, and the odour permeates milk, farmers call it a detestable weed.

GOOD KING HENRY   *Chenopodium bonus-henricus* [*p.* 150

This hardy perennial plant, known variously as Fat Hen, Smearwort, English Mercury and Mercury Goosefoot, was formerly cultivated in Britain as a garden pot-herb, and is now found growing wild in waste places on the outskirts of villages and farmsteads. It is a darkish green plant, about two feet high, with arrow-shaped leaves and dull spikes of small greenish flowers. In earlier centuries the leaves were cooked as a green vegetable and put into the broth-pot; the cultivation of this Goosefoot persisted in parts of Suffolk and Lincolnshire until World War I.

It is sown in seedboxes in February, and germination will be expedited if the boxes are exposed to frost for a week or two, then brought into gentle heat. The seedlings are pricked out, hardened off, and planted in open ground a foot apart in June or July. A small quantity of foliage and young shoots may be gathered during the first autumn, provided that the plant is not stripped bare. It will then continue to produce 'greens' for many years, but ungrateful users sometimes referred to it as 'Blite' (from the Greek *bliton*, insipid), and the flavour is greatly inferior to that of Spinach.

The name Good King Henry has nothing to do with Good King Hal, but some obscure connection with two German elves named Heinz and Heinrich; another Goosefoot was *Malus henricus*, the bad or poisonous one. 'Fat Hen' also comes from Germany, where the plant was traditionally used to fatten poultry. Our own country name of Smearwort refers to the old use of Chenopodium in ointment. The leaves were also applied in the form of a poultice to heal chronic sores. A decoction of the leaves was taken internally as a remedy for indigestion, and the roots were fed to sheep as a cough cure.

GROUND IVY   *Glechoma hederacea*

This is one of the commonest wild plants in all parts of Britain. The root is perennial, and it throws long trailing square stems which run and root all over the ground. They bear kidney-shaped leaves on long stalks, hairy and aromatic, which, because of a fancied resemblance to the true Ivy, gave the plant its current name. I find it hard to perceive any likeness. The two-lipped flowers of brilliant purplish blue open early in April, and the plant continues to bloom throughout the summer and often well into the autumn. It is found on waste ground, hedge-banks and in woods, and merits examination, both for the clear colour of its flowers and for the finely shaped leaves and their gradation in size towards the tips of the trailing stems. They will stay green throughout all but the most severe winters. Usually disregarded because of our familiarity with it, this plant would have its beauties extolled at once if it became less common. The flower colour varies from place to place, but in some specimens is as vivid and clear a blue as that of any Gentian.

> And 'buzz, buzz, buzz'
> Gaily hums Sir Pandarus,
> As blue ground-ivy blossom
> Bends with the weight of a bee in its bosom.
> Andrew Young

Among the many vernacular names of this plant are four indicative of one of its uses: Alehoof, Tun-hoof, Gill-go-over-the-Ground and Hedgemaids. Before the cultivation of hops in Britain, Ground Ivy was used to clarify and flavour ale, and it continued in regular use for these purposes until the close of the reign of Henry VIII. Hops and Heresy, so the saying goes, came into Britain together. So, apparently, did the word 'beer', which is brewed with the Hop. The name Gill-go-by-the-ground came from the French word *guiller*, to ferment ale; but as Gill also meant a girl it was transmuted in Britain into 'Hedgemaids' or 'Haymaids'. Early alehouses in these Islands were called 'Gill houses'.

In some modern herbals, Chaucer's lines about the *Parvenke*, ending 'Men call it the ivy of the ground' are quoted as a description of *Glechoma hederacea*. This is incorrect, for *Parvenke* was in fact the Periwinkle, as the lines

> The lef is thicke, schinende and styf
> As is the grene ivy lef

suggest. Our Ground Ivy does not have thick, shining and stiff leaves.

As the Periwinkle was often called Ground Ivy in Chaucer's day, no more need be said.

Other names for *Glechoma* are, or were, Cat's Foot, Devil's Candlesticks, Lizzy-run-by-the-Hedge, Thunder Vine and Benth. The plant was used in the past for making wreaths for the dead, possibly because its habit of growth readily fits it to be woven into a circular from. It is an excellent bee-plant, but farmers discourage it in pasture land, because cattle and horses are not fond of it.

In medicine, the whole herb is used, gathered in May when most flowers are still in fresh condition. The action is diuretic, astringent, tonic and gently stimulant. It has been employed in the treatment of kidney disease, indigestion, coughs and nervous headaches, and as a wash for sore eyes. A good tonic drink known as Gill tea is made by infusing two handfuls of fresh Ground Ivy in a pint of boiling water until cool. This is strained, sweetened with honey or liquorice, and taken in doses of a wineglassful three times a day. 'Ground Ivy' was at one time among the Cries of London, being sold in the streets to make this tonic tea to purify the blood.

HELLEBORE, BLACK *Helleborus niger* [*p.* 135

This Hellebore is our well-loved Christmas Rose and a native of Central and Southern Europe as well as of Asia Minor, and it is grown in Britain as a garden plant and by some florists for cutting. Two allied species, *H. foetidus* and *H. viridis*, found wild in this country, have similar properties and the rhizomes were sometimes substituted for those of *H. niger* imported from Europe, mostly from Germany. Others now popular as garden subjects are *H. corsicus* (or *H. argutifolius*), with glaucous foliage, and *H. orientalis*, the Lenten Rose.

The Black Hellebore was formerly known as Melampode, after Melampus, a physician of 1400 B.C. who, according to Pliny, used it to treat nervous disorders and hysteria. In his *Shepherd's Calendar* (1579) Spenser refers to the veterinary use of Melampode.

This plant gathered many superstitious beliefs around it, and at one time people blessed their cattle with it to avert evil spells, having dug it up with elaborate ritual. In an old French legend a sorcerer, to make himself invisible when passing though the enemy's camp, scatters powdered Hellebore in the air as he goes.

Most Hellebores will thrive in ordinary garden soil, if given good drainage. They like a fairly damp place in partial shade, and should improve without lifting for about seven years. Propagation is by seed or by root division in July. In favourable situations self-sown seedlings will abound, and these should bloom in their third year.

Medicinally the rhizome is used, collected and dried in autumn. It contains two crystalline glycosides, Helleborin and Helleborein, both poisons. These were formerly prescribed in cases of dropsy and amenorrhoea, as well as for the treatment of hysteria and nervous disorders, but must be given with the greatest care.

The American Green Hellebore (*Veratrum viride*) and White Hellebore (*Veratrum album*) are listed in this country as 'False' Hellebores. They belong to the Natural Order *Liliaceae*, and also yield poisonous drugs akin to those provided by *H. niger*, which is a member of the Natural Order *Ranunculaceae*.

HEMLOCK   *Conium maculatum*   [*p.* 151

The tall (up to eight feet), branched and red-blotched stem of this European herb bears finely cut leaves and white flowers in umbels. It has a foetid, repellent smell. The whole plant contains the alkaloid Coniine, but there is a greater concentration in the leaves and seed. It is found growing wild in hedgerows, by the borders of streams, and on waste land in most parts of England, and on similar sites throughout most of Europe. It has been introduced into both north and south America.

This plant's acrid juice is so narcotic in its effects that a few drops will kill a small animal. Hemlock provides a poison which was known in ancient Greece and Rome, and it formed the fatal draught that Socrates had to drink, this being the state method of execution. It was then known as *Cicuta*, but in the sixteenth century the name of *Cicuta virosa* was given to the Water Hemlock, and so Linnaeus allotted to this Hemlock the name *Conium maculatum*, derived from the Greek word *konos*, spinning top, because the poison causes vertigo and then death. *Maculatum*, spotted, refers to the distinctive mottling of the stems. Our vernacular name, Hemlock, may have come from the Anglo-Saxon *hem*, border, or shore, and *leac*, leek or plant. Another suggestion is that it comes from *healm*, straw, from which the current English word haulm is derived.

Many illnesses, some fatal, have occurred through people having eaten the leaves of Hemlock in mistake for Parsley, or the small, ridged fruits in the belief that these were Caraways. Even the roots have been mistakenly dug up and cooked as 'parsnips'. Any tall, evil-smelling plant with a red-blotched stem and leaves like Parsley is best left alone.

Fresh green Hemlock is used for the preparation of the juice of Conium, Conium ointment and green extract of Conium. The British Pharmacopoeia requires that leaves and young branches should be gathered from wild plants in this country when the flowers are fully matured and the fruits just beginning to form. This is the most power-ful stage, and occurs towards the end of June. As a medicine Conium is sedative and antispasmodic. The drug has to be administered with great care, as narcotic poisoning may result from any excess taken. The drug coniine comes into Part I of the British Poisons List.

The Water Hemlock (*Cicuta virosa*) is also poisonous, but in this case most of the drug is concentrated in the root of the plant.

HENBANE *Hyoscyamus niger* [*p.* 134

This curious looking (and poisonous) herb takes two forms—one annual, the other biennial—and both forms will appear from the same batch of seed. The first grows to a height of eighteen inches or two feet and will produce flowers and seed in one season. The other forms a large rosette of leaves the first year, and throws a branched flowering stem in the second season, usually much larger and more vigorous than that of the annual form. The rosette leaves of the biennial plant are a foot or more in length, grey-green, sticky and hairy; but foliage on the next year's flower stalk, which clasp the stem, are smaller and of a pale green colour, with a raised centre rib. The flowers are a mustard yellow with evil-looking purple streaks, and the whole plant exudes a sickening smell.

The official preparation of Henbane is obtained from fresh or dried leaves, flowering tops and branches of the biennial form of *H. niger*. The chief constituents are the alkaloid Hyoscyamine, Atropine and Hyoscine. The medicinal action is hypnotic, antispasmodic and mildly diuretic, similar to that of stramonium and belladonna, but milder in effect. It has been employed in the method of assisting mothers in childbirth known as Twilight Sleep, and in tablets taken to prevent seasickness.

In the first century A.D. it was commended by Dioscorides, who used it to alleviate insomnia and pains, though Pliny declared that it was offensive to the understanding. The herb was used in magic, for its power of throwing victims into convulsions; it was added to the midnight brews of witches, and a sorcerers' ointment was prepared from it.

It is included in Part I of the British Poisons List.

HOREHOUND, BLACK *Ballota nigra* ssp. *foetida* [*p.* 135

The botanical name of this species of Horehound is derived from the Greek *ballo*, strike the senses, which it acquired in the time of Dioscorides on account of its vile smell. Because it was anciently supposed to be an antidote to rabies it was named Madweed, and an old American recipe alleges that an infusion of the herb, taken hot, will be efficacious if you are 'poisoned by your stepmother'.

The plant has stout, branched stems, hairy, egg-shaped wrinkled leaves, and whorls of sickly purple flowers in July and August. It is usually found near habitations, and has accompanied settlers to many a colony overseas. Medicinally it is antispasmodic, stimulant and a vermifuge.

A related herb, Gipsywort (*Lycopus europaeus*) is sometimes called Water Horehound. Gipsies put this into washing water to keep flies from settling on their skin.

HOREHOUND, WHITE *Marrubium vulgare*

The White Horehound, like its Black relative, is a member of the Natural Order *Labiatae*, but, instead of the foul odour of the Black variety, its leaves (when fresh) exude a pleasant musky smell. It is a perennial, indigenous to Britain, and particularly common in eastern England, where country people have for centuries cultivated it in their cottage gardens for use in Horehound drinks and in candy administered to soothe sore throats and relieve coughs.

The plant will grow to a foot or eighteen inches in height, has wrinkled hairy leaves, and produces axillary whorls of white flowers in August. Hippocrates, born 450 B.C. and known as 'the father of medicine', listed this as a valuable herb. Priests in ancient Egypt valued it under the names 'Seed of Horus' and, rather beautifully,

'Eye of the Star'. The Romans, too, knew all about its medicinal properties.

Cultivation is easy. The plant is hardy, and flourishes best in poor, dry soil. It may be sown in spring, or increased by cuttings or by root division. Horehound does not flower until the second season after sowing.

Medicinally, it is an expectorant and tonic, given for chronic coughs, asthma and in some cases of tuberculosis. The powdered leaves have also been employed as a vermifuge and at one time Horehound ointment was used in the treatment of wounds. For the common cold, a tea made by infusing an ounce of fresh herb in one pint of boiling water is effective. The best mixture for a stubborn cough is made as follows: Simmer a good handful of the fresh leaves in a quart of water for twenty minutes, then strain and press out the juice, add honey and lemon juice to taste, and cool. In Norfolk and Suffolk, Horehound Ale was popular in earlier times. In 1967 I heard an old Norfolk farm worker describe the hot summers and long working hours of his youth, which were tempered by the 'lovely drink Mother used to make with Horehound'.

HORSERADISH
Armoracia rusticana (syn. *Cochlearia armorica*)

This coarse and invasive herb has been cultivated for its root since very early times. Its exact place of origin seems to be in doubt. Pliny refers to it under the name *Armoracia*, although at a later period it became known as *Cochlearia*; now the earlier name has been restored. It seems to have been used wholly for its medicinal qualities until the Germans, towards the end of the sixteenth century, invented Horseradish sauce to eat with fish. Perhaps this was valued particularly by Catholics on the Friday fast. By 1640 a taste for this condiment had spread to England, although Parkinson described it as being 'too strong for tender and gentle stomachs'. In France it was called *Moutarde des Allemands*.

In cultivation it requires well manured and deeply dug soil, the compost or stable manure being put down at a depth of eighteen inches or two feet. Root cuttings are planted in this prepared ground in February, dibbled into holes twelve to eighteen inches deep and the same distance apart. The holes are filled in lightly with fine soil, and no more attention will be necessary. In winter the entire crop may be lifted and stored in boxes of sand, or single roots dug as required for use. For really good crops it is advisable to replant the bed every three years. The flavour of this root is hot and biting, but at the same time decidedly sweet. The large leaves often remind people of the Dock plant, but the small white flowers are less familiar.

Medicinally, Horseradish is stimulant, diuretic, antiseptic and aperient. It acts as a stimulant to the digestive organs and is valuable when eaten with oily fish or rich meat. Infused in wine, the root will stimulate the whole nervous system and promote perspiration. Horseradish syrup, made by infusing one drachm of fresh, scraped root in four ounces of water for two hours, then boiling it with double its weight in sugar to make a syrup, will be efficacious in cases of hoarseness. The dose is one teaspoonful at intervals of an hour or two.

An old remedy for flatulence directs the sufferer to put two ounces of scraped Horseradish and half an ounce of crushed Mustard seed, together with a little salt, into a bottle, and cover these ingredients with hot—not boiling—vinegar. This mixture must be kept well corked. The dose is one teaspoonful in half a cupful of boiling water. Stir, and sip slowly. At one time scraped Horseradish was applied to chilblains, under a light bandage.

Horseradish is best confined within a brick enclosure to keep it from spreading wildly, and if the ground does have to be cleared, even the smallest fragment of root must be removed—otherwise each fragment will grow.

HYSSOP   *Hyssopus officinalis*   *[p.* 54

This aromatic and attractive little sub-shrub is almost evergreen and may be trimmed into a neat edging for herb garden or flower border. The flower is usually blue, but pink and white varieties are obtainable also. It is a native of southern Europe, and came to Britain in the sixteenth century. Mazes of that date were frequently 'set with Isope'. The name *Hyssopos*, of Greek origin and used by Dioscorides, was derived from *Ezob*, holy herb, because the plant was used for purifying sacred places.

It is propagated by seed sown in April, or by cuttings made in spring and rooted in semi-shade. When rooted, the plant succeeds best in a light, fairly dry and warm soil. If required to form a clipped edging,

Hyssop should be spaced at intervals of about one foot. The clipping may be done in late March. The plant has narrow leaves, square stems and lipped flowers, and it is a member of the Natural Order *Labiatae*.

Some cooks like to put a tiny sprig in stews and broth, but as the flavour is very pungent this herb should be used with caution in the kitchen. Medicinally, Hyssop is diaphoretic, stimulant, pectoral and carminative, and it is particularly valuable in cases of chronic catarrh. For this complaint it is usually given in a warm infusion, sometimes mixed with White Horehound. Hyssop Tea, made from the dried flowers (a quarter of an ounce, infused in one pint of boiling water, sweetened with honey) is taken three times daily in doses of a wine-glassful, for chest troubles. An infusion made from the green tops is a remedy for catarrh, and is also reputed to be helpful in cases of rheumatism. Pliny mentions *Hyssopites*, a wine made from Hyssop.

Hyssop is a favourite bee plant, and honey made from it has a delicious aroma. It was formerly popular as a 'strewing herb', and the essential oil distilled from this plant's leaves, stems and flowers is valuable in perfumery. It was also used in liqueurs, notably in Chartreuse.

There has been considerable discussion about the 'Hyssop' of the Bible; it seems likely that this was not in fact *Hyssopus* but a species of *Origanum* (Marjoram) or possibly the Caper Plant (*Capparis spinosa*), which is known to the Arabs as 'Azaf'.

A smaller plant, *H. aristatus*, the Rock Hyssop, is suitable for either rock or herb garden. It has blue flowers which open considerably later than those of *H. officinalis*, namely, in late August or September.

INDIGO   *Indigofera tinctoria*

The rich blue dye obtained from the Indigo plant does not exist ready formed, but is produced during a process of fermentation. We know that this dye was used in the ancient world several centuries before Christ, because Herodotus mentions it. Textiles dyed with Indigo have been identified in Egyptian tombs and in Inca graves. At the close of the seventeenth century, seeds of the plant were sent to the United States of America by a Lt.-Col. George Lucas, from Antigua in the West Indies, and by 1747 crops of the dye-plant were flourishing in Carolina and over a million pounds of it came to Britain annually.

Before that, ever since the opening up of routes from Europe to India in the sixteenth century, Indigo had been imported from the Far East. It supplanted the Woad which had hitherto provided most of the blues worn by the Western world. To the Greeks it was known as *Indikon*, Indian dye.

The *Indigofera* is a delicate looking shrub of the Natural Order *Leguminosae*, with small oval leaves and reddish-yellow pea flowers. It is not hardy in U.K. At one time it was used in medicine as an emetic.

The dyestuff known as Indigo is prepared by fermenting leafy branches in tubs of water. The paste that settles on the bottom of the tubs is made into balls or cakes, which must be finely ground before use. According to Mrs Ethel Mairet there are two ways of dyeing with Indigo. The powder is insoluble in water, but may be dissolved in sulphuric acid or oil of vitriol, thereby making an Indigo extract. This gives good blue colours on wool; but is not very permanent, nor will it dye cotton or linen.

The other method, the Indigo vat process, produces fast colours but is complicated and difficult. In order to obtain colour with Indigo it must be deprived of its oxygen. The deoxydized Indigo is yellow, and in this state it penetrates the fabric, or fibre. The more perfectly the Indigo in the vat is deoxydized, the brighter and faster will be the colour. For wool, dyeing vats are heated to fifty degrees Centigrade, but cotton and linen are generally dyed cold.

An old recipe from the Outer Hebrides for dyeing with Lump Indigo is given by Winifred Shand in a handbook *Dye Plants and Dyeing* issued by the Brooklyn Botanic Garden, New York.

Lump Indigo: Boil wool with onion skins till clear yellow, then let wool dry. Have an old pail filled with urine at least two weeks old, or until a skin forms on top. Use a wooden tub for dyeing. Put the Lump Indigo in a muslin bag, heat the 'bree' to hand warmth by placing a hot stone in it, and squeeze in the blue bag. Wet the wool and place in the liquid. Cover the wooden vessel and place it where it will keep warm. After twenty-four hours take the wool out and shake it, do not wring or squeeze. Heat the stone again in the fire and place in the 'bree' until hand-heat again; replace wool and cover as before, repeat shaking and reheating every twenty-four hours for at least seven days. For navy blue, eleven to twenty-one days are required. Fix with boiled sorrel roots in rinsing water, but do not boil the 'bree' or it loses its properties.

There are also two hardy plants, known as Wild Indigo (*Baptisia tinctoria*) and False Indigo (*B. australis*), named from the Greek *bapto* to dye, which are natives of North America from Canada to Carolina; both produce from their woody stems a blue dye, inferior to Indigo. The young shoots were used by New England settlers as substitutes for asparagus, and the root of the Wild Indigo had medicinal uses as an antiseptic gargle and emetic. Both plants are also members of the Natural Order *Leguminosae*.

IRIS   *Iris florentina*

Since ancient times the Iris has been a symbol of power and kingship. It was dedicated to Juno, and its silhouette gave rise to the sceptre, the trifoliate shape signifying faith, wisdom and valour. The Iris—or 'Orris'-root—at one time of great economic value because of its delicious violet scent, was used in perfumery, in sachet powders, in cachous and dentifrices; the dried rhizome was chewed to counteract halitosis, and the dried and powdered root made a kind of snuff. The fragrance, so closely resembling that of the Violet, is not apparent in the fresh root: it develops when the rhizome is dried.

In Tuscany the cultivation of this Iris was at one time a major industry. It took three years for the root to attain maturity, and by that time the flowering plant might stand as high as a man's shoulder. The white flower of the Florentine Iris, known as 'Flower-de-Luce of Florence', or as 'White Flower-de-Luce', appears in the ancient arms of the City for which it is named. It is sometimes mistaken for a Lily. A writer in Bologna in the thirteenth century described the cultivation of this Florentine Iris, and gave the season for harvesting the rhizome. Orris root was also used in ancient Greece and Rome; Elis and Corinth were renowned for their unguents made from Iris.

Theophrastus was acquainted with the root, and Dioscorides and Pliny too. They mentioned that Illyricum (later Dalmatia) produced the best quality. It seems likely that the Illyrian plant was the related and very similar plant *I. germanica*, which has blue flowers. Another Iris with a fragrant rhizome is *I. pallida*.

The rhizomes of these Irises, when fresh, were also employed in medicine, being cathartic, and effective in the treatment of dropsy. In England, Orris root mixed with Anise was used as a perfume for linen about five hundred years ago. It is listed in the accounts of Edward IV.

In the reign of Queen Elizabeth I a 'swete clothe' was produced, and is believed to have been scented with Orris by the clothworkers who made it.

IRIS *Iris pseudacorus*

This wild British Iris, whose yellow flowers edge so many ponds, ditches and marshy places all over the country, has been given a variety of names, including Dragon Flower, Myrtle Flower, Fliggers, Daggers, Jacob's Sword, Gladyne, Meklin, Segg, Sheggs, Livers and Shalder. At the present time most of us call it Yellow Flag.

Segg, Sheggs, Skeggs and Cegg are all of Anglo-Saxon origin. Segg = a small sword, and this obviously relates to the blade-shaped foliage. Gladyne dates from Chaucer's day. Another country name, 'Cheiper', describes the shrill sound made by small boys who blow against a taut leaf, and 'Cucumber' refers to the appearance of the seed-vessels.

The Romans called this plant *Consecratrix*, because it was used in purification ceremonies, and Pliny mentions the rites used when it was gathered. Medicinally, the uses of the rhizome of this native Iris are similar to those of *Iris florentina*, for it is a powerful cathartic, but it has no fragrance to compare with the first, and therefore was not valued by the perfumery trade.

Early in the last century a French chemist discovered that the ripe seeds made a palatable coffee-like drink, if well roasted before being ground and infused.

The flowers yield a good yellow dye, and the roots, with sulphate of iron mordant, black. In the Outer Hebrides of Scotland the rhizomes of this plant were formerly in great demand for the strong black dye they produced. This was in regular use for the 'Sabbath black' clothing worn by everybody on Sundays and other great occasions. This dye-plant is called *Bun Sealasdair* in the Gaelic.

JUNIPER *Juniperus communis* [*p.* 150

This Juniper, which may grow to thirty feet, but is seldom seen much above the height of a man in this country, thrives on chalky soils, and is common on the North Downs near London and in the limestone hills of the Lake District. Although it is a member of the Natural

Order *Coniferae*, it bears fruits which appear to resemble berries rather than cones, and it is these Juniper 'berries' which yield the volatile oil used in medicine and in the production of gin—a word derived from the French *Genévrier*, Juniper. These fruits take several years to ripen, so that berries in the green, unripe state are frequently seen in company with ripe, blue ones. In Sweden they are used for brewing a Juniper beer, and in hotter countries the tree exudes a kind of varnish or gum through incisions made in the bark.

Medicinally, the distilled Oil of Juniper has been used as a diuretic, stomachic and carminative, in the treatment of diseases of kidney and bladder, and to alleviate indigestion. In France it has been prescribed for chest complaints and scrofula.

Most animals will eat the fruit, and it is said to prevent and cure dropsy in sheep.

The Juniper, with its blue-grey spiky 'needles', is an attractive garden subject and easily grown in suitable soil and situations. It thrives in chalk and limestone districts, and requires good drainage. Propagation is by seed, which is sown half an inch deep in beds of light soil in a cold frame in April; seedlings are transplanted into pots when two inches high, and put outdoors a year later. Or cuttings of young branches may be struck in sandy soil in a cold frame in September or October.

There is a small species, *J. sabina*, five to ten feet in height, whose fresh tops, gathered and dried, produce the 'Savin' which is employed in an ointment used externally for blisters and skin troubles. The oil of Savin is included in Part I of the British Poisons List.

LADY'S MANTLE *Alchemilla mollis, A. vulgaris*

This hardy perennial is described by Margaret Brownlow as 'a quiet member of the Rose family'. Quiet and unshowy this member of the Natural Order *Rosaceae* certainly is, with its soft, green fan-shaped foliage, whose seven- or nine-lobed edges are supposed to resemble the scalloped edges of a mantle, and its small, lime-green flowers in corymbs terminating long, branching stems of graceful habit from June to July. *Alchemilla mollis* is usually cultivated in gardens.

Alchemilla vulgaris may be found growing wild all over Britain, but prefers high-lying districts and the colder climates of the north—such as the Yorkshire Dales or the Scottish Highlands, where it thrives at altitudes of up to 3,500 feet. Further afield it flourishes within the Arctic Circle, in Europe and Asia and in Greenland and Labrador. This species reaches to between a foot and eighteen inches in height. Another kind, *A. alpina*, with green flowers and silvery foliage, is less than half that size.

The name *Alchemilla* is derived from the Arabic word for alchemy, ascribed by some writers to the miraculous healing power of the plant. Others connect alchemy with the dewdrops that lie in the plant's curiously pleated leaves, and in the little cup made by its stipules, which clasp the stem. These drops were of old collected to play a part in wonder-working potions. The name Lady's Mantle, given to this Alchemilla in the Middle Ages, began, as did so many similar names, as *Our* Lady's Mantle, with reference to the Virgin Mary. It is therefore incorrect to write it as 'Ladies' Mantle'. Another name, Lion's Foot—and the French *Pied-de-Lion*—came from a supposed resemblance between the outspread lower leaves to a lion's pug mark on the ground.

In medicine the whole herb is used, gathered in June or July when the flower is out and the leaves are at their best. The root, fresh, was sometimes used medicinally too. The properties of this plant are astringent and styptic, and it was formerly considered to be one of the finest wound herbs. As an old herbal puts it: 'It quickly healeth green wounds, not suffering any corruption to remain behind, and cureth old sores although fistulous and hollow.'

In times past a small bag or 'pillow' filled with Lady's Mantle was believed to promote sound sleep. In modern herbal work, an infusion made with one ounce of the dried herb put into one pint of boiling water is taken, in doses of a teacupful when needed, to lessen excessive menstruation.

Another species of Alchemilla, or Aphanes, *A. arvensis*, known as Parsley Piert, is common in most parts of Great Britain, particularly in dry places such as gravel pits and the tops of walls, but it is not found above the 1,500 foot contour. It is inconspicuous, seldom above four inches in height, with dark green wedge-shaped leaves, each with three deeply cut lobes. The plant is downy, and the tiny green flowers have no stalks. This annual plant blooms from May to August.

It has for centuries been prized in herbal medicine as a cure for stone in the bladder, which gave it the old vernacular name of Parsley Breakstone (or Parsley Piercestone), the latter word now abbreviated to 'Piert'. It is not related to the true Parsley, but some folk see a likeness. The whole herb is used medicinally, either fresh or dried. It has an astringent effect on the mouth, but no taste or smell. It is diuretic, demulcent and refrigerant, acting on bladder and kidneys powerfully but safely. It also removes obstructions of the liver, and is useful in cases of jaundice.

A simple infusion may be made from a handful of the fresh herb in a pint of boiling water. This is taken three or four times daily, in doses of half a teacupful; but to cure stubborn cases its best action is seen when it is compounded by the skilled herbalist with demulcents such as Comfrey or Slippery Elm bark.

Juliette Levy says in her interesting *Herbal Handbook for Farm and Stable* that both species of Alchemilla are valued by Arab and gipsy herbalists and herdsmen. Horses, sheep and goats seek out the wild *Alchemilla mollis*, which has a tonic effect on them, and *A. arvensis* is much used by gipsies for curing stone and as an after-tonic in the treatment of colic.

LAVENDER   *Lavandula officinalis*

Lavenders were formerly classified as *Lavandula vera* and *L. spica*, but as both species have seemingly contributed to the making of our modern garden hybrids, these are now often grouped together under *L. officinalis*, although Sanders's *Encyclopaedia of Gardening* quotes *spica* as a synonym for *officinalis*, without mention of *L. vera*.

The raising of Lavenders from seed is difficult, and germination very slow. As cuttings root so easily, this method of propagation is the one commonly used. Root division in spring is also possible. When taking cuttings of Lavender the mistake of selecting large woody branches is often made; better results are achieved by using smaller and newer shoots, about six inches long. Remove the lower leaves and place the cut end firmly in a sandy bed. Rooting takes place most rapidly in spring, but cuttings will be successful at almost any season when the mother plant can provide strong little shoots.

Mature plants of Lavender should be cut hard back directly the flower stalks have been picked. Some gardeners, who prefer to leave these on the plant until the autumn for interest, not wishing to utilize the 'pips' for sachets, are then afraid to cut into the wood of their bushes as late as the end of September. If bushes never receive vigorous pruning they become misshapen and straggly in time. The best solution to this problem is to forfeit spikes on alternate plants every year, cutting the stripped bush hard back in July or August and leaving its neighbour in bloom until the end of the season. In the West of England I have carried out very hard pruning in early October without causing damage, but this will not succeed in every district.

The Lavender is indigenous to the hilly regions bordering the western Mediterranean, and in view of the fact that it has for centuries been a familiar feature of English gardens, it is interesting to discover that in the late sixteenth century some herbalists considered that it was not hardy enough to stand the climate of Britain. It reached England in 1568, and this opinion must soon have been rejected, for it quickly became a favourite garden plant, and was taken to America by the Pilgrim Fathers.

The Greeks gave the name *nardos* to Lavender, from Naarda in Syria, and from that it became known as 'Nard'. In Pliny's day blossoms sold for a hundred Roman denarii per pound. Some authorities believe that this 'Nard' was the Spikenard of the Bible, *Lavandula spica*. Another species *Lavandula stoechas*, often called French Lavender, was probably the plant used by the Romans as a bath perfume, which gave rise to the name Lavandula, from *lavare*, to wash. *Lavandula stoechas* is referred to in the old herbals as 'Sticadore'. Its flowers were an ingredient of the notorious 'Vinegar of the Four Thieves', already mentioned under GARLIC.

Lavender inspired some of the best-known Cries of London, including:

> Here's your sweet Lavender, sixteen sprigs a penny,
> Which you'll find, my ladies, will smell as sweet as any,

and:

> Lavender, sweet blooming Lavender,
> Six bunches a penny today.
> Lavender, sweet blooming Lavender,
> Ladies, buy it while you may!

Most of us know that this is a good bee plant, and that it was of old used as a strewing-herb, but it surprises some people to hear that this fragrant herb has had medicinal virtues ascribed to it. According to Mrs Grieve the Essential Oil, or a Spirit of Lavender made from it, has carminative and nervine properties. Her friend Mrs Leyel wrote that a *tisane* of Lavender, or even a spray of the plant worn under one's hat, would get rid of a nervous headache, while a few drops of Essence of Lavender in a hot footbath would relieve fatigue. These virtues of Lavender were known to the early Welsh physicians of Myddfai, who called the herb *Llafant*.

Having been born and brought up in Carshalton and Wallington in Surrey, where in the early years of this century a small residue of cultivation left over from the once famous Mitcham Lavender Fields could still be seen, I have felt an almost proprietary interest in Lavender ever since, and find bottles of Lavender Water hard to resist. As a girl I liked to think that the gardens of houses recently built on the Lavender fields must retain some traces of the fragrance which once they nurtured in such abundance—a fancy that was never substantiated.

The late Eleanour Sinclair Rohde wrote in *The Scented Garden* of her 'beautiful white Lavender with pearl-like flowers . . . just as strongly scented as the mauve'. This plant, supposed to be vulnerable to cold winds, 'survived the bitterly cold winter of 1928, when many hardy plants succumbed'. She mentions the Lavender-scented sugar made in olden days by pounding Lavender flowers together with three times their weight of sugar. In *The Queen's Closet Opened*, Queen Henrietta Maria's cook states that this 'conserve' will keep for a year.

Many good Lavenders are now obtainable for garden use. The following selection has been divided into three heights.

1 DWARF LAVENDERS—under 2 feet

Munstead—18 inches. Grey foliage, deep purple flowers.

Folgate Blue—18 inches. Green-grey foliage, the bluest mauve flowers of all Lavenders.

Pink Lavender—Lavandula nana rosa—18 inches. Grey-green foliage.

Lavandula atropurpurea nana—15 inches. Neat, compact growth, silvery foliage, purple-violet flowers.

Dwarf White—Lavandula nana alba—6–8 inches. Needs shelter.

2 SEMI-DWARF LAVENDERS 2–2½ feet

Hidcote Purple—Free-flowering (June), a rich purple, silver-grey foliage. An excellent plant of good, compact habit.

Twickle Purple—The most fragrant of all dwarf and semi-dwarf kinds. Long spikes carried fan-wise over green-grey foliage. Mauve flowers with bluish lights in them. Good for sachets.

3 TALL LAVENDERS—3 feet or more

Old English or 'Mitcham' types—Flower-spikes thick and close, deep bluish-mauve flowers, green-grey foliage. In flower mid-July to early August.
Grey Hedge Lavender—Narrow silver-grey foliage, soft mauve flowers. In bloom late July and August.
Dutch Lavender—This may be either semi-dwarf or tall, but it belongs to the Grey Hedge group, with pale and pointed spikes rather sparsely produced, and silver-grey foliage.

4 FRENCH LAVENDER—*Lavandula stoechas*

The inflorescence has purplish-black flowers with little gold 'eyes', arranged in neat rows, as Margaret Brownlow puts it, 'like corn on the cob', and the spike is topped by a quaint purple bract which suggests a ribbon bow. This plant is slightly tender and needs a sheltered position and well-drained, light soil. It flowers before any other Lavender—in the month of May.

Some recipes for sweet-bags and pot-pourri, using Lavender, will be found on pages 168–171.

LINSEED   see FLAX

LIQUORICE   *Glycyrrhiza glabra*   [*p.* 54

This perennial shrub, a native of south-east Europe and south-west Asia, with racemes of mauve or cream coloured pea-flowers and graceful pinnate leaves of a pale green rather like Laburnum, blooms from July to September and has been in cultivation by man since ancient times. It is valued for its sweet root, used in both medicine and confectionery.

Dioscorides, who was familiar with the uses of Liquorice Extract, named the plant *Glycyrrhiza* from the Greek *glukus*, sweet and *rhiza*, a root. The Greeks are supposed to have learnt the uses of the plant from the Scythians, and Theophrastus in the third century B.C. spoke of the 'sweet Scythian root' found growing in the vicinity of the Sea of

Azov, a root with curative properties in cases of asthma and coughs.
A Latin name for it, *Liquiritia officinalis* (a corruption of *Glycyrrhiza*),
seemingly gave rise to the English 'Liquorice', which is spelt 'Lycorys'
in the wardrobe accounts of Henry IV dated 1264. Cultivation of the
plant began in England early in the reign of Queen Elizabeth I, and
by 1597 the well-known herbalists had it growing in their physic
gardens.

Liquorice is official in all pharmacopoeias, which differ only in the
varieties recognized, the botanical names used, and in requiring root
supplies to be in the peeled or unpeeled state. The British Pharmacopoeia stipulates that the root shall be peeled.

This plant grows best on sandy soil near streams; it does not like
clay, and prefers deep, fine soil in river valleys. It requires moisture
during the growing period, and hard-baked soil in late summer, when
dry heat helps to form the sweetness of the root. It cannot survive
much frost, and cool weather is apt to make the root woody and to
inhibit the formation of juice.

The root of Liquorice penetrates to a very great depth, and for this
reason the plant needs ground well cultivated and manured down to
two-and-a-half or three feet. It is best planted in March, when small,
young runners left over from the root harvest, each piece about six
inches long, are dibbled in four inches below the surface and three feet
apart, with eighteen inches or more between the rows. Growth during
the next two years is not very great above ground, but in the third and
fourth years the plant reaches maturity and the root is then ready for
harvesting.

English Liquorice is taken up in late autumn. Every part of the
subterranean growth, consisting of runners and roots, is saved. The
root and all older, harder runners form the crop, while younger, softer
runners are kept for replanting. This plant was formerly grown in
large quantities by commercial cultivators in Surrey and around
Pontefract in Yorkshire, a place that gave its name to the Liquorice
sweetmeat known as 'Pontefract cakes', popular with children in my
youth. Long 'bootlaces' of Liquorice were then to be seen in every
sweet shop, retailing at two a penny.

The medicinal properties of Liquorice are demulcent, emollient and
moderately pectoral. It is an ingredient of many cough mixtures and
enters into the composition of cough lozenges and pastilles. Fluid
Extract of Liquorice is often used to disguise the unpalatable taste of

bitter drugs such as Quinine and Cascara. It was prescribed by early physicians, beginning with Hippocrates, in cases of dropsy. It is the only sweet substance with thirst-quenching effect. The sugar of Liquorice is said to be safe for diabetic sufferers. According to Juliette Levy it is employed in some countries to promote female fertility.

A drink made from one ounce of the peeled and bruised root, infused in one pint of boiling water for five or ten minutes, is useful in cases of sore throat and of catarrhal conditions occurring in the urinary intestinal tracts.

Brewers have made use of Liquorice to give substance and dark colour to stout and porter.

LOVAGE *Levisticum officinale* (syn. *Ligusticum levisticum*)
[*p.* 150

The Lovage plant was brought to Britain from the Mediterranean at an early date and became a popular herb in gardens. It is now largely neglected, but deserves to be propagated for its delicate aroma, refreshing flavour (if not overdone by the cook), and because it is easy to grow. The plant is a perennial belonging to the enormous Natural Order *Umbelliferae*, with thick and fleshy roots, stout, erect stems—up to four feet high—and dark green leaves not unlike those of Celery in shape although darker in colour. When crushed, their scent is reminiscent of both Celery and Angelica. Umbels of small yellow flowers in June and July are similar to those of Fennel, and they are followed by small, very aromatic fruits. One of this plant's botanical names, *Ligusticum*, is thought to have come from the Italian Province of Liguria, where the herb flourishes in abundance.

Propagation is by root division in early spring, or by seed sown in late summer and transplanted into permanent quarters in autumn or early spring. Lovage does well in moist, rich soil and in semi-shade. It was quietly popular as a medicinal herb in the fourteenth century; the roots and fruit are aromatic and stimulant, and have some diuretic and carminative action, but extravagant claims have never been made for it.

At one time the leaf stalk and stem bases were blanched like Celery and used as a vegetable. Freshly gathered leaf stalks, split lengthways, are employed in cookery, also the leaves—fresh or dried. The flavour of Lovage is potent, and it should be used with caution at first. It goes into soups, stews and salads, and blends extremely well with tomatoes.

The roots and seeds were once used as a kind of pepper, to season meat and broth.

A herbal tea may be made from dried leaves of Lovage, one ounce infused in a pint of boiling water. The cordial drink known as 'Lovage', which was formerly brewed and sold in country inns all over Britain, contained not only this herb but Tansy and Yarrow also.

The name 'Lovage' has been misapplied to several plants, but 'Scotch Lovage' really is a *Ligusticum* (*scoticum*). It is a garden escape, now growing wild on cliffs, sea-shores and beside estuaries in Northumberland and Scotland. It is also seen near monastic ruins, where the monks once cultivated the plant as a potherb. It has a strong and not very agreeable taste. In the Hebrides the leaves were formerly eaten, raw or boiled, as a vegetable. It was there called *Shunis*.

Another harmless and edible plant, Smallage (*Apium graveolens*), is occasionally confused with Lovage and called by that name. It is in fact Wild Celery, found growing in salt marshes, and is valuable in the treatment of rheumatism. This herb is also a good nervine and promotes sleep.

The so-called 'Water Lovage' is in a different category altogether. This is the Common Water Dropwort (*Oenanthe fistulosa*) and it is a poisonous relative of the even more dangerous Hemlock Water Dropwort (*Oenanthe crocata*). Both plants are very common in Britain, found growing wild in ditches and beside streams. As these tall umbelliferous plants are difficult to identify with certainty, except by experienced botanists, it is probably wiser for the rest of us to refrain from eating any of them when in the wild state.

LUNGWORT *Pulmonaria officinalis* [*p.* 150

A favourite old country plant this, with many rural-sounding names: Soldiers and Sailors, Adam and Eve, Joseph and Mary, Hundreds and Thousands, Jerusalem Cowslip. The vernacular and Latin names both relate to the curious pale blotches on the leaves, which were of old thought to resemble the appearance of lungs. From this idea, under what was known in the seventeenth century as the 'Doctrine of Signatures', the use of this herb in treating pulmonary complaints had been divinely indicated to mankind.

Lungwort is a hardy perennial, twelve to eighteen inches high, a member of the Natural Order *Boraginaceae*. The blossoms of *P.*

officinalis are usually rosy at first, changing through mauve to blue as they mature; but, with a succession of them opening throughout the flowering season (March to May), the plant is a kaleidoscope of pink, mauve and blue. I have always thought these colours too soft and delicate to warrant the Somerset name of 'Bloody Butcher', which refers to the blood-stained apron of 'butcher's blue' formerly worn by the man in the village butchery. This easily grown and lusty plant makes excellent ground cover, doing well in semi-shade, and the type with leaves so generously blotched that the general appearance is silvery gives a particularly charming effect.

In her delightful book, *Cottage Garden Flowers*, Margery Fish describes the fun of being a Pulmonaria fancier:

Connoisseurs are choosy about them. They want the one known as *P. saccharata*, because its leaves are longer and more heavily spotted. Collecting good forms is a regular gardening sport, and some of those found are so heavily covered with spots that they are practically silver. There is one good Pulmonaria in this family called *P. saccharata* 'Mrs Moon', with very good foliage and flowers that open pink, then turn blue, but I have never found out who Mrs Moon was or where she lived.

The red Pulmonaria *P. rubra* comes out very early, often before the blue-and-pink. It is a fine reward for facing the draughty air of a February day, to come face to face with little clusters of tight coral flowers tucked into cups of soft green foliage. *P. rubra* has no markings on its leaves, and its flowers are the brightest shade of pure coral. Sometimes this plant is called Bethlehem Sage, and I have heard country folk refer to it as the Christmas Cowslip . . .

The blue Pulmonarias are a little higher in the social scale and are sometimes considered worthy of a place in the rock garden. There is a little confusion about the names. *P. angustifolia* appears to be the same as *P. azurea*, with *P. angustifolia azurea* as the name for one with light-blue flowers. They divide again into Mawson's Blue and Munstead Blue, which must have come from Miss Gertrude Jekyll's garden, and is, I think, the more refined plant. It is deciduous and slow-growing. The leaves appear before the flowers as little folded pricks of bright green, and the intensely blue flowers are carried on six-inch stems.

Propagation of all these subjects is by seed or by division of the rootstock, which may be done after flowering in moist weather in late spring, or in the autumn. Lungworts do well in almost any soil so long as it does not dry out too much in a hot summer.

The plant contains a large amount of mucilage, and an infusion made from one teaspoonful of the dried herb in a cup of boiling water, strained and taken three times a day, has undoubtedly some soothing and healing power in chest complaints and whooping-cough.

MACE see NUTMEG

MADDER, DYER'S *Rubia tinctorum*

This plant was cultivated in great quantity in Europe, notably in France and Holland, and in Britain too, before the introduction in the nineteenth century of the aniline dyes which superseded vegetable dyestuffs in all but a few hand-weaving industries. In the Middle Ages Madder (*Garancia, Warancia*), was the commonest red dyestuff, and the Madder trade equalled in volume and importance that of Woad. *Mediaeval Merchant Venturers*, by E. M. Carus-Wilson, quotes the records of tolls imposed on cartloads of Madder coming into the town of Winchester. The dried roots of this plant yield a rich red dye, when used on white wool mordanted with cream of tartar and tin. With an alum mordant the colour is more rusty, and with chrome a reddish brown, while a purplish brown is obtained with iron mordant. Other red dyes, all of which had to be imported into Britain, were 'brasil' (derived from the East Indian tree *Caesalpinia sappan*), 'vermilion' (a mineral dye derived from a crystalline substance found on the shores of the Red Sea), and 'grain', derived from dried bodies of the kermes insect, *coccus ilicis*.

Rubia tinctorum is not naturalized in the U.K., but a close relative, Wild Madder (*Rubia peregrina*), is found in places, usually on cliffs along our south and west coasts, and a good rose-pink may be obtained from the root. Another wild British plant, the yellow Lady's Bedstraw (*Galium verum*), gives a rust colour from the roots. I have also tried roots of the white-flowered Hedge Bedstraw (*Galium mollugo*) and found that they, too, yield a pleasing rusty red which appears to be reasonably fast.

Rubia peregrina is a perennial plant with straggling four-angled prickly stems, and whorls of dark, shining, evergreen leaves. The flowers (June–August) are small and yellowish-green, and they are succeeded by black berries about the size of a pea. Some directions for dyeing with the Bedstraws are given on page 182.

MALLOW, MARSH   *Althaea officinalis*   [*pp.* 135, 151

This attractive hardy perennial Mallow, growing up to four feet in height, has velvety greyish foliage and very pale coloured mauve-pink flowers. It is found in most European countries; in Britain it is common to the south of a line from the Wash to Shrewsbury. It appears in salt marshes by the sea, on the banks of tidal rivers and in ditches. It has been known by the country names of Mallards, Mauls, Cheeses and Mortification Root.

The common Mallow is frequently alluded to as 'Marsh' Mallow, but the true Marsh Mallow is distinguishable by its hoary appearance—stems and leaves thickly covered with downy hairs—and by the bluish hue of the flowers, which are also paler than those of the Common Mallow. The plant contains much mucilage, which is highly emollient and superior to that of the Common Mallow. The generic name *Althaea* is derived from the Greek *althaino*, heal; the healing power of this plant was well known to the ancients, and *Malvaceae* comes from *malakos*, soft, from its emollient properties.

Most of the Mallows have also been used as food, and the Romans esteemed the Marsh Mallow as a succulent vegetable. Similar uses of various Mallows have been recorded in China, Syria and Egypt, in times past; and in France today the fresh young tops are still put into salads. The roots, when first boiled and then fried with onions and butter, are said to form a palatable dish which has often been valuable in times of food shortage. A Biblical reference to 'Mallow' in this connection is now thought to be a mistranslation; it is probable that a saline plant, either Orache or Sea-purslane, should be substituted for 'Mallow' in Job xxx. 4.

For medicinal use, the leaves are picked in August when the plants are beginning to flower. The root is also harvested for use in herbal medicine. According to Mrs Grieve this plant contains starch, mucilage, pectin, oil, sugar, asparagin (found too in Asparagus), phosphate of lime, glutinous matter and cellulose. It is useful in inflammation and irritation of the alimentary canal and of respiratory and urinary organs. Juliette Levy writes that the fruits, known as 'cheeses' by peasant children, are highly tonic. 'The leaves and flowers yield a healing lotion, the roots make a useful poultice, and were once used to check mortification, one ancient name for mallow being "Mortification Plant".'

The roots of this plant, being boiled in water, produce over half their weight in sweet-tasting mucilage with soothing and healing properties. The decoction may be made by boiling a quarter of a pound of the dried root in five pints of water until it is reduced to three pints. Boiled in wine or milk, Marsh Mallow was once a popular remedy for coughs, bronchitis and similar troubles. In France the Marsh Mallow flower forms one part of the *Tisane de quatre fleurs* taken for colds.

The real 'Marshmallow' confectionery is made from the dried, powdered roots. Two ounces of this powder is mixed with 14 ounces of fine sugar, a little mucilage or gum tragacanth and water of orange flowers is added to bind the mixture together; balls are shaped from it and left to dry. The so-called 'Marshmallows' sold today in sweet shops do not contain any Mallow root, but are compounded of flour, gum, egg-albumen and flavouring.

Although the Marsh Mallow is superior to all other plants of this family, species with somewhat similar virtues have been utilized in place of it at times. These are: Musk Mallow (*Malva moschata*), one to two feet high, with rose-pink flowers in July and August; Common Mallow (*Malva sylvestris*), up to three feet high, with crinkled Ivy-shaped leaves, often with a small spot near the base. (Flowers of this species are an inch or more across, with narrow pinky-purple petals; these often show darker veins.) The Dwarf Mallow (*Malva rotundifolia*) has prostrate stems and pale lilac flowers; and the tall, branching Tree Mallow (*Lavatera arborea*) is a downy biennial with many branches bearing flowers up to two inches across, pinky-purple, in July, August and September.

The Marsh Mallow is sometimes cultivated in herb gardens; good clumps of it look well at the back of a border or surrounded by Hyssop and Lavender. Propagation is by seed sown in spring or summer, or by division of the root in autumn. This plant will grow in fairly light soil, if planted with a good supply of compost, put in at considerable depth, so that the roots are kept cool.

MARIGOLD *Calendula officinalis*

This plant is the queen of cottage gardens, and as children we knew that if all else failed we could count on it to spring up and provide brightness in our small plots of ground. Its generic name *Calendula* is said to derive from the fact that it may be found in bloom, somewhere, in every month. The modern Italian name, *Fiore d'ogni mese*, repeats this belief.

The old English herbalists referred to the plant as Golds or Ruddes. A *Herball* of 1578 states: 'It hath pleasant, bright and shining yellow flowers, the which do close at the setting downe of the sunne, and do spread and open againe at the sunne rising.' In *The Winter's Tale* Shakespeare expresses the same idea: 'The Marigold that goes to bed wi' th' sun, and with him rises weeping.' A contemporary writer referred to the use of the plant as a dye: 'Of Marygold we learn that summe used to make theyr here yelow with the floure of this herbe, not beyng content with the naturall colour which God hath geven them.'

Curiously enough, this most popular of all cottage garden flowers has received few vernacular names. Margery Fish does not quote any; Mrs Grieve, apart from the ancient Golds and Ruddes, gives us only Jackanapes-on-horseback and the corruption Mary Gowles. Mrs Leyel, in *Cinquefoil*, adds to these the English name Pot Marigold and the Latin *Verrucaria*.

As a domestic medicine [she writes] the Marigold is one of the best herbs available to man, and is so easy to grow that no garden should ever be without it.

After accidents, for cuts and inflammation of any kind, when the skin has been broken, it would never be wrong to apply it locally, or to take internally a hot decoction of these flowers, made with a pint of boiling water to two handfuls of the flowers and leaves. It promotes healthy granulation. It is a cordial herb, and as such excellent for the heart and circulation . . . The old name *Verrucaria* denotes its efficacy as a cure for warts.

Only the common, deep orange-flowered variety is of medicinal value. Both leaves and ray florets of the flowers are used; the latter need quick drying in a good current of warm air in a shady spot. The florets must be laid out on sheets of clean paper, loosely without touching, or they will become discoloured. Of old these were used in cookery as well as medicine, being put into salads, broths and soups. The flower also provides a good yellow dye.

Cultivation is easy. Although the plant is a native of southern Europe, it is hardy and seeds germinate readily in almost any soil and conditions. The seedlings should be thinned to about nine inches apart. Flowering begins in June, and if seedheads are culled the plants will continue to bloom until severe weather kills them. If a few seed-heads are left on the plant, a supply of self-sown seedlings will be ensured for the next season. Margery Fish tells an amusing story about a child who thought her garden was bewitched. Given various packets of seeds each year, which she sowed, she found that they always came up as Marigolds. It never occurred to her that the seeds were in the ground beforehand, and smothered everything else before later arrivals had a chance to grow.

MARJORAM *Origanum vulgare*

The name Origanum is derived from the Greek *oros*, mountain, and *ganos*, joy, which describes the gaiety given to the hillsides in countries bordering the Mediterranean by quantities of this herb, which grows in profusion and scents the warm air for months on end. Marjoram is a small perennial plant with a very long record of service to man. The Greeks used it extensively in medicine, taking it internally for narcotic poisoning and dropsy, and applying it externally as a fomentation. They also crowned newly married couples with wreaths of Marjoram, and if it sprang up on a grave it was considered an augury of happiness in a future state for the person buried there. One species of Marjoram is believed to be the plant called *amarakos* by some of the old Greek writers.

In Britain *Origanum vulgare* grows wild in many parts, especially favouring chalk downs. In July and August it produces pink blossom, with rich purple bracts; it often has plum-coloured stems, and reaches a height of twelve to eighteen inches. The leaves are oval and darkish green, with hairy undersides. The whole plant gives out a warm fragrance. Occasionally a type with lighter green foliage and white flowers makes an appearance. Marjoram is eaten by goats and sheep, but horses and cattle do not seem to care for it.

This wild Marjoram is the species generally used in medicine; the extracted oil is stimulant, carminative, diaphoretic and mildly tonic in effect. A few drops on a plug of cottonwool have often been used to relieve toothache, and dried leaves and tops, heated, are applied in bags as fomentations for swellings and to dispel colic. An infusion made from a handful of fresh tops in one pint of boiling water helps to relieve nervous headaches. The strong balsamic flavour and fragrance of this plant are well preserved for a considerable time after the harvested tops have been dried and stored; of old, country folk took advantage of this and hung up bunches of the wild herb to use as

Marjoram Tea. In Tudor and Stuart days it was popular as a 'strewing herb', and it was constantly used for 'swete bags', 'swete powders' and 'swete washing waters'. Our forefathers also cleaned their household furniture with its aromatic juices, so the perfumed polish manufactured today is no new thing. But refrigeration is comparatively new; no longer do dairymaids, anxious about the keeping of milk in thundery weather, have to run out to the fields for bunches of Marjoram to place beside pans and pails of new milk in the dairy. It was firmly held that this plant could assist to preserve the sweetness of dairy products.

The flowering tops of Marjoram were also used for colouring cloth. The dye is purple on wool, and a reddish brown on linen. It is not a fast or very satisfactory material, but the poorer folk who could not obtain Madder would have to make do with it at times.

Marjoram is easily cultivated in the garden, being raised from seed or propagated by division of the fibrous rootstock in spring or autumn. It does best in full sun and in moderately rich soil, which must be well drained. The tops are cut just before the plant comes into full flower, and then hung up in bunches in a current of warm air to dry, before being rubbed down and stored in airtight jars. This herb is used, fresh or dried, in *bouquet garni*; in mixed herb flavouring; in stuffings for poultry, pork and veal; in omelettes, cheese dishes and salads. (Recipes: pp. 172–180.) Although our native species may be used in the kitchen, there are others even more popular for culinary purposes.

French or 'Pot' Marjoram (*O. onites*) has grass-green foliage and pinky-mauve flowers. It is more sweetly aromatic than *O. vulgare*.

Sweet or Knotted Marjoram (*O. marjorana*) has small greyish leaves and is very aromatic. It is a native of Portugal and usually treated as half-hardy in the United Kingdom, where it is sown under glass in March or April and planted outside in June. It will also make good pot-plants, and if kept in a cool greenhouse will flourish for years to keep the cook supplied with fresh sprigs. It likes a sandy soil, blended with compost.

For garden interest, the Golden Marjoram (*O. aureum*) with its rounded oval, slightly crinkled leaves will make a glorious clump of pale, shining gold wherever lightness is required in a scheme of colour. Provided it has a sunny position it will keep its brightness for many months, and the pale pink flower-heads in summer blend with the foliage to create a 'sunrise' effect. In addition, this variety serves equally well in the kitchen—if you can spare a few sprigs for mundane purposes. The golden form of *O. vulgare* is not quite as rich as *O. aureum*, but none the less useful, and a stronger grower.

All the Marjorams are excellent bee-plants. This herb was praised by Izaak Walton, who refers in *The Compleat Angler* to 'Sweet Margerome'.

MEADOWSWEET *Filipendula ulmaria*

This fragrant and lovely wild native plant is so common in damp woods, ditches and on moist banks that an exile is apt to think first of its fernlike foliage and creamy foam of blossom when recalling overseas the delights of an English summer scene. On such nostalgic occasions it seems to have bloomed for half the year, but in reality it begins to flower in June and continues until September is half through.

The blossom smells of almonds, and the whole plant is so fragrant that it became one of the most popular 'strewing-herbs' in the sixteenth and seventeenth centuries, and was a great favourite with Queen Elizabeth I. The office of King's Herb-strewer, after being in abeyance for many years, was revived at the coronation of George IV. The woman appointed for this office wore the old costume, consisting of a white gown and scarlet mantle with gold lace. On her head she had a wreath of laurel and oak leaves, and round her neck a badge of office. She was attended by six maidens in white, adorned with flowers and greenery. Each pair carried a two-handled basket from which they took this and other herbs to strew in the path of the king.

In company with Vervain, Mistletoe and Water-mint it was held sacred by the Druids.

Meadowsweet is not usually considered to be a culinary herb, but according to Eleanour Sinclair Rohde a sprig of it adds a good flavour to soups. In country places the flowering tops were formerly dried to make an infusion popular with those suffering from cold in the head. Meadowsweet Tea is made by infusing an ounce of the dried flowers and leaves in one pint of boiling water. Chaucer mentions a drink made from 'Meadwort' called 'Save'. Queen-of-the Meadow, Dolloff and Bridewort are other vernacular names used.

Juliette Levy states that this plant is a proved fever herb, of use also in dysentery, and will improve the complexion. (For the latter, Somerset gypsies, she says, make a lotion by steeping flower-heads in shallow dishes of rainwater placed in the sun. Dew collected from

Teasel and other water-holding plants is added to improve this.) For tea, a handful of the flowers, nipped off the stalks, placed in a steel, enamel or earthenware pan, is covered with two cups of cold water and heated gently until it reaches nearly—but not quite—boiling point. This is kept on the heat for three minutes, but not permitted to boil. It is then taken off and left to cool and steep for at least three hours. A wineglassful of this tea, sweetened with honey, may be taken night and morning for blood disorders, fevers, dysentery, diarrhoea and colic. She also recommends that bunches of Meadowsweet be placed in linen cupboards and wardrobes to make them fragrant.

MELILOT   *Melilotus officinalis*   [*p.* 151

This biennial herb of the Natural Order *Leguminosae* has smooth, erect and branching stems up to three feet in height, with trifoliate leaves, bright green; and long racemes of sweet-scented yellow (occasionally a white form is seen) 'pea' flowers, rather like a delicate version of Laburnum. When dried it emits a powerful and lasting perfume of new-mown hay, due to the substance called *coumarin* which it contains. The plant is said to have been brought to Britain as a fodder crop, and become naturalized here. In the fields it was superseded by clovers, sainfoin and lucerne, but the Melilot still flourishes in quantity on pieces of waste ground and along our railway embankments.

The name of this genus comes from *mel*, honey, and *lotus*: that is, honey-lotus, which refers to the great attraction it has for bees.

The whole herb is dried for medicine; it has aromatic, emollient and carminative properties. As a fomentation it is an old-fashioned country remedy for the relief of abdominal and rheumatic pains. Taken internally, Melilot relieves flatulence. In Switzerland this herb is used to flavour cheese, and in other countries of Europe it is laid away between furs and woollens to prevent moth.

A still-room book issued in 1651 gives the following recipe:

To make a bath for Melancholy. Take Mallowes, Pellitory-of-the-wall, of each three handfuls; Camomell Flowers, Mellilot Flowers, of each one handful, senerick seed one ounce, and boil them in nine gallons of Water untill they come to three, then put in a quart of newe milke and go into it bloud warme or something warmer.

MINT, GARDEN *Mentha viridis*

In *A Modern Herbal* Mrs Grieve sums up the complicated genus *Mentha* in these words: 'There are three chief species of Mint in cultivation and general use: Spearmint (*Mentha viridis*), Peppermint (*M. piperita*) and Pennyroyal (*M. pulegium*), the first being the one ordinarily used for cooking. The various species of Mint have much in common and have all been held in high medical repute.' Dr Westmacott, the author of a work on plants published in 1694, mentioning the different kinds of Mint, states that they are well known to 'the young Botanists and Herb Women belonging to Apothecarys' shops'.

In gardens of today people interested in herbs may grow a bewildering variety of culinary Mints, Peppermints and Pennyroyal, from the enormous 'Bowles' Mint (*Mentha rotundifolia* var. Bowles), with large woolly grey leaves, borne on stout stems of up to five feet in height, to the tiny *Mentha requienii*—only one inch high, but yielding a terrifically pungent aroma of peppermint. It is a native of Corsica—but is sometimes referred to as 'Spanish Mint'. The late Vita Sackville-West planted a seat with this little mint in her garden at Sissinghurst Castle in Kent, where in the herb enclosure it flourished and made a soft felty cushion for her. It is a little temperamental, and must be given a sheltered site with warmth and moisture. It is sometimes mistaken for Helxine ('Baby's Tears'), until its strong scent reaches the nostrils.

The commonest Mint is Spearmint (*Mentha viridis*), found in nearly every garden at castle or cottage. This favourite kitchen herb, put into every pan of new potatoes and with green peas, was in times past called Our Lady's Mint, Spire Mint or Fish Mint, although few cook it with fish now. The Mints take their name from *Menthe*, a nymph who was loved by Pluto. His jealous wife, Proserpina, turned the girl into the green herb we call Mint. In France they called it '*Menthe de Notre Dame*', and in Italy '*Erba da Santa Maria*'.

Spearmint is a native of the Mediterranean region, and was brought to Britain by the Romans, who esteemed it greatly. Pliny wrote of Mint that it 'would not suffer milk to cruddle', and in his time people scented their baths with it. Mints were also employed much as Victorian ladies used bottles of smelling-salts—to revive anyone in danger of swooning. In Greece the ancients were given to scenting their persons with a different perfume for each part of the body, and they reserved Mint for the arms.

There are Biblical references to tithes of Mint, Anise and Cumin, and Chaucer wrote of 'a little path of mintes full and fenill greene'. An old herbal contains this appreciation of the scent: 'The smelle rejoiceth the heart of man, for which cause they used to strew it in chambers and places of recreation, pleasure and repose, where feasts and banquets are made.' In Britain, too, the seventeenth-century herbalist Parkinson wrote of mints 'put into baths with Balm and other herbs as a help to comfort and strengthen the nerves and sinews'. Another virtue praised in old herbals is that of curing chapped hands—the result of applying a strong decoction of Spearmint to the skin.

As Mrs Grieve remarks, Mint 'has in fact been so universally esteemed that it is to be found wild in nearly all the countries to which civilization has extended, and in America (where the Pilgrim Fathers took it) for three hundred years it has been known as an escape from gardens, growing in most soils and proving sometimes as troublesome as a weed'.

The common Spearmint has erect, square stems up to two feet in height, with lance-shaped, finely toothed leaves of a brilliant green. A form with curled leaves is also obtainable, *M. spicata crispata*. This is attractive in appearance, but very few examples of the plant have the true Spearmint flavour. When the more rank taste of Corn-mint (*M. arvensis*) creeps into any Mint, the plant becomes inferior for culinary purposes.

Most Mints grow easily in Britain, and the difficulty is to keep them within bounds. While living in Canada, where the motorist obtains a new set of number-plates each time the licence is renewed, I came upon a hoard of discarded plates in a basement and found these ideal for fencing in my bed of Mint. All kinds of Mint like rich, moist soil and will do well in partial shade. This perennial plant spreads by means of underground creeping stems, and it is easily increased by division of the runners in February or March. Cuttings may be taken at almost any time during the summer; young shoots will root quickly if kept moist in a shady bed of light soil, or in a frame. Most Mints are susceptible to a disease known as rust, and when signs of this appear the affected plants should be destroyed and a new start made with fresh plants on a different site.

Spearmint, 'Bowles' Mint and Horsemint (*M. sylvestris*) are the best culinary types. The variegated Applemint (*M. rotundifolia variegata*) is good in a drink known as Mintale, and it is very attractive as a garden subject. For pot-pourri and sweet-bags the vigorous Eau-de-Cologne Mint (*Mentha × piperita, var. citrata*) is good, and its bronze foliage and purple stems are also of decorative value in the garden—as is the Ginger Mint (*M. gentilis*), with its gold-splashed leaves. The most exciting non-culinary Mint known to me is the Buddleia Mint (*M. longifolia var. mollisima*) with grey leaves and pale mauve spikes of blossom. Recipes: pp. 176–77.

MULLEIN, GREAT *Verbascum thapsus*   [*p.* 55

Of the six species of Mullein native to Britain, the Great Mullein is, as its name implies, the tallest, measuring four or five feet in the wild and up to eight feet when cultivated in good garden soil. Given the right setting, its grey woolly spires are so effective that it seems a pity so few gardeners choose to grow this stately herb. After visiting one old Cotswold house (Daneway, open to the public from time to time), I remembered for years the picture of a grand procession of Great Mullein 'torches', all shining as though alight, against a dark background of evergreen hedge.

This Mullein, in addition to its medicinal virtues, was of everyday practical use before the days of electricity. Being resinous, it was dipped in tallow and made into torches or 'link' for lighting travellers on dark nights. The whole plant is covered in whitish hairs which, being dried, once formed valuable tinder for kindling with flint and steel. It was used also for lamp and candle wicks. Some of the many vernacular names record these customs: Candlewick Plant, Hag's Taper, High Taper, Hedge Taper, Our Lady's Candle and Torches. Other country names were Velvet Dock, Clown's Lungwort, Bullock's Lungwort, Aaron's Rod, Jupiter's Staff, Shepherd's Staff, Cuddy's Lungs, Feltwort, Fluffweed, Hare's Beard, Blanket Herb and Old Man's Flannel. In France it is called *Herbe de St. Fiacre*; he was one of the patron saints of gardeners.

This plant is found all over Europe and in the temperate parts of Asia; it is now abundant in eastern states of America, having become a naturalized weed there. In Britain it grows everywhere except the extreme north of Scotland, and is found in Ireland and the Channel Isles. It is usually seen on gravel or chalk, on hedge banks, waste ground and roadside verges, flowering in the month of August. In its first season it makes only a rosette of large leaves, six to fifteen inches long, rather

like those of a Foxglove but thicker and much more hairy. In the
following spring a stout, pale-coloured stem rises from the centre of
the rosette, a stiff, erect stalk whose rigidity accounts for the use of
'rod' or 'staff' in several country names.

The leaves become smaller as they ascend the stem, and are arranged
on alternate sides, so placed as to steer raindrops from apex to foot,
and so direct to the roots. This is vital for the plant, which is adapted
to very dry soils. The hairs in which it is so plentifully covered help to
reduce evaporation of the plant's essential moisture, and act as a
defence against insects and grazing animals. Towards the apex of the
stem the smallest leaves merge into a woolly flower spike, about twelve
inches long, where sulphur yellow flowers open at random, and not in
orderly fashion from the base upwards as blossoms of the Foxglove do.

In his book *Popular Names of British Plants* Dr Prior says that the
word Mullein was *Moleyn* in Anglo-Saxon and *Malen* in Old French,
derived from the Latin *Malandrium*, The Malanders, or Leprosy. The
term *Malandre* also became applicable to cattle diseases (lung troubles
among others), and so the plant remedy for these afflictions acquired
the names of Mullein and Bullock's Lungwort. In the year 1657 it was
recorded in Kent as a specific against 'the cough of the lungs in cattle'.
The name of Clown's Lungwort referred to its use for the same trouble
in the humble folk who tended the beasts of the field.

The generic name *Verbascum* is said to be a corruption of *barbascum*,
from *barba*, a beard, in allusion to the plant's shaggy appearance.
Mullein was of old believed to possess the power of driving away evil
spirits, and Ulysses employed it against the wiles of Circe.

Other British species are: *V. nigrum* (Dark Mullein), *V. blattaria*
(Moth Mullein), *V. lychnitis* (White Mullein), *V. pulverulentum* (Hoary
Mullein) and *V. virgatum* (*Large-flowerd Mullein*). All these possess
similar medicinal properties, but *V. thapsus* has been most employed
by the herbalists. In her *Herbal Handbook for Everyone* Juliette de
Bairacli Levy recommends Mullein as a valuable inhalant for asthma,
hay fever, congestion of the nose and all sinus troubles. A heaped
tablespoonful of the leaves, cut fine, is put into an old kettle and
covered with boiling water. Steam is inhaled from the spout, keeping
the head beneath a towel.

In olden days a poultice made of Mullein seeds and leaves, boiled
in wine, was used to 'draw forth speedily thorns or splinters gotten
into the flesh'. These same seeds are said to intoxicate fish when they

are thrown into the water, being slightly narcotic—a trick utilized by poachers. Roman ladies, more circumspectly, used an infusion of yellow Mullein flowers to dye their hair.

Cultivation is easy. Mullein seed may be sown in boxes or directly where the plants are to grow, in late spring or in summer. The plant, a hardy biennial, needs a well-drained site and will grow in very poor soil. Slugs appear to like the young plants very particularly, and traps or slug pellets should be placed around these. All the Mulleins are attractive garden subjects. Mrs Margery Fish makes splendid use of them in her garden at Lambrook, and propagates various species in her nursery.

MYRTLE *Myrtus communis* [*p*. 134

This fragrant evergreen shrub is reasonably hardy in sheltered places, although a very sharp frost can turn it brown overnight. It is a real cottage-garden plant, for in the old days every country bride must have a sprig of Myrtle in her bouquet along with 'orange-blossom' and Rosemary, and when the ceremony was over, a bridesmaid (*never* the bride) had to plant the sprig of Myrtle in a warm corner outdoors. Very often these cuttings, planted snugly against the cottage wall in a crowded border, would happily strike and in time grow into quite large bushes.

The association with weddings springs from ancient mythology. Venus took shelter behind a Myrtle tree on the island of Cytherea, where satyrs disturbed her while she was bathing. She wore a wreath of Myrtle when Paris gave her the golden apple; and her attendants, the Graces, also wore chaplets of this fragrant shrub. The Myrtle tree is dedicated to Venus, and in the Language of Flowers its message is of love.

Another plant which is given the name of Myrtle, the fragrant Bog Myrtle or Sweet Gale (*Myrica gale*), is really a member of the Bayberry family and not a *Myrtus*. This low-growing plant of wild moorlands is seldom above two feet high, with lanceolate leaves, small greenish flowers, and little waxy catkins. That connoisseur of herbal aromas, Margaret Brownlow, has described its fragrance as 'a subtle blend of vanilla, incense and allspice'. Bog Myrtle flourishes on peaty, wet ground in the Lake District, in Scotland and on similar land elsewhere. To those who know and love the remote hills of Argyllshire,

Inverness-shire and Ross-shire in particular, one whiff of this tough little plant is sufficient to evoke panoramas of magnificent scenery.

It happens to be the clan badge of the Campbells, but despite lingering traces of ancient feuds the plant now seems to be loved by most Scots as an emblem of their beautiful country. In Scotland and in countries of northern continental Europe it has been used as a substitute for hops (in brewing a beverage known as Gale Beer), and as a dyestuff too, for the good yellow colour it yields, while the fruits have been added to broth as a flavouring. Dried sprigs of Sweet Gale have for centuries been used by Highland women to scent their linen, just as their English sisters employed Lavender, and it is credited with the power of deterring moths and other insects. In China this herb was infused to make a kind of tea.

That other *Myrica*, called Bayberry (*Myrica cerifera*), is a native of the eastern states of North America, and is known also as Candle Berry and Tallow Shrub. This plant, three to eight feet in height, grows in low-lying thickets near the Atlantic coast and on the shores of Lake Erie. It has fragrant lanceolate leaves, glossy and resinous, and small berries crusted with greenish-grey wax, which persist for several years. When these are boiled in water the wax they contain floats to the top and may be skimmed off. It is harder and more brittle than beeswax, and was formerly used to make aromatic candles, said to be smokeless. Four pounds of berries yield about one pound of wax.

Herbalists regard the Bayberry as astringent and stimulant, and use the bark of the root to treat cases of diarrhoea, jaundice and scrofula.

NETTLE, STINGING   *Urtica dioica*

The Saxon name for this herb, *Wergulu*, seemed appropriate to me in my youth, when it was seen in a herbal; for the memory of having fallen at a very tender age head first into a bed of nettles was still painfully vivid. This Saxon word had a suitably baleful appearance. Yet the Nettle is a plant which improves on acquaintance, provided that it is not too close. It is possible—indeed desirable—to end by crediting this irritating herb with more virtues than the sweet and saintly Angelica. Not, perhaps, as a garden subject—how that horticultural monk Walafred Strabo complained of its invasive tactics a thousand years ago:

When last winter had passed and spring renewed the face of the earth, when the days grew longer and milder, when flowers and herbs were stirred by the west wind, when green leaves clothed the trees, then my little plot was overgrown with nettles. What was I to do? Deep down the roots were matted and linked and rivetted like basket-work or the wattled hurdles of a fold . . .

Had he lived contemporaneously with Sir Albert Howard, Strabo might have learned how to make first-rate compost with his nettles; used this way they are great improvers of the soil. Often the smaller annual species, *Urtica urens*, is the greater nuisance to gardeners, being, as Margaret Brownlow puts it, 'even more aggressive than the perennial Nettle'.

But, when the complaints of gardeners and badly hurt children are put behind us, how much virtue shines out from this cross green plant! It yields an excellent fibre for textiles, similar to that of Flax, for weaving strong bedsheets and tablecloths. The poet Campbell said: 'In Scotland I have eaten Nettles, slept in Nettle sheets, and dined off a Nettle tablecloth. My mother thought Nettle cloth more durable than any other species of linen.' It was from Nettle fibre, too, that the princess in Hans Andersen's story was made to weave the linen shirts for her eleven brothers who had been turned into swans. Nettle stalks and leaves yield a good green dye. (See page 182.)

In the kitchen, Nettle tops, picked when young and tender, make a splendid green vegetable. According to John Gay they were once cried in the streets of London: 'Nettles with tender shoots to cleanse the blood!' Nettle soup and Nettle Tea make alkaline spring tonics, particularly valuable for sufferers from rheumatic complaints. Later in the year the plant grows bitter and loses much of its medicinal virtue. The method of cooking Nettles is similar to the conservative way with Spinach. The vegetable is thrown into fast-boiling water, only just sufficient to keep it from sticking to the pan, and cooked for about ten minutes. The result is sieved, and served with butter, pepper and salt. Nettle Tea is brewed by pouring boiling water on the Nettle tops, about a pint to an ounce of the herb. Nettle seed may be used in the same fashion.

A rougher way of dealing with rheumatic aches was to whip the patient with Nettles. Seed of the Roman species, *U. pilulifera*, is said to have been brought to England by the Roman soldiery, who cultivated the plant and used it to flagellate each other 'as a warming exercise' in our cold northern winters. Or so it is said, but one wonders if these exercises had sexual significance. 'The Roman Nettle burns more severely than either of the indigenous species,' says Mrs Leyel in her book *Herbal Delights*. She adds that in Siberia Nettles are made into paper, Nettle oil may be burnt instead of paraffin, and a decoction of Nettle is used instead of rennet to curdle milk. Nettle juice can be made to coagulate and fill up interstices in leaky tubs; and Nettle seeds, when fed to hens, increase egg production.

Another, unexpected, use for this plant is to pack stone fruit with it. No other wrapping so well retains the bloom on such delicate skins as those of plum and peach.

Andrew Young in *A Retrospect of Flowers* writes that Nettle broth 'cured Catullus, when a cough was shaking him to pieces'. He quotes a piece of minute observation from Kerner's *Natural History of Plants*: ' "Anyone standing in front of a bed of stinging nettles on a bright summer morning, and waiting until the first rays of the sunshine fall on the flowers, will be surprised to see small, pale-coloured clouds of dust ascending here and there from amidst the dark foliage." The Nettle is a fascinating plant when it puffs out its pollen.'

Edward Thomas praised a different kind of dust seen on the Nettle.

> As well as any bloom upon a flower
> I like the dust on nettles, never lost
> Except to prove the sweetness of a shower.

And did not Shakespeare himself write of nettles in one of his most-quoted passages, words that (to me) only the voice of some member of the distinguished Terry family can render in purest spine-thrilling perfection:

> There is a willow grows aslant a brook,
> That shows his hoar leaves in the glassy stream;
> There with fantastic garlands did she come
> Of crow-flowers, nettles, daisies, and long purples . . .

These plants were chosen to represent Ophelia's tragedy. Crow-flowers indicate purity and faithfulness; Nettles, stung to the quick; Daisies signify innocence and virginity; and Long Purples, the cold hand of death. From Chaucer's day until the eighteenth century the Language of Flowers was known in eastern countries as well as those of the west. Now it has gone completely out of fashion, unless the young who call themselves 'Flower People' choose to revive it.

NUTMEG TREE *Myristica fragrans*

This tropical tree grows to about twenty-five feet in height and is indigenous to the Molucca Islands and the Malayan archipelago. It is cultivated in Sumatra and in French Guiana. The leaves are dark green and glossy, with paler undersides; both the 'Mace' and the 'Nutmeg' of commerce are prepared from the fruit of this tree. The thin mace arillus which covers the hard centre 'nut' is a brilliant scarlet when fresh-picked, as I saw when some fruits were plucked for me in the Peradeniya Botanic Gardens in Ceylon. Few people realize that the nutmeg used in cookery was originally wrapped in a shawl of the finest scarlet silk. This 'mace' is detached and dried separately from the 'nut', and when dry the scarlet hue of the aril turns to a cinnamon yellow.

Medicinally, nutmeg was seldom used alone; but it entered into a number of compounds, including the *Emplastrum picis*. It was at one time applied externally as a gentle stimulant.

In the kitchen, grated nutmeg has for ages been popular on custards and junkets, and in many spicy flavourings for sweetmeats, cakes and curries. Mace, whose properties are said to be identical to those of nutmeg, went into sauces, ketchups, etc. It is less used today in the home; but my edition of Mrs Beeton's *Everyday Cookery* dated 1900 contains a picture of a spice-box with receptacles for Cloves, Cinnamon, Nutmeg, Allspice and Mace.

The mace obtained from *Myristica fragrans* should not be confused with the leaves of the hardy perennial plant Alecost or Costmary, which are sometimes referred to in old herbals and cookery books as 'blades of Mace', as also are those of *Achillea decolorans*, a relative of the Yarrow.

ORACH *Atriplex hortensis*

This plant, known also as Arrach, Garden Orache or Mountain Spinach, is a tall, erect, hardy annual, obtainable in white, green and crimson varieties. It comes from central Asia and was introduced into Britain in the sixteenth century. From that time until the nineteenth century it was commonly grown for use as a vegeable, cooked like Spinach. The French still cultivate it, for use with Sorrel, to correct the acidity of that plant. In French it is called *Arroche*.

For culinary purposes it requires a good, rich soil, and should, like Spinach, be grown quickly; but in Britain it is seldom seen nowadays in the vegetable garden, where it has been superseded by Spinach. Medicinally, the plant was formerly applied externally as a remedy for gout, heated with vinegar, honey and salt. Eaten, after boiling without water in its own juice, this herb was of old considered to be good for the womb.

As an ornamental garden subject and for use in flower arrangements, the Red Orach is increasingly valued for the 'stained glass' effect given by the transparent crimson arrow-shaped foliage when seen against the sunlight. Propagation is by seed, sown under glass early in April or outdoors in late May. This variety is not completely hardy. In rich soil it will grow to five feet, but it is equally attractive in hot, poor soil on top of a dry wall or bank, where it may not exceed eighteen inches in height. It self-sows freely.

PARSLEY *Petroselinum crispum*

The Garden Parsley, so familiar an inmate of every vegetable plot, is not a native of Britain. It is believed to have been introduced in the middle of the sixteenth century; but various authorities differ as to its primary wild habitat. Sardinia, Turkey, Algeria and Lebanon have all been named.

The name *Petroselinum* is of classical origin, said to have been given to the plant by Dioscorides. At that time there were two plants called *selinon*; the first, our Celery (*Apium graveolens*) was known as *Heleioselinon* or Marsh Selinon, and our Parsley as *Oreoselinon*, Mountain Selinon or *Petroselinon*, Rock Selinon. In the Middle Ages this became *Petrocilium*, which was anglicized as Petersylinge, Persele and Persely, from whence came Parsley. The herb was originally dedicated to Persephone and to funeral rites by the Greeks. In later, Christian, times the herb was re-dedicated to St Peter in his capacity of successor to Charon. Sixteenth-century botanists named the plant *Apium hortense*, Linnaeus in the eighteenth century called it *A. petroselinum*, later it was known as *Carum petroselinum*, now as *Petroselinum crispum*.

Parsley has been venerated for centuries. The Greeks crowned victors at the Isthmian Games with chaplets of 'Parsley', and made wreaths of it for tombs. There are, however, arguments as to whether *Heleioselinon* or *Petroselinon* was in truth the sacred herb of the Greeks.

It does seem clear that the sacred herb, whichever that was, could not be brought to table. It is known that Greek gardens contained borders of Parsley and Rue.

Mrs Grieve says that the plant is harmful to small birds and domestic fowls and deadly to parrots, but that hares and rabbits travel long distances to obtain it. Given in quantity, it was believed to prevent footrot in sheep. One eighteenth-century herbalist advocates feeding Parsley to sick fish in a pond, to cure their ills.

This herb has a remarkable gift for overcoming strong odours. Even the powerful Garlic is largely neutralized by the scent of Parsley. In cookery, the finely chopped fresh leaves are commonly used as flavouring for sauces, stews, soups, rissoles, minces and the like, also sprinkled over vegetables and in green salads. In winter, when fresh leaves are scarce, the dried herb is similarly employed. (Recipes, pp. 176, 179.)

Medicinally, the two-year-old roots, the dried leaves (for making Parsley Tea) and the seeds, from which an oil called Apiol is extracted, were all considered to have curative powers, Apiol being used in the treatment of ague and malaria. Parsley Tea was utilized in World War I, when men in the trenches developed kidney trouble while suffering from dysentery. In France an ointment made from green Parsley and snails was a popular application for scrofulous swellings, and the bruised leaves have been applied externally to tumours.

In cultivation, Parsley has the reputation of going down to visit the devil seven times before it appears above ground. It is very slow to germinate, and because of this gardeners sometimes wait over-long for the seedlings to show, not realizing that they have been sold seed that is too old to germinate. This seed should be sown within a year after being harvested. The superstitious never care to transplant Parsley, as this is said to bring bad luck. Another country belief is that where the Parsley flourishes, 'Missus is master'.

The soil should be warm and moist for sowing, conditions sometimes provided by the pouring of hot water along the drills. In warm places a slightly shaded site may be selected. Seed should be very lightly covered—an eighth of an inch of fine soil is sufficient—and drills prepared ten inches apart. Seedlings should be thinned to six inches in the rows. It is useful to make one sowing in April or May and another in July or August, for use the following spring.

Parsley is a hardy biennial and will normally flower and go to seed in the spring after it has been sown, although in hot summers it has a tendency to 'bolt'. There are many forms, but the curled, crisp-leaved types are most popular in Britain for table use. French Parsley is broad-leaved and uncrisped, and Hamburg Parsley is turnip-rooted, with large edible tap-roots. Garden Parsley leaves are rich in iron, and this herb, eaten fresh, is good for anaemia.

To preserve the foliage for winter use, it should be gathered when dry, spread out on trays and put into a cool oven at about one hundred degrees, and left just long enough to become crisp. It is then rubbed down immediately and stored in airtight opaque jars or tins to preserve the colour, which will speedily fade if light reaches the product.

Fool's Parsley (*Anthriscus cynapium*) is a poisonous weed of garden and field, and must not be confused with Garden Parsley. The leaves are a darker green and more finely divided; when bruised they give out an unpleasant smell.

PARSLEY PIERT   see LADY'S MANTLE

PERIWINKLE, GREATER   *Vinca major*
PERIWINKLE, LESSER   *Vinca minor*

The Periwinkles belong to the Natural Order *Apocynaceae*, which includes a number of tropical plants with handsome flowers, many of them poisonous. Periwinkle is the sole representative of this Order in Britain, and there is doubt about its right to be claimed as a native plant. Here it seldom ripens seed, although in more southern lands it does so freely—which is taken by some as proof that it is not indigenous.

The Periwinkle is a hardy perennial, evergreen, and its shining leaves make valuable ground-cover in wintertime. It propagates itself here by means of long, trailing stems which root readily wherever they can find a foothold. In cultivation silver-variegated forms appear which are strikingly decorative in the flower garden or on hedge banks and in woodlands. The Lesser Periwinkle (*Vinca minor*) may be had with white, blue or purple flowers, sometimes double, but the usual colour of *Vinca major* is a beautiful blue-mauve.

Periwinkle is believed to be the *Vinca pervinca* of Pliny. Of old in

Britain this flower, sometimes called Sorcerer's Violet, or Joy of the Ground, was used in love-philtres and charms, and was supposedly powerful against wicked spirits. The plant was well known in Chaucer's day.

> Parvenke is an erbe grene of colour
> In tyme of May he beryth blo flour,
> His stalkys ain so feynt and feye
> Yet never more growyth he hey.
> On the ground he runneth and growe
> As doth the erbe that hath turnhow,
> The lef is thicke, schinende and styf
> As is the grene ivy lef . . .

Medicinally, Periwinkles are valued for their acid, astringent and tonic properties. Both Dioscorides and Galen prescribed this herb for use 'against the fluxes'. It was at one time considered to be a good remedy for cramp; Bacon wrote that bands of green Periwinkle tied round a limb would cure this affliction. An ointment prepared from bruised leaves and lard was once popular for treating skin inflammations and bleeding haemorrhoids. Bruised leaves were also placed in the nostrils to stop nose-bleeding.

The plant was of old considered to be a potent aphrodisiac. In *The Boke of Albertus Magnus* we find: 'Perwynke when it is beate unto pouder with worms of ye earth wrapped about it and with an erbe called houslyke, it induceth love between man and wyfe if it bee used in their meales.'

The Periwinkles are easily increased by division and tip-layers, and —given a cool, moist site—cultivation is simple, and the ground cover provided by closely matted trailing stems becomes almost weed-proof in time.

In the nineteen-twenties it was announced that the Madagascar Periwinkle, *Vinca rosea* (syn. *Lochnera rosea*, now reclassified as *Catharanthus roseus*), a small shrub with red flowers, had been found efficacious in cases of diabetes and might be expected to supersede insulin. So far this does not seem to have happened, although herbalists have for long used *Vinca major* and *Vinca minor* in the treatment of diabetics.

POKE ROOT *Phytolacca americana* (syn. *P. decandra*)

[p. 70

This plant has long been popular with the 'Red' Indians of North America, where it is indigenous. Among the vernacular names for it, Pigeonberry, Bear's Grape, Dyer's Grape, Skoke, Crowberry, Chongras, Red Ink Plant, Virginian Poke, Pocan or Cokan, Jalap, Garget and American Spinach were all in common use at different times.

It is a hardy perennial in sheltered places, and has a striking appearance, growing to a height of four or five feet, with spikes of cream flowers followed by handsome purplish-black berries set in fairly close formation on the stem. The young shoots in springtime are eaten, having a flavour resembling asparagus; but in its later stages the foliage of the plant is poisonous. The root and the berry are employed medicinally; both, according to Mrs Leyel, must be used fresh and not dried. Preparations of the root are suggested for nasal catarrh and infected sinus, but a warning is given that reactions can be violent and alarming; amateurs should not experiment with this plant. The berries have been used to reduce obesity, also an extract of Poke Root has been found efficacious in some types of chronic rheumatic affliction.

As a dyestuff the flower is said by some to yield a red colour and the berries a purplish magenta; but according to the handbook *Dyeplants and Dyeing* issued by the Brooklyn Botanic Garden, the aboriginal Indians of Canada obtained a red dye from the berries, while at Harlow Old Fort House in Plymouth, Massachusetts, 'Pokeberry with its magenta juice fades to an unremarkable brown when applied to woolen yarn, although it can be used to give a reddish stain for basket materials'. It may easily be grown from seed, and it flourishes in the herb garden of the American Museum in Britain at Claverton Manor near Bath.

PURSLANE, GREEN *Portulaca oleracea*
PURSLANE, GOLDEN *Portulaca sativa*

Purslane is a herbaceous annual, native to many parts of Europe but not indigenous in Britain. It has a round, smooth, procumbent stem; the Golden Purslane, with yellow leaves, is less hardy than the Green. (It is most decorative in herb borders, and possesses similar qualities.) Both these plants are good salad herbs, with anti-scorbutic properties. The young shoots are cooling in spring salads, the older ones may be cooked as a pot herb, and the thick stems are usefully pickled in salt and vinegar for winter salading. Purslane and Sorrel together go into the French soup *bonne femme*.

Medicinally, Purslane was of old said to cure 'heat in the liver', to be good for 'hot agues' and 'pains in the head proceeding from heat, want of sleep, and the frenzy'. The old herbalists recommended Juice of Purslane, with Oil of Roses, for sore |mouths, swollen gums and 'to fasten loose teeth'. The leaves, eaten raw, were said to be excellent for 'teeth that are set on edge with eating sharpe things'.

Propagation is by seed, sown in drills on light but good soil from May onwards. These herbs require more water than most.

At one time the Purslane was regarded as 'a Protection against Evil Spirits, blastings by Lightening or Planets, and burning of Gunpowder'.

ROSEMARY *Rosmarinus officinalis*

'Rosemary for Remembrance'—it is not generally known that herbalists do in fact use this herb medicinally to treat forgetfulness. Like Lavender and Peppermint, it grows better and is more sweetly aromatic in England than anywhere else. It flourished at Hampton Court in Tudor and Stuart days, and Sir Thomas More allowed it to ramp all over his garden walls because it is an emblem of friendship and a good bee-plant. Rosemary was popular then as a strewing-herb, too. It is mentioned in a tenth-century Anglo-Saxon herbal, *The Leech Book of Bald*, and is generally believed to have been lost in Britain and re-introduced in the fourteenth century by Queen Philippa, who was sent plants of Rosemary by her mother, the Countess of Hainault.

Parkinson, in his *Paradisi in Sole*, says that Rosemary wood was used to make lutes 'and suchlike instruments'. Sprigs of Rosemary were included in wedding bouquets and carried at funerals, used in spells to ward off black magic, burnt in sickrooms to dispel infection, and employed in church decorations for festivals. The old French name for this plant, *Incensier*, commemorates its use as incense when the latter could not be procured.

A Spanish legend says that the flowers were originally white, but turned blue when the Virgin Mary threw her cloak over a bush of Rosemary, and have preserved the memory of this honour by coming blue ever since. The Spanish name for this plant, *Romero* (Pilgrim's

Flower), is said to be related to the legend that the Holy Family
sheltered under a bush of Rosemary during the flight into Egypt.

In *The Bible in Spain* George Borrow describes the belief of
Spanish peasants in the power of Rosemary to ward off the evil eye.

Anne Pratt, in her book *Flowers and their Associations*, quotes one
Roger Hackett, D.D., as saying in a sermon: 'Speaking of the powers
of Rosemary, it overtoppeth all the flowers in the garden . . . It
helpeth the brain, strengtheneth the memorie, and is very medicinable
in the head. Another property of the Rosemary is, it affects the heart.
Let this Rosmarinus, this flower of men, ensigne of your wisdom, love
and loyaltie, be carried not only in your hands, but in your hearts
and heads.'

Use of the plant in Christmas decorations is mentioned by the poet
Herrick:

> Down with the rosemary, and so
> Down with the baies and mistletoe,
> Down with the holly, ivye all
> Wherewith ye deck the Christmas Hall.

Together with a clove orange, a branch of Rosemary decked with
silken ribands was a traditional New Year's gift in the time of Ben
Jonson, who alluded to this custom. At the annual distribution of
specially minted silver coins on Maundy Thursday in Westminster
Abbey, the Queen is presented with a nosegay of herbs prepared by
the Queen's Herbalist. This includes Rosemary and Thyme, white
Stock, primroses, daffodils and violets. The custom is a reminder o,
the days when herbs were believed to give protection against infectionf
particularly against the dreaded plague.

Rosemary flourishes best in a warm, light, limy, well-drained soil,
in full sun, and is propagated by seed sown in late spring; by cuttings,
about six inches long, taken in late May or June; and by layering lower
branches under sandy soil in summer. Cuttings made in late summer
will probably need to be wintered in a cold frame or under cloches.
Bushes should be carefully clipped in summer after flowering to ensure
a neat appearance and prevent weak, straggly growths.

Rosmarinus officinalis has narrow, deep green leaves, silver underneath; its misty blue flowers open in April and May on last year's
wood. In sheltered places a bush may reach a height of six feet and live
for twenty years. Miss Jessup's variety, popularized by the late E. A.
Bowles, is upright in habit and has golden-green foliage; it is con-

sidered to be slightly less hardy than the type, while *R. corsicus* has narrower foliage and brighter blue flowers. Prostrate Rosemary, some six to twelve inches high, is good in a snug sunk-garden or rockery.

The gilded Rosemary is now very scarce in U.K., many plants having succumbed to the bitter winter of 1963. Some people imagine that this is merely *R. officinalis* with some gold paint on it—a sacrilege sometimes committed, but the real thing is a gold-variegated plant in its natural state. Margery Fish in *Cottage Garden Flowers* refers to a silver-variegated Rosemary of which she has heard. She would like to see this plant, and so should I.

Medicinally, the Oil of Rosemary, distilled from flowering tops, appears in the British Pharmacopoeia. From a hundred pounds of tops about eight ounces of oil are obtained, which makes it very costly. The Oil of Rosemary has carminative properties and is an excellent stomachic and nervine, curing many severe headaches. It is employed externally in hair lotions. An infusion of the dried leaves and flowers, combined with borax and used when cold, makes an effective hair wash for prevention of dandruff. The Oil of Rosemary is also used externally as a rubefacient and is added to liniment.

Hungary Water, for outward application to restore vitality to paralysed limbs, was first prepared for a Queen of Hungary who was said to have been completely cured by its use. It is made by putting one and a half pounds of fresh Rosemary tops in full flower into one gallon of spirits of wine. This should be allowed to stand for four days, after which it is distilled. Hungary Water was also considered to be a remedy for gout.

In cookery, a fresh sprig of Rosemary stuck into a joint of lamb, veal or poultry before roasting, or dried leaves sprinkled over the meat, will impart a delicious flavour. Rosemary Wine, made by chopping up sprigs of green Rosemary and pouring on them white wine, which is strained off after a few days, stimulates the brain and nervous system. Rosemary Tea, made by infusing one ounce of flowering tops in a pint of boiling water, is good for headaches, colds, colics and nervous troubles. Care should be taken to prevent the escape of steam while the brew is standing. 'Rosemary Flowers, made up into Plates with Double Refined Sugar after the manner of Sugar Possets, Comfort the heart and make it Merry, Quicken the Spirits and make them more Lively' (from a manuscript book of receipts by Thomas Newington dated 1719). Recipe, page 177.

RUE *Ruta graveolens*

Called Herb of Grace, or Herb of Repentance, because holy water was at one time sprinkled from bunches of Rue at a ceremony preceding High Mass on Sundays, this plant was well known to the ancients, long before Christianity. The name *Ruta* is probably derived from the Greek *rhusis*, deliverance, because the herb was regarded as an antidote to poisons and a protection against witchcraft, as well as a remedy for a number of diseases. The Romans believed that it had power to bestow the gift of second sight. It was almost certainly brought to the British Isles by them. It is one of our oldest and most revered garden plants.

This hardy perennial will grow in various types of soil, but lives longer and is less liable to frost damage when established on poor, dry land, where it makes fewer lush shoots to winter-kill. It is easily propagated by seed, sown in spring, or by cuttings of young wood taken from May to July and placed in a shady spot out of doors. In severe winters it is noticeable that old bushes tend to shed their leaves, while the younger ones are well covered. The foliage is of a metallic bluegreen hue, beloved by flower-arrangers, and a particularly good form, Jackman's Blue, is the best for a flower border. There is also a variegated Rue with creamy sprays of young foliage, becoming dappled with blue at a later stage. It is less robust than the ordinary blue form, but its seed has the uncommon attribute of coming true to the variegation.

All the Rues have rather insignificant greenish-yellow flowers from June to September, which some gardeners remove because they prefer the colour of the foliage by itself.

The pungent odour of this herb has been variously described as disagreeable—'like a musty old church', or 'like very old Gorgonzola cheese', and, with more warmth, as 'sharply aromatic—like gorse in bloom amid salt spray on a sea-cliff'. Bacon wrote that 'Rew doth prosper much and become stronger if set by a fig-tree'; but perhaps he was merely recording the fact that a sheltered site agreed with Rue, rather than divining an affinity between this herb and the Fig. The bouquets still presented in some places to judges at assizes were originally composed of aromatic herbs, including Rue, which were supposed to ward off Plague and gaol-fever. Rue is an ingredient of the 'Vinegar of the Four Thieves', which a quartet of notorious robbers made to protect themselves while stripping valuables from the corpses of Plague victims. Their recipe is given in old herbals as follows: one and a half ounces each of tops of Sea and Roman Wormwood, Rosemary, Sage, Mint and Rue; two ounces of Lavender flowers; a quarter of an ounce each of *Calamus aromaticus*, cinnamon, cloves, nutmeg and garlic; half an ounce of camphor; all these added to one gallon of red wine vinegar.

Rue is one of the few herbs employed in heraldry. In Britain it may be seen intertwined in the collar of the Order of the Thistle, and there is a Saxon Order called the *Rautenkrone* (Crown of Rue).

Medicinally, Rue is considered to be stimulant and anti-spasmodic, often employed as an emmenagogue. The flowers are used in a lotion for eye ailments. The tops of young shoots, gathered before flowering begins, are the most potent parts of the plant; the whole may be used either fresh or dried. Oil of Rue is distilled from the fresh herb, while infusions in water may be made from either fresh or dried foliage. Rue Tea is administered for coughs, croup and flatulence; also for hysterical conditions. Externally, Rue is employed as a rubefacient. It is an active irritant, and some gardeners find that handling the plant unprotected by gloves gives them a skin rash. Rue formed an old and popular remedy for croup in poultry, and it has been used also in the treatment of certain diseases of cattle.

SAGE   *Salvia officinalis*

This herb is to be found in most country gardens, and not a few city ones, yet it is surprising how seldom the growing plant is harvested for culinary purposes today. So many friends keep a packet or a jar of grocers' dried Sage in the cupboard, often several years old, while their home-grown product languishes, neglected by cook and gardener alike. This useful and attractive plant soon turns into an eyesore if it is not cared for and trimmed to an elegant shape each year. As it is so easily propagated—by seed sown outdoors in March to May, or by cuttings taken in summer—it is well worth the small trouble of raising young and vigorous plants every few years to replace bushes which have become over-large and woody, perhaps with less flavour than they possessed in their youth.

Not only does the traditional sage-and-onion stuffing for goose, duck, pork or vegetarian roast taste better when newly picked Sage or fresh home-dried product are used, but the home-grown Sage also provides material for a health-giving and palatable tea. This may be made simply by the infusion of a handful of fresh leaves in a pint of boiling water. A more elaborate, old-fashioned recipe for making Sage Tea is as follows: one ounce of fresh leaves, an ounce of sugar, juice of a lemon; infuse in a quart of boiling water for thirty minutes before straining off the liquid. This beverage was once used for debility and digestive weakness, for liver and kidney trouble, for fevers and cold-in-the-head. The first recipe, with a couple of leaves of Lemon Balm added to the Sage leaves, makes a pleasant change from the usual Indian, Ceylon or China Tea in the pot. Red Sage is just as good if not better for this brew, as compared with the commoner grey-green form.

There are many varieties of *Salvia officinalis*. The so-called broad-leaved Sage is popular with professional growers of culinary herbs. Because it seldom flowers, all the plant's vigour goes into the foliage, which is of excellent flavour. The narrow-leaved Sage has, however, the advantage as a garden subject, particularly the form with rich bluish-mauve flowers. There are also pink and white-flowered forms, and one with washy mauve blossoms which is best avoided. The handsome purple-leaved variety *Salvia officinalis*, var. *purpurea*, known as Red Sage, is equally at home in the garden border and in the kitchen. There are flowerless forms of this kind, as well as the better one for decorative use, which bears good purple blossoms. There is also a Golden Sage, which rarely blooms but makes a fine contrast of foliage against the Red and grey Sages, and a Red variegated (or 'painted') Sage which is gaily splashed with random patches of red, cream and green.

Salvia officinalis is a native of Syria, Italy and southern France. It needs warm, well-drained soil, for in damp ground it is prone to rot in winter. It thrives in partial shade, but does not like to be directly under trees where it will be dripped upon. It has been in cultivation in the British Isles since the fifteenth century at least, and was probably introduced long before that. It is evergreen, and reasonably hardy. All the fancy forms are easily propagated by cuttings of the best shoots taken in spring or summer, but they will not come true from seed.

For medicinal purposes the Red and Broad-leaved Sages are usually selected by herbalists. The plant has stimulant, astringent, tonic and carminative properties. Sage Tea has for long been prescribed for dyspepsia, and the centuries-old practice of cooking Sage with rich meats such as pork and goose has good sense behind it, because the herb is a digestive.

The Latin name *Salvia* is derived from *salvere*, to save; in the Middle Ages the plant was sometimes referred to as *Salvia salvatrix*, 'Sage the saviour', and there was a saying, Why should a man die while Sage grows in his garden? Later this became the well-known rhyming couplet:

> He that would live for aye
> Must eat Sage in May.

The herb was at one time supposed to soothe grief, and Pepys referred to a little churchyard between Gosport and Southampton where it was customary to sow all the graves with Sage. The herbalist known as 'Sir' John Hill, who had a famous garden in Bayswater in the later years of the eighteenth century, wrote in his book *Vertues of British Herbs* that the chief goodness of Sage was to be found in the flowers when they began to open. (He also remarked that the leaves were at their best in May, 'before the flower stalks rise'.) He made these rather extravagant claims for the plant:

Sage will retard that rapid progress of decay that treads upon our heels so fast in the latter years of life, will preserve the faculties and memory, more valuable to the rational mind than life itself without them; and will relieve under that faintness, strengthen under that weakness, and prevent absolutely that sad depression of spirits, which age often feels and always fears; it will long prevent the hands from trembling and the eyes from dimness and make the lamp of life, so long as nature lets it burn, burn brightly.

The harvesting of Sage for culinary purposes begins just before the herb comes into flower in May, and if the plants are well established shoots may be taken off several times during the summer months. For winter culinary use, the herb is bunched and dried in a current of warm air—at about seventy degrees Fahrenheit it will take six or seven days. The dried leaves should then be removed from stalks and stored, either whole or rubbed down, in airtight and opaque jars. This dried product may also be burnt on a shovel or in an incense-burner to dispel the odours of cooking, smoking, or sick-room.

A seventeenth-century Herbal gives some unusual recipes, such as: FOR THE TEETH: If you would keep your teeth from rotting, or aching, wash your Mouth continually every Morning with juyce of lemmons; afterwards rub your teeth with a Sage-leaf, and wash them after Meat with fair water. FOR ONE THAT HATH NO SPEECH IN SICKNESS: Take the juyce of Sage and put it in the Patient's Mouth, and by the Grace of God it shall make him speak.

Culinary recipes of a modern kind are given on pp. 175, 178.

SAGE, CLARY *Salvia sclarea*

This Sage, a biennial, sometimes remains in its first-year rosette form in the second year, and does not flower until the third season. On one occasion some of my seedlings of *Salvia sclarea*, var. *turkestanica* came up and grew into good rosettes in the first year, all of equal size. Suddenly one of these shot up and flowered that same autumn, while the rest behaved normally and bloomed the following year. The variety called *turkestanica*—sometimes known as the Vatican Sage— has very handsome rosy-purple bracts and grows to a height of six feet. The ordinary Clary Sage is usually smaller, about three feet and a half as a rule, with paler mauve bracts; much less colourful as a garden subject.

The vernacular names, Clear Eye and See Bright, are a reminder that the seeds of Clary had a reputation for soothing inflammation of the eyes and for improving the sight.

Clary was at one time employed as a substitute for hops in brewing beer, or as an additive to hop beer. An early eighteenth-century writer tells us that 'Some brewers of Ale and Beere doe put it into their drinke to make it more heady, fit to please drunkards, who thereby, according to their several dispositions, become either dead drunke, or foolish drunke, or madde drunke.'

SAGE, SPECIES

There are numerous attractive species for use in the flower border in addition to those already named. The following are purely decorative and not medicinal or culinary. *Salvia ambigens* is a hardy perennial, three feet high, with royal blue flowers; it is aromatic. *Salvia grahami* is a deciduous shrubby plant, needing shelter, when it may reach four feet; it has glowing scarlet flowers over a long period. *S. greggei* is similar but with carmine flowers. These should be pruned in March or April, if frost has not cut them to the ground.

S. haematodes is regarded as a hardy perennial; it is a favourite for the herbaceous border, but is seldom very long-lived. It has wrinkled leaves and lavender blue flowers on stems two to four feet in height. The biennial Meadow Sage, *S. pratensis*, has translucent blue and mauve-pink blossoms; the colour veers between blue and pink in random fashion on the same stem, which is attractive. There is also *S. pratensis rosea*, a more consistently pink form. *S. superba* (syn. *S. virgata nemorosa*) makes a fine show in July and August with its crimson-purple bracts and violet coloured flowers. *S. rutilans*, the Pineapple Sage, has a delicious fruit scent, but is not hardy and needs to be wintered under glass. There are many others to choose from.

SAVORY, SUMMER *Satureia hortensis*

Satureia is the name given by Pliny to over a dozen aromatic herbs of the Mediterranean region, which were supposed to belong to the Satyrs. Of these only two, *S. montana* and *S. hortensis*, are commonly grown in Britain. Both species were mentioned by Virgil, who described them as being amongst the most fragrant of herbs; he recommended them as bee-plants. The earliest settlers took with them Savory for their herb gardens in the New World.

Summer Savory is a hardy annual with slender, erect stems about twelve inches high. It bears flowers of a washy pink in July, and is raised from seed sown in shallow drills in April, preferably in a sunny position. The seedlings should be thinned to six inches apart and kept well watered. Germination is slow. The plants may be topped early in June for use in the kitchen as fresh flavouring, and by the time they come into flower they will be ready to pull up and dry in bunches for winter use. A sprig of this herb is good cooked with broad beans, and it is an ingredient of *bouquets aromatiques*—Basil, Chervil, Celery (or Lovage), Rosemary, Savory, Tarragon. This flavouring is used by French cooks to give warmth to soups and stews. The herbs are tied up in a muslin bag, and removed from the dish before it is served. The exact amount of each herb, and the time the bag is permitted to steep, are matters for individual choice. An excellent Savory Butter is made by blending three tablespoons of finely-chopped herb in half a pound of salted butter. This is used on small biscuits as cocktail accompaniments, or with broad beans. Both the Summer Savory and Winter Savory are popular in sauces, meat dishes, soups, sausages, stuffings, egg dishes and salads. Summer Savory has the more delicate flavour of the two.

Medicinally, Summer Savory has been used as a carminative; a sprig of either *S. hortensis* or *S. montana* is an old remedy for sting of bee or wasp, applied to the spot after being bruised to release the juice of the herb.

SAVORY, WINTER *Satureia montana* [*p.* 70

This low-growing, evergreen, hardy perennial shrub, twelve to eighteen inches high, is occasionally mistaken for a bushy plant of Thyme with rather longer leaves than usual. The foliage of Savory has a pleasantly pungent scent and flavour, and it is useful in the kitchen, but being among the most powerful herbs it should be used with discretion. The plant is an old inhabitant of our British herb gardens, having been popular here since the days of Queen Elizabeth I.

It may be propagated from seed, sown outdoors in April, or by cuttings of young side-shoots taken (with a heel) in early summer and rooted in a shady plot. It is also possible to divide plants; but, as the younger less woody specimens yield the best shoots for harvesting, it is preferable to replace this herb with new and vigorous examples every other year. It flourishes on poor, well-drained and warm soil, and should be kept well clipped. Older plants, additional to those grown for culinary purposes, make pleasing small hedges for dividing up sections of a large herb garden.

In ancient times Savory was used in place of the spices from the East which we employ today. The Romans made a vinegar sauce for meats with it, in the style of our modern Mint sauce. Some of the old English herbals described how the Winter Savory, dried and powdered, was mixed with bread crumbs 'to breade meate, be it fish or flesh'. It was often used to dress trout. (Recipes, pp. 175, 176, 179.)

SELF-HEAL *Prunella vulgaris* [*p.* 135

This common perennial plant of the British countryside is found, too, all over Europe—chiefly in open and exposed places, where it is seldom more than six inches high. On more sheltered and lush sites it grows considerably taller. This wildflower has found its way to North America, where it is known as Heart-of-the-Earth, or Blue Curls. It has oblong, blunt, hairy leaves set on short stalks in pairs upon the square stem; the lipped flowers are bluish purple as a rule (occasionally

LEMON BALM

HENBANE

BOG MYRTLE

FOXGLOVE

GREEN HELLEBORE **MONKSHOOD** **WORMWOOD**

COMMON MALLOW **SELF-HEAL** **BLACK HOREHOU**

pink), with large purple calyces. This plant is easily distinguished from others of the Natural Order *Labiatae* because on the top of the flowering stem the blooms are 'Thicke set together like an eare or spiky knap', as an old Herbal puts it.

The generic name *Prunella* is thought to be a corruption of *Brunella*, from the German *Brunellen*, which relates to the power this herb possesses of curing an inflammation of the mouth known as *die Brellen*.

Medicinally, the whole herb is used, collected at midsummer when it is at its most potent. It is astringent, styptic and tonic. It was prized in former centuries as a wound herb, and is still used by herbalists as an astringent for both internal and external use. An infusion of one ounce of the herb to one pint of boiling water, sweetened with honey and taken in doses of a wineglassful, is good for a sore throat, and may be used as a gargle also.

SOAPWORT *Saponaria officinalis*

This herb belongs to the Natural Order *Caryophyllaceae*, and according to some works of reference it was introduced into Britain in the sixteenth century; though the Romans were conversant with its value, and it seems likely that they grew it in the British Isles during their period of occupation. It is certain that some Roman introductions were lost, and subsequently reintroduced in later centuries; but, knowing how invasive the *Saponaria* can be, it is hard to imagine it dying out. If only plants could speak!

Soapwort is a stout, herbaceous perennial, two to three feet in height as a rule, though some cultivators claim considerably larger specimens. It is 'inordinately hardy', says one authority; with creeping rhizomes, and thick, brittle stems bearing smooth lanceolate leaves and pink flowers—about an inch across—varying from a pale hue to deep rose, and sometimes double. Margaret Brownlow states, succinctly, that it is 'propagated by its own territorial claims'. It may be planted from October to April, and needs plenty of water in dry weather.

The vernacular names, Soapwort, Soaproot, Latherwort, Fuller's Herb and Crow Soap speak of the chief use to which this plant was put, that of producing a saponaceous lather. It was also credited with some medicinal value, and the name Bruisewort commemorates one prescription. According to Mrs Grieve (*A Modern Herbal*) a decoction was used in the treatment of jaundice; as a cure for 'the itch'; and in long-standing cases of venereal disease, when mercury had failed to effect a cure. Mrs Grieve describes its medicinal properties as tonic, diaphoretic and alterative, adding that it should be used internally with caution owing to its saponin content.

Mrs Margery Fish tells an amusing story of the plant, which grows freely in her Lambrook garden. Years ago her friend the late Mrs Clive of Brympton d'Evercy coveted this *Saponaria*, and so she was given a basketful of the rhizomes. Not one survived the move. Every time Mrs Fish, who found her Soapwort altogether too invasive, dragged up handfuls of it she carted the unwanted roots over to Brympton d'Evercy, but that fine gardener Mrs Clive failed to establish it. Those of us who have experience of this lusty subject usually imagine that it will thrive anywhere, but seemingly it has likes and dislikes. At Lambrook it has now staked a claim outside one of the entrance gates, and makes a pink fringe round a stone step there. The vigorous habit of *Saponaria* is implied in one of the country names, Bouncing Bet. Others call it Wild Sweet William. In some places it has a sweet scent, in others it is practically scentless. It blooms from July to September.

The value of Soapwort as a cleansing agent for old and delicate fabrics had long been known to me in theory; but not until I visited Lady Meade-Fetherstonhaugh at the great house of Uppark near Petersfield and was shown the 'before' and 'after' exhibits of brocade curtain material, which she restored from filthy and colourless decrepitude to rich and useful beauty, did I appreciate the miraculous powers of this simple herb.

There were numbers of these great curtains at Uppark, drawn up on cords to form draped pelmets above the long windows, and when the late Admiral Meade-Fetherstonhaugh inherited the house his friends and relatives all said that the shabby old curtains must be taken down and thrown away. Lady Meade-Fetherstonhaugh, in her charming 'Epilogue' at the end of the book *Uppark and its People*, describes her own feelings in the matter.

'Those curtains' were not going to be thrown away, though they hung like depressing wreaths of damp distressed pink seaweed, for I was going to mend them . . . There were over 30 curtains, each measuring 16 to 18 feet high and 6 feet wide, which could not be let down: the sight was too shocking. They were made of Italian brocade of 1740, and I knew of no other house which had them.

SOAPWORT

Our family was blessed with two maiden aunts, of immortal fame, who fulfilled all the Beatitudes for all the family all their lives, and they brought to Uppark one day a little old lady who taught me how to make soap from a herb called *Saponaria officinalis*. She smiled at me kindly after she had taken in the magnitude of the restoration needed.

'You can do it, only it needs work,' she said. A bundle of herbs was sent for from Norfolk. Pascal, the chef, provided a cauldron for the initiation in the old still-room kitchen. It was impossible not to think of Macbeth's witches as we watched muslin bags bobbing on the seething spring water in the cauldron, but—as the ritual proceeded—my faith knew no bounds as the air became pervaded with the subtle unforgettable scent that filled my nostrils for the first time, and proved to be my novice introduction to the miracles of nature therapy. The soap was a brown liquid with a meaningful lather, which covered the surface of the copper like a foaming tankard of beer. The scent that arose to eager nostrils was aromatic and rather exciting.

The Prince Regent's bed and a curtain from the Little Parlour were tackled at once. An alarming process of what was called 'loosening the dirt' took place in a big bath. The water turned inkpot black, and dustbin dirt hid the objects of ablution. If the ragged curtain had entered the bath a sorry mess of powdered rags, it emerged looking more than ever like seaweed which had been dragged from the bed of the ocean!

The little old lady was never daunted and was an inspiring teacher. Would she meet her Waterloo over this Stygian mass of weeds, red and dripping? I was relieved to find she appeared quite unmoved . . . By the time our lives were once more disrupted by war we had mended and re-hung twenty eight brocade curtains, three Queen Anne four-poster beds, and a set of chairs, besides much other restoration. The work of restoration has gone on for thirty years, and new techniques have been developed over this period in applying the *Saponaria* to textiles which have been sent to Uppark for repair from Europe and America as well as in Britain.

This simple statement gives little idea of the complete transformation that occurred. Not only were the ancient fabrics cleaned gently and efficiently by the *Saponaria* extract: the herb actually put new life into the fibres from which they were woven. The colour of the dye, too, seemed more than cleaned—it was in truth restored to its original brilliance and depth. Uppark, a place of loveliness within and without, was well worth a visit for the sake of witnessing this unique work alone.

Unhappily, for family reasons over which the National Trust had no control, Lady Meade-Fetherstonhaugh was obliged to leave Uppark in 1968. Suitable premises for her and for the textile restoration work have been found in the same locality, where the pure spring water essential to release the vital powers of the herb *Saponaria* is available—the plant cannot function in chemically treated tap-water— together with convenient access for the trained craftswomen who have built up this skilled work so successfully.

For the sake of posterity, it may be hoped that Lady Meade-Fetherstonhaugh, who is President of the Society of Herbalists, will leave to that Society a full description of the method which she has discovered and developed over the years. She deserves great honour for applying herself to this unique work, in order that later generations may see ancient and lovely textiles restored to much of their original beauty.

Having been trained in the nineteen-thirties as a tapestry weaver at the Central School of Arts and Crafts in London, under a tutor who was himself taught by William Morris, I am particularly excited by the effect of *Saponaria* cleaning. Too often the hangings in our great houses and museums are dull and lifeless, because dirt and age combined have erased the depth from their pictorial designs, and flatness where none was intended results in dreariness and boredom for the beholder—although few are outspoken enough to say so. With *Saponaria*, in skilled hands, we are allowed to see the original planes restored—foreground, middle distance and distance being clearly delineated once more. The restored tapestry picture then springs to life in all its original vigour. Modern chemical cleaners cannot achieve this result. The method—believed to be of German origin—in use by too many of our great collections is as detrimental to the treasures of tapestry as are some of those now commonly employed for the 'cleaning' of famous paintings.

It is not unknown in these islands for people of the finest sensibility to be found pursuing their original ideas in some quiet corner, unpublicized, while officialdom makes do with the second-best. If an exhibit could be staged in London, showing a tapestry treated by Lady Meade-Fetherstonhaugh alongside one from a national collection where chemical cleaning is employed, there can be little doubt that the vote would be cast overwhelmingly in favour of the result produced by *Saponaria*.

SORREL, FRENCH   *Rumex scutatus*   [*p.* 70

The Sorrels share the cooling virtues of the Docks, and belong to the same family. Sorrel leaves contain oxalate of potash, and this gives the sharp taste which makes the herb acceptable in salad, soup and sauce; although the French kind is less acrid than the indigenous Garden Sorrel more commonly grown in England. The acidity strengthens towards the end of summer, when the flowers are a deep bronze-purple and the foliage tinged with russet. As green vegetables both Sorrels may be boiled in the same way as Spinach. French Sorrel, said to have been introduced into Britain at the end of the sixteenth century, is often known as Buckler-leaved Sorrel.

SORREL, GARDEN   *Rumex acetosa*   [*p.* 54

Known as Green Sauce, Sour Suds, Cuckoo Sorrow, Cuckoo's Meate and Gowk-meat, this plant grows wild in abundance in our English meadows, usually on soil that contains iron. The leaves of Garden Sorrel, a hardy perennial two or two and a half feet tall, are oblong and slightly arrow-shaped; the upper ones clasp the stem. The country names of Cuckoo's Meate (in Scotland, Gowk-meat), come from an old tradition that the bird used this herb to strengthen his voice.

In the time of Henry the Eighth Garden Sorrel was a very popular salad herb and used, too, as a pot herb or green vegetable; but after the introduction of French Sorrel it lost ground. John Evelyn wrote in the seventeenth century 'Sorrel imparts so grateful a quickness to the salad that it should never be left out'. Country folk in his day used to beat the herb to a mash, mix it with vinegar and sugar, and take it as a sauce with cold meat—hence the name Green Sauce for the plant. Some cooks wrap tough meat in a covering of Sorrel, tie it tightly, then cook. The acidity in the Sorrel helps to make the meat tender. If fish is stuffed with Sorrel before cooking, the smaller bones will be softened and become edible.

Medicinally, the Sorrels are refrigerant and diuretic, employed as a cooling drink in fevers, and at one time much in demand as anti-scorbutics.

Propagation of both species is by seed, sown outside in drills a quarter-inch deep in April and May, in fairly good soil. Seedlings may be thinned to eight inches apart, or, better still, transplanted into well composted holes, and watered copiously. Established plants may be divided in spring or autumn.

Some recipes will be found on pp. 178, 179.

Sheep's Sorrel (*Rumex acetosella*) and Mountain Sorrel (*Oxyria reniformis*, syn. *Oxyria digyna*) have also been used as pot herbs and in medicine; they share the same acid quality and have anti-scorbutic properties.

SOUTHERNWOOD   *Artemisia abrotanum*

This is a real cottage garden plant, a favourite bush to place near the gate or front door, where the aromatic foliage will emit a delicious scent when passers-by pinch or brush against it. The name means 'Southern Wormwood'; this Artemisia is a native of southern Europe, while the Wormwood (*Artemisia absinthium*) is a British native.

One of the vernacular names, Lad's Love, comes from the use that adolescent males used to make of the herb to encourage the growth of their beards, so as to appear older than they really were. It had a great vogue at one time in a pomade, which was believed to stimulate the hair on the head and prevent baldness.

Southernwood, introduced into this country in the mid-sixteenth century, has lacy grey-green foliage, very finely cut, and is never seen in flower here. Other country names for the plant are Old Man, Boy's Love, and (in Scotland) Apple Ringie, while in France they call it *Garde Robe*, because it discourages the attacks of clothes-moth. In earlier centuries it was used as a strewing-herb.

In medicine, it was well known as a wound herb, and considered also to be valuable as a tonic, antiseptic and anthelmintic. A teaspoonful of the powdered herb was given in treacle to children suffering from intestinal worms. To make a tonic tea, one ounce of the herb should be infused in one pint of boiling water; the vessel must be kept covered during the infusion. The plant was also used as a dyestuff, giving a good yellow colour on wool.

Propagation is by cuttings: green, taken in summer, or hardwood, taken in autumn. The plant flourishes in full sun, on light to medium soil, and it makes a good low hedge if clipped back in March and again in July. Margery Fish cuts hers down to ground level every spring. Southernwood requires hard, regular clipping if it is not to become the straggly misshapen bush we too often see athwart the path in country gardens.

SPURGE, CAPER *Euphorbia lathyrus*

This stiff, angular, biennial plant, with its glaucous foliage and nasturtium-like ridged seeds, has an architectural charm which can be valuable when the plant is carefully sited in the gardener's scheme. It has a centuries-old reputation as a mole-repellent, but a nurseryman friend who is bedevilled by these industrious tunnellers has allowed the Caper Spurge to seed itself all over his land, without the slightest effect on the exploding population of moles.

The seeds, which resemble true capers—these are buds of the *Capparis spinosa*, an Eastern plant—are said by Mrs Leyel to be an exception to the poisonous nature of the Euphorbia family in general. The so-called 'capers', she says, 'may be pickled and eaten with meat without harmful effects'. I am not sure that this advice is sound, for I came across a village child who became violently ill after eating a few seeds of Caper Spurge. Margaret Brownlow cautiously suggests that it is inadvisable for more than a few fruits of this plant to be eaten at a time. I prefer to leave it alone.

This Spurge is easily raised from seed, sown in summer to produce mature plants the following year, for it is a biennial. After that the plant is certain to self-sow in abundance, and it will grow to four feet in good conditions.

There are many species of Euphorbia, and most of them contain a poisonous, acrid, milky juice which has often been employed externally to remove warts. The plant takes its name from Euphorbus, physician to Juba, king of Mauretania. Curiously enough, the most deadly of all the Spurges, in its raw state, is the South American plant known as Manioc; but after the acrid juice has been extracted, the root of this species is manufactured into a wholesome and nourishing food, whence comes the tapioca we use in milk puddings.

The Euphorbias had a reputation as medicinal herbs in ancient Greece. Mrs Leyel, seeing a green-flowered variety growing near the sacred fountain of Vesalia, wondered if this could be the *Euphorbia antiquorum* of India and Ceylon, known as a powerful alterative medicine. Another Spurge, *E. neriifolia*, is employed medicinally in Malaya, boiled with rice to relieve coughs, and its juice mixed with

Sesame oil to cure earache; while the American Spurge, *E. coroldata*, is applied externally to relieve rheumatic pains.

For most people in Britain today the Euphorbias are chiefly of interest for their value as foliage plants in the garden. From the formidable *E. wulfenii* and the slightly less imposing *E. characias*, the glowing orange-stemmed *E. griffithi* and the greeny-gold springtime clumps of *E. epithymoides* and *E. polychroma*, to the delicate green creeping *E. cyparissias*, this family includes something suitable for everyone's taste and type of garden.

SWEET CICELY *Myrrhis odorata*

This fragrant perennial herb, three feet high, with a thick root and fern-like foliage, has a Latin name which is derived from the Greek word for perfume. It is found wild in many parts of Britain, often in the neighbourhood of buildings, and has for centuries been used fresh in green salads, and as a pot herb, when the root, leaves and seed were all cooked and eaten. Although the plant has a distinct taste of Anise, the smell of it is more suggestive of Lovage. The leaves are delicately lacy, the white flowers in umbels appear in early summer, and are succeeded by inch-long blackish-brown fruits which are full of flavour.

The plant is attractive to bees, and in an old herbal is described as being so harmless that nobody could use it amiss. The roots were thought to be especially good for old people, when boiled and eaten with oil and vinegar: 'This food rejoiceth and comforteth the heart of them that are dull and without courage, and increaseth their lust and strength.'

Some country names of Sweet Cicely are rather confusing: Anise, Sweet Chervil and Cow Chervil. Others, such as Smooth Cicely, Sweet Fern, Shepherd's Needle, British Myrrh and The Roman Plant are more distinctive.

In medicine this herb was classed as stomachic, carminative and expectorant. Herbalists employ it to relieve coughs and flatulence; as a gentle stimulant for debilitated stomachs; and as a tonic for adolescent girls. The distilled water is diuretic, useful in cases of pleurisy, and the essence was considered to be aphrodisiac.

Propagation may be by seed, sown outdoors in spring, or by root division early in the year. The plant enjoys a fairly moist site in semi-shade. Authorities differ on whether it should be claimed as a true

British native, or is, as one vernacular name suggests, a Roman importation. In the north of England people used to employ the seeds in an unexpected manner, to polish and scent oaken floors and furniture, but I have so far been unable to find explicit directions for making Sweet Cicely polish.

TANSY *Tanacetum vulgare*

The common Tansy, sometimes called Athanasia, or Buttons, was at first dedicated to St Athanasius and later to the Virgin Mary. It is a familiar wild plant of our banks, hedgerows and waste places in Britain. The stem is tough and erect, some three feet high, grooved and angular, bearing alternate pinnate leaves of a bright green, with yellow button flowers in August and September. The scent of the whole plant is powerful, some say unpleasant; out-of-doors it is not as a rule sufficiently concentrated to offend. At one time it was popular as a flavouring herb, recognized as a suitable accompaniment to roast lamb before Mint took its place; but today, if we cooked with it at all, this pungent flavour would of necessity be introduced in very small amounts. The difficulty of keeping fish and flesh sweet in earlier times led to a lavish use of strong herbs and spices to disguise the unpleasing taste of tainted food. Today, the growing fashion of using certain herbs in the kitchen proceeds less from a need to cover up bad flavours than from the tastelessness of many dishes made from frozen, 'oven ready', processed or otherwise de-natured products.

Tansy was also regularly employed of old in a cake or pudding—the latter seems to have been more of a thick sauce—traditionally eaten at Easter, when most people were expected to gorge themselves after their Lenten fast. This herb was regarded as a stomachic to assist overburdened systems to cope with the sudden excess of rich food. Others maintain that it was more often taken to purify the humours of the human body after the diet of salt fish consumed during Lent. Others, again, say that the true reason for eating 'tansies', as the cakes or puddings were called, was to symbolize the bitter herbs eaten by the Jews at the Passover. One recipe for this food—a rich mixture of eggs, cream, brandy, sugar and crumbs—seems far from bitter. It is given on page 179.

The name Tansy, some suppose, is derived from the Greek *athanatos*, immortal, which may have sprung from the long-lasting nature of

TANSY

this plant's blossom, or from the custom of using it to preserve corpses from corruption. Then there is the story of Jupiter ordering Mercury to give Ganymede this herb in the cup that was to make him immortal, and so fit to become the cup-bearer of the gods. It is assuredly a plant with a long history, and many legends have accumulated round it in the course of centuries.

Common Tansy is often cultivated in gardens, though the old

herbals insist that in the wild it develops greater virtue in both leaves and flowers. There is some doubt as to whether it is truly indigenous in Britain. It seems likely that in the first place it was cultivated in monastic herb gardens, whence it escaped to naturalize in great quantities. In the fifteenth century it was esteemed as a wound-herb, and in the time of Elizabeth I it was a favourite strewing herb, used in beds and bedding to discourage vermin. An old country habit may still be seen in farm kitchens, where a bunch of Elder and Tansy is placed on the window-ledge to repel flies. Tansy was propagated in the herb garden of Charlemagne, and at the Benedictine monastry of St Gall in Switzerland a thousand years ago.

Medicinally, Tansy is anthelmintic, tonic, stimulant and emmenagogic. For expelling worms in children, Tansy Tea (one ounce of the herb infused in a pint of boiling water) was given to the child when fasting, in doses of a teacupful night and morning. This infusion has also been used to treat hysteria, kidney weaknesses and cases of ague. In Scotland, an infusion of the dried flowers and seeds was formerly given to relieve sufferers from gout. Applied hot as a fomentation, Tansy is recommended for sprains and rheumatic aches. Leaves and tops are harvested by being cut close above the root just when the flowers first open. This crop is easily dried and stored, and retains its power for a couple of years at least.

The plant may also be used as a dyestuff. On wool, the leaves will give a clear yellowish green, using a chrome mordant; the flowering tops yield a bright golden yellow on wool mordanted with alum, and with chrome and cream of tartar for mordant the same dye-bath produces a rich orange or tan colour. It is said that the roots will give a good green, too, but this I have not tried. It seems preferable to take only the tops of a perennial wild plant, leaving the roots for crops in subsequent years.

A few years ago I was asked to draw up a guide to the herb garden at the American Museum in Britain, at Claverton Manor near Bath. There were four categories of herb: the culinary, medicinal, fragrant and dye-plants. It was of interest that Tansy alone, of those grown at Claverton, came into all four sections. Appropriately enough, it grows wild in profusion along the valley of the Bristol Avon, which is in view from the Museum grounds.

As a garden subject, the fern-leaved Tansy, *Tanacetum vulgare*, var. *crispum*, cherished by the great Gertrude Jekyll, is well worth having. It has the most enchanting lacy foliage, and is slightly less rampant than the common kind.

TARRAGON   *Artemisia dracunculus* (French)
A. dracunculoides (Russian)   [p. 71

This popular member of the Artemisia tribe has for long been cultivated in herb gardens for its sharply aromatic leaves, used in salads, seasonings and in the preparation of Tarragon vinegar. The name Tarragon is said to be a corruption of the French *Esdragon*, from *dracunculus*, a little dragon. The herb was once known as Dragon's Mugwort; to this, as to the other 'dragon' herbs* was imputed the power of curing sufferers from venomous stings and the bites of rabid dogs. Many curious fables have grown up around the plant. That which instructs credulous gardeners to place a seed of Flax within a radish in order to produce a root of Tarragon cannot be substantiated.

Of the two sorts of Tarragon in cultivation, the French is usually considered to be so far superior in flavour that few who have tried both will bother to cook with the Russian kind. I heard an amusing story from a professional grower, who was particularly requested to supply a bunch of *Russian* Tarragon along with vegetables for a dinner-party to which some Russian diplomats had been invited. The vendor had difficulty in convincing the overwrought hostess that *French* Tarragon would prove suitable, even to Russian palates.

Miss Carola Cochrane, author of *Two Acres Unlimited*, who sends many vegetable delights from her Court Lodge Farm near Ashford in Kent to Covent Garden, as well as superb flowers, once found this peculiar request written on her telephone pad: 'Six chips of Russian *Paragon* for a very important client.'

These perennial plants rarely produce seed in this country, and are propagated by root division, preferably when new shoots are appearing in May, or by cuttings taken when the spring growth is under way. A sheltered, sunny position and well-drained, composted soil are required for the slightly tender French Tarragon, and a little protection in winter may be necessary. It is a native of southern Europe, while the Russian Tarragon comes from Siberia and stands much

* Wormwoods traditionally sprang up in the path of the serpent after that reptile's banishment from Eden.

colder conditions. Both plants are unlike other members of the genus in having leaves that are entire, not divided up with the feathery effect so characteristic of Wormwood, Southernwood and the other Artemisias. The French kind is a bushy plant with smooth dark green leaves; the Russian Tarragon is taller, with willowy leaves of paler green, less glossy.

As soon as plants have become well established, leaves may be plucked for use, fresh, in the kitchen—a practice which continues throughout the summer. For winter storage, the foliage is harvested in autumn, when plants may be cut quite low. Bunches are dried in a temperature of seventy or eighty degrees Fahrenheit—if wire trays are available, so much the better, for when thinly spread the herb will dry very quickly, and retain its full flavour. It must be stored at once in stoppered containers away from light. The flavour of French Tarragon is at once warm and biting; that of the Russian kind is insipid by comparison.

This herb is used in cookery, fresh or dried, in the traditional *fines herbes* mixture for omelettes; also cooked with steak and chops; sprinkled in soups and salads; in poultry stuffings; egg dishes; and in pickles and sauces. Recipes for Tarragon Vinegar and Tarragon Sauce are on pp. 179, 180.

Tarragon was a favourite herb of Charlemagne; but it did not arrive in Britain until Tudor days, and at first it was grown only in royal gardens. The diarist John Evelyn gave his opinion that young shoots of Tarragon must never be excluded from 'sallets'. Of its medicinal action he wrote ' 'tis highly cordial and friend to the head, heart and liver'. The root of this plant was at one time used to relieve toothache.

THORNAPPLE *Datura stramonium*

This poisonous plant is occasionally found growing wild in Britain, although it is not a native. The place of origin is in some doubt. In America it has been regarded as an import from Europe, while some European botanists describe it as belonging to North America. It flourishes in many parts of Russia and far north into Siberia. The seed is viable over long periods and in many climates, so that it is thought to have spread far and wide in ships' cargoes and ballast. The derivation of *stramonium* is uncertain, while *Datura* is supposed to have come from the Sanskrit, after many changes.

Thornapple is a large, coarse herb with irregularly toothed leaves. With its bushy habit, rising to three feet or more in height with spreading branches, it does not look in the least like an annual plant—which it is. It is in bloom nearly all the summer, and its large white Convolvulus-shaped flowers are followed by thorny seed capsules variously described as being like green walnuts, Spanish chestnuts and little leathery apples—no doubt the latter fancy provided the vernacular name of Thornapple. These 'apples' contain the black seed. The foliage emits an unpleasant, foetid smell and the sweet-scented flowers are narcotic if inhaled for too long. The whole plant is poisonous, but the seed contains the most active principle, which neither drying nor boiling will destroy. It comes in Part I of the British Poisons List.

The effects of Stramonium poisoning are dimness of sight, dilation of the pupil of the eye, giddiness, delirium and death. At times those who but lightly rub their eyes with hands that have come into contact with the plant find their pupils dilating. Medicinally, *D. stramonium* leaves and seeds are official in many pharmacopoeias; the constituents are similar, except that the seeds contain oil. This drug is antispasmodic, anodyne and narcotic; it is similar to Belladonna in action, but without the constipating effect. It has been largely employed as an ingredient of asthma powder and cigarettes. It is also put into ointments, plasters and the like for the relief of neuralgia, rheumatism and haemorrhoids. There are advocates for its use in treating cases of hydrophobia.

Thornapple figures in legend and superstition in many parts of the world, which is not surprising in view of its strange appearance, vile smell, narcotic powers and quick action. It is said to have been used by the priests of Apollo at Delphi, to assist them in their prophesying; by the Arabs of Central Asia; by Thugs and other practitioners of evil arts in India; by witches and sorcerers in Europe. It is, or was, smoked by poor Turks in lieu of opium. It is not surprising that the country name of this plant in America is the Devil's Apple. It is said that early settlers, not knowing of its dangers, ate some of the leaves and suffered such ill effects that the name of the devil was given to the plant. If anyone wishes to grow this fruit of the Evil One, it is easily raised from seed, sown in May in an open, sunny situation; or it may be raised earlier under glass and transplanted.

According to the sixteenth-century herbalist John Gerard, the 'Thornie apple' was first seen in Britain when 'seeds I rescieued of the

Right Honourable Lord Edward Zouch, which he brought from Constantinople'.

THYME, WILD   *Thymus serpyllum*   [*p.* 71

This aromatic creeping perennial herb is commonly seen on chalky downs and sandy heaths: it is said that the delicate flavour of South-down mutton is due to the large amount of Thyme consumed by the sheep. As far back as the early years of the twelfth century Thyme was used as a culinary herb in these islands; but it is difficult to ascertain whether this was the native species or one imported from the Continent and cultivated in monastic herb gardens. The wild Thyme, known also as Mother O'Thyme, Brotherwort and Creeping Thyme, is indigenous to the greater part of Europe. It is found up to a considerable height in the Alps, and in the valleys; on rocks; in stony, abandoned fields and along ditches; and at times in damp, clayey places.

The specific name *serpyllum* means 'creeping', and describes the usual procumbent, trailing habit of this plant; but Thyme is very adaptable, and when growing protected amid whin bushes it will sometimes throw up a tall stalk, which gives it an unfamiliar appearance. The root of this herb is fibrous and woody, and the many stems are tough and branched, usually of a reddish-brown colour and bearing many small, oval leaves of a bright green set in pairs. The purple flowers, in whorls, appear in late May and June and continue until the autumn, and are much visited by bees.

In cultivation it will grow in almost any soil, but is at its best in light and well-drained beds in the sun, or on rockeries or between paving stones. Propagation is by seed sown in April or May, by cuttings made in spring and summer, and by root division in spring or early autumn when the soil is warm. The herb is harvested just before the tops break into flower, and a succession of cuts will be obtainable between May and September. The crop is dried in bunches, hung up in a current of warm air.

Medicinally, it is aromatic, antiseptic, stimulant, antispasmodic, diuretic and emmenagogic. An infusion has been prescribed for chest maladies, convulsive coughs and weak digestion—being good for flatulence. A sound remedy for obstinate coughs, including whooping-cough: Take a tablespoonful of whole linseed, bring to the boil in a quart of water and simmer for half an hour. While still boiling, pour the liquid (in the proportion of one pint to an ounce of Thyme) on to fresh or dried Thyme and some slices of lemon. Sweeten with honey or barley sugar, strain when cold, and give a tablespoonful of the mixture five or six times a day. The simpler Wild Thyme Tea, made by infusing an ounce of the herb in a pint of boiling water, is an old remedy for headache. Some prefer it with the addition of a sprig of Rosemary.

In the garden this small plant is ideal for making paths or aromatic lawns, which have a pleasant feel to the foot and give out delicious fragrance when crushed. The plants will stand up to considerable wear if allowed to grow together into a mat before being walked upon. Cultivated forms include *T. serpyllum coccineus*, which has rich crimson flowers and very small bronze-green leaves. It blooms in June and July, but has very little scent. *T. serpyllum citriodorus* has mauve flowers and a lemon scent, with green leaves. *T. serpyllum lanuginosus* makes clumps of grey, woolly foliage and has pale mauve blossoms. *T. serpyllum* 'Pink Chintz' has hairy grey-green leaves and pink flowers. Small, rooted pieces of any of these, planted six inches apart in spring, should meet and form a carpet by late summer. A solid path to take constant treading may be made by sinking some form of paving slab about half an inch below the surface of the soil, with creeping Thymes planted between the stones and running on top of them.

THYME, GARDEN *Thymus vulgaris*

This is another woody, perennial herb with a fibrous root, but of more upright growth, usually nine or ten inches in height. The very small green leaves are set in pairs on the stalks, and the two-lipped flowers, of pale purple, open from May to August. The whole herb is highly aromatic. The type with narrow greyish-green leaves is the most pungent: it is sometimes called Winter, or German Thyme. Lemon Thyme (*T. citriodorus*) has rather broader leaves than the ordinary kind, and a sharp lemon flavour which is excellent for cooking.

Then there are the attractive silver Thymes: *T. vulgaris* 'Silver Posie', very hardy and of warm Thyme flavour, equally valuable as a decorative garden subject and in the kitchen; *T. citriodorus* 'Silver Queen', less hardy and with the lemon flavour. This plant has charming pink leaf-buds in winter, and is well worth growing in a warm, sheltered place. The golden Thymes are also decorative. *T. vulgaris*

LIVÈCHE OFFICINALE.

LOVAGE

DILL

Stachara alterantis

Rimon Alkanet

ALKANET

LUNGWORT

JUNIPER

Chenopodium Bonus Henricus

GOOD KING HENRY

HEMLOCK

COLTSFOOT

MELILOT

MARSH MALLOW

aureus is ordinary Garden Thyme with golden foliage, very hardy, and *T. citriodorus aureus* has the lemon flavour and green leaves variegated with golden streaks. There is a third form, all-gold foliage resembling ordinary golden Garden Thyme, but with the lemon scent. This is sometimes differentiated by the name *T. aureus citriodorus*.

There are too many Garden Thymes to list in full here, but *T. fragrantissimus* has a scent that reminds one of oranges ripening in the sun, and the so-called 'Caraway Thyme', *T. herba-barona*, smells like Caraway and was at one time rubbed on the joint known as baron of beef. The growth is semi-prostrate, with small, shiny green leaves and rosy-purple flowers in June and July. This is a good herb for the rock garden. Thymes flourish wherever Rosemary and Lavender thrive.

It seems strange that a plant of such long-standing popularity in these islands has no real vernacular name: Thyme being but an anglicized version of the Greek *thumon*. This old favourite was grown in bee-gardens in the days when honey was the major sweetening agent, and is mentioned by Pliny. Gervase Markham gave instructions to seventeenth-century English bee-keepers for perfuming hives with Fennel, Hyssop and 'Time-flowers', also 'the stone upon which the beehive shall stand'. So far as is known, the Romans did not use this herb in cookery, although they put it into cheeses and liqueurs. To the ancient Greeks *thumon*, Thyme, was a symbol of *thumos*, courage, and they believed that the plant had invigorating properties. In the Middle Ages a piece of Thyme was given to knights by their ladies, to keep up their spirits, and a design depicting a sprig of Thyme was commonly embroidered on the scarf offered as a farewell gift to lord or lover before his departure on a Crusade or other high enterprise.

Of old, Thyme had many uses. A recipe dated 1600 in the Ashmolean Museum at Oxford is headed '*To enable one to see the Fairies.*—A pint of sallet oyle put into a vial glasse; first wash it with Rose-water and Marygolde water; the flowers to be gathered towards the east. Warm it till the oyle becomes white, then put it into the glasse, and then put thereto the budds of Hollyhocke, the flowers of Marygolde, the flowers or toppes of wild Thyme, the budds of young Hazle; and the Thyme must be gathered near the side of a hill where fairies used to be; and take the grasse of a fairy throne; then all these put into the oyle in the glasse and sette it to dissolve three dayes in the sunne and then keep it for thy use.' The very look and sound of those words are of themselves almost sufficient to evoke the fairies, if we live in remote and unspoilt country, whence they have not yet been driven away.

In most of the western world Thyme is now put to more mundane uses. The traditional *bouquet garni* of the cookery books consists of one sprig of Parsley, one Bay leaf, two sprigs of Thyme. The herbs are tied in a bunch or placed in a muslin bag, and plunged into the soup or stew while it is cooking. The herbs are of course removed before the dish is brought to table.

For other recipes, see pp. 172–179.

The antiseptic oil known as Thymol is obtainable from both Garden and Wild Thyme, also from certain species of Mint and Caraway. Thymol is a powerful antiseptic for internal and external use; most of us know it best as an ingredient of a well-known gargle and mouth-wash. Perhaps the herb-doctors who invented the Holy Herbs Charm centuries ago were wiser than they knew—or than their quaint way of expressing knowledge might suggest at first glance today:

> Thyme and Fennel, two exceeding mighty ones,
> These herbs the wise Lord made
> Holy in the Heavens; He let them down,
> Placed them, and sent them into the seven worlds
> As a cure for all, the poor and the rich.

VALERIAN *Valeriana officinalis*

To most people 'Valerian' is that plant which grows in profusion on walls and banks, on sea-cliffs and along many a railway embankment, its domed heads of crimson, pink or white flowers very attractive to butterflies. This, however, is not the true Valerian of the herbalist. The botanical name of what has become so commonly known as 'Valerian' is *Centranthus ruber*.

Valeriana officinalis is at first sight a little dull by comparison, with tall, erect stems up to four feet in height, bearing pinnate leaves in shape, size and colour rather like those of the Ash tree, and small flower-heads from June to September of a washy lilac-pink colour. These emit a peculiar sickly scent, likened by imaginative sniffers to that of the Heliotrope, but definitely a poor imitation. The rest of the plant smells even less like that favourite old garden flower, while the roots, when dried for use in medicine, stink like bad drains. 'The chief preparation of the British Pharmacopoeia,' says Mrs Grieve, 'is the

VALERIAN

Tincture *Valerianae ammoniata*, containing Valerian, oil of Nutmeg, oil of Lemon and ammonia; it is an extremely nauseous and offensive preparation.' As it was once prescribed for me at a time of great stress, and was so repulsive that I preferred to face the ills life brought without its help, I can endorse her description. It is considered to be a powerful nervine, stimulant, carminative and anti-spasmodic, and, according to Mrs Leyel, it is a cure for noises in the head.

In view of these strictures it may surprise readers to hear that the Anglo-Saxons used the plant as a salad-herb. Even more astonishing, in the Middle Ages the root was prized, not only as a medicine but as a spice and even as a perfume, being laid among linen and clothing. In our time it is mainly attractive to cats, throwing them into a frenzy. It has been used by old-fashioned rat-catchers to bait traps, and it is sometimes said that the Pied Piper of Hamelin secreted roots of Valerian in his garments, which so attracted the rat population that he was able to lead them all away without trouble—the music being just a blind.

In Chaucer's time humble folk in the north of England and in Scotland used Setewale or Setwall—an old country name for the true Valerian—in their broths.

> Then springen herbes grete and smale,
> The Licoris and the Setewale.

The derivation of Valerian is ascribed to various sources. Some attribute it to an ancient physician named Valerius, who is said to have been the first to use it in medicine. Others suggest that it comes from the Latin *valere*, to be in health. The name *Valeriana* does not seem to have emerged until about the tenth century, when it was often written in conjunction with the expression *Phu!* or *Fu!*—an ejaculation which seems so remarkably descriptive that we might well revive it.

VERBENA, LEMON   *Lippia citriodora*

This deciduous shrub was brought to England in the eighteenth century. Its foliage has the most delicious fragrance of all the lemon-scented herbs, but the plant is tender, needing a warm, sheltered site, and it does not succeed everywhere. The leaves are lanceolate and pale green; the mauve flowers appear in slender spikes in August. The foliage should be harvested at this time, and will retain its fragrance for years in sachets and pot-pourri.

Medicinally, a decoction has been used as a stomachic and anti-spasmodic in cases of dyspepsia and indigestion.

As a culinary herb, the dried and powdered leaves, sparingly used, add a lemon tang to stuffings for poultry or fish, and are even pleasant in cakes and puddings if lemon is missing from the shelf.

This plant is propagated by cuttings of new young shoots taken in summer. Pruning is done in the spring. The shrub often alarms gardeners by looking utterly spent and dead, until green buds suddenly break out in April. If outdoor cultivation is not a success, it is possible to raise the shrub in tubs, putting these out of doors in plunge beds in summer and returning them under cover in September. *Lippia citriodora* should not be confused with the common hardy perennial Lemon Balm (*Melissa officinalis*), or with the Lemon Grass (*Andropogon schoenanthus*).

WATERCRESS
Nasturtium officinale (syn. *Rorippa nasturtium-aquaticum*)

This common creeping herb grows in Europe and in Russian Asia, and is found near open watercourses and springs. It has smooth, shining pinnate leaves and ovate leaflets; usually the foliage is a bright green, but one variety has a bronze tinge. The white flowers, which open in June, are inconspicuous. Unfortunately this very valuable edible plant sometimes accompanies the poisonous Marshwort or Fool's Cress. This latter subject may be distinguished by its finely toothed leaves of a paler green, and white flowers in umbels; but the risk of a mixture occurring in bunches of Watercress picked in the wild, added to the possibility of the water being contaminated, makes it generally preferable to obtain the cultivated crop from a reputable grower or retailer.

The Latin name, *Nasturtium*, means a wry nose, and was invented for this genus because of its pungent smell. The garden annual, known as Nasturtium or Indian Cress, is properly not a Nasturtium but a Tropaeolum. This favourite plant of our gardens in childhood has caper-like seeds which, unlike those of the Caper Spurge, are quite harmless and may safely be eaten to flavour sandwiches or salads, together with the young, hot, leaves.

The true Watercress, cultivated in pure spring water and eaten when fresh, is one of the most prized additions made by herbs to our diet, especially for those who suffer from impurities of the blood. It improves the complexion, is powerfully anti-scorbutic and promotes appetite. The bruised leaves (or the expressed juice) assist in clearing away spots and blemishes from the skin. If adolescents cared more for this article of food and less for sweets, they would suffer from fewer embarrassments of blotchy and pimpled face and neck. The active and beneficent principles of Watercress are at their best when the plant is just coming into flower.

It has a long history of service to mankind, and was anciently listed as one of the Nine Sacred Herbs. The poet Herrick wrote of it:

> Lord, I confess too when I dine,
> The pulse is thine:
> And all these other bits that be
> There placed by Thee:
> The worts, the Perslane, and the mess
> Of Watercress.

'Eat cresses and get wit' was said in Greece long ago. In England, the herb was of old known as *Stime*.

WILLOW HERB *Epilobium*

There are nine native species of this, perhaps the commonest herb plant in Britain, and one of the few that have the actual word 'herb' as part of the vernacular name. Willow Herbs belong to the Natural Order *Onagraceae*, and are related to the Evening Primrose and Enchanter's Nightshade. The very tall (6–8 ft) *Epilobium angustifolium*, commonly called Rosebay or Fireweed, has of old been used a substitute for tea in these islands and in Russia also, where it was named Kaporie Tea. An ale brewed from Rosebay with the addition of Fly Agaric (*Agaricus muscarius*) is said to be highly intoxicating. Few who saw how this plant ramped over the ruins of war-torn London in the nineteen-forties thought of using it in this manner.

Medicinally, the root and leaves are demulcent, tonic, astringent and antispasmodic, and were used to treat whooping-cough, asthma and the hiccough. The American names Wickup and Wicopy probably allude to the latter ailment.

The Great Hairy Willow Herb (*E. hirsutum*) is equally common but less useful medicinally; powerfully astringent, it has been known to cause poisoning and convulsions when misused. To the gardener it is highly unpopular as an invasive weed, but in the wild it has charm. The name of Codlins and Cream was given to it by countryfolk who discovered that the young shoots, bruised in the hand, gave out a delicious aroma akin to that of roasted apples. An artist who saw the shadow photograph below described the seeding Willow Herb as a peerless exponent of the art of doodling.

WILLOW HERB

WINTERGREEN *Gaultheria procumbens*

This small shrubby evergreen plant is a native of the United States and Canada, from Georgia to Newfoundland. It is found in quantity growing wild beneath trees and larger shrubs, particularly under evergreens such as Rhododendrons and Kalmias. The oil obtained from the leaves of this Wintergreen has been valued as an external application for rheumatic pains, and in tooth-powders. It is readily absorbed by the skin, but as it sometimes causes irritation it has been largely superseded by a synthetic product (methyl salicylate) with the characteristic Wintergreen scent.

As a garden subject, this little creeping plant with its dark glossy leaves, small white flowers and red berries makes attractive ground cover for shady places; but it prefers peaty lime-free soils, such as its favourite companions of the Rhododendron genus require. It may be propagated by seed or by root division. It provides valuable winter berries as food for deer and partridge in America, where vernacular names include Partridge Berry, Deer Berry, Checkerberry, Boxberry, Teaberry and Mountain Tea.

The British Wintergreen, *Pyrola rotundifolia*, is also a member of the Natural Order *Ericaceae*, but is of very different habit, bearing little white bell flowers on erect and slender stems above rosettes of small, rounded leaves. The plant has at times been mistaken for Lily-of-the-Valley. It was of old prized as a wound herb.

WITCH HAZEL *Hamamelis virginiana*

Most gardeners wish to grow the nurseryman's favourite species of this shrub, *H. mollis* from China, even if their soil and aspect are not particularly suited to it. The sweet-scented spidery yellow flowers with maroon centres burst out of leafless branches with astonishing swiftness and charm in the bleakest of January weather, by which they seem to be undaunted. The real Witch Hazel is an autumn flowering kind, a native of the eastern United States and Canada, where its medicinal virtues were first demonstrated to settlers by the 'Red' Indians. It is now much used by herbalists and others in simple medicine here. The clean, fresh smell of 'Pond's Extract' (of Witch Hazel) calls to mind many a sprain and bruise of childhood; pains so quickly alleviated by the application of this friendly plant's cooling essence.

H. virginiana reaches a height of some twelve feet and throws several branching trunks from the one root, with smooth grey bark; the leaves drop in autumn before its yellow flowers come. These are followed by blackish nuts containing edible white seeds. When ripe, the nuts fly open and eject their contents, a habit which procured the name of Snapping Hazelnut for the parent shrub. Seed is seldom produced in Britain, and in America it often fails to ripen until the succeeding summer. Leaves and bark yield astringent, tonic and sedative extracts, long familiar in pharmacopoeias on both sides of the Atlantic. It is still used today for bruises and sprains, swellings, scalds and skin inflammations, as an external application.

According to most gardening handbooks, both species are quite hardy and require good rich loam; but the finest specimens of *H. mollis* known to me are found in peaty soil, in rhododendron gardens such as Rowallane and Guincho in Northern Ireland.

H. mollis is slow-growing. It is rather expensive to buy, because it must be grafted on seedlings of *H. virginiana*. There is also a variety with pale primrose-yellow blossom, *H. pallida*.

WOAD *Isatis tinctoria* [*p.* 71

This is the one herb that everybody seems to have heard about, although few, perhaps, think of it as a herb. Woad (some say it is named from the Saxon *Wad* or *Waad*) is to most of us that blue dye we learnt in childhood to picture as the main garment worn by the Ancient Britons whom Caesar found in residence here. When, at a later date, we are shown the plant growing, it is disappointing to find little evidence of that rich blueness which we had for so long seen in the mind's eye. The spoon-shaped leaves are admittedly of a glaucous hue, but no more so than Eucalyptus and far less azure than the Jackman's Blue Rue. The flowers do nothing for us, either, being of a crude greenish-yellow. When ripe, the pendant blackish-brown seeds have a sinister look, like little black tongues, and here perhaps we may feel that the famous old plant lives up to its rich, legendary past.

Before the development of Indigo dyeing in the sixteenth century, Woad was cultivated as a dye-plant in various parts of Britain. Tewkesbury, Wisbech and Glastonbury are all mentioned as well-known centres of the industry, and the *Glas* in Glastonbury is said to be a Celtic word meaning 'grey-blue', with reference to the colouring of fields of Woad surrounding that small Somerset town. Pliny writes of Woad as *Glastum*, both plant and dye bearing the same name.

By the fifteenth century it is thought that the culture of Woad was fast dwindling in Britain, though as a dyestuff it was still in great demand. To fulfil this need the shippers (and in particular the 'Merchant Venturers' of Bristol) imported quantities, chiefly from Bayonne and Bordeaux. The value of this trade is shown by mention of Woad in wills of that period. One Bristol merchant left stocks of Woad to pay for his burial in St Mary Redcliffe Church, and another bequeathed 'eight measures of Woad towards a new pair of organs in St Werburgh's Church'. It is interesting to see that the French cloth-weaving industry of Languedoc declined (although woad-growing did not) at a time when British cloth production was on the increase. The dwindling crops of home-grown Woad made Britain a good customer for the French Woad—a neat piece of economic dove-tailing.

In her book *Mediaeval Merchant Venturers*, E. M. Carus-Wilson mentions woad (*waida, gaida*) as being 'the most important of dyestuffs, not only for blue cloth but as a foundation for other colours too. The best deep blue, perse, was properly dyed in woad alone on white wool mordanted with ashes, although some dyers, not succeeding in that way, tried to achieve the correct shade by putting wool dyed with woad into madder' (and other dyes) 'to make the colour darker'.

They got into trouble for this, for it was then an offence to describe as 'perse' cloth not dyed solely with woad on white wool. Perse was 'a high quality cloth fetching up to six shillings a yard in the thirteenth century'. The importance of this European industry in mediaeval times is commemorated in the cathedral of Amiens, where inscriptions may be seen to *maieurs de waidiers*, and a sculpture of two woad-men standing with a sack of woad balls between them. Similar roughly spherical balls of woad, prepared for use as a dyestuff, may be seen in a museum at Kew Gardens.

Preparation of this plant for dyeing is a complicated and messy business. After being dried in the sun, the foliage is crushed into a paste and then exposed to the air until it ferments. When this state has been reached the crust is broken and the material is formed into cakes, which are later broken up into powder, moistened, and again fermented—a process called 'couching'. During the eight or nine weeks taken to complete this treatment the paste first grows heated and steams, then cools, giving out a smell of ammonia. It is said that every nine pounds of leaves produced but one pound of the dye. In the great days of this industry in Britain, up to and including the sixteenth century, the working of woad was handed down in families, who were familiar with traditional chants appropriate to the various stages of the process.

A cruciferous plant, about three feet in height, *Isatis tinctoria* is not unlike some species of Wild Cabbage, but the one unmistakable feature of Woad is its pendant black seeds, now becoming popular with flower arrangers.

The garden culture of Woad is by seed, sown in May and June; it germinates readily, but as the plant is a biennial the seedlings will not flower until the following summer. It does best in deep, warm loam, but will tolerate frost, also drought, and lime, if obliged to do so. According to Mrs Grieve crops of this plant should not be grown for more than two years in succession on the same soil, so that the early professional cultivators of this crop were nomadic, hiring parcels of land here and there and travelling the country with their families, as some gipsies still do today.

At a later stage, settled farmers took to cultivating the plant in rotation with grain and root crops. On good land leaves can be harvested several times in one season; on the first occasion most of the growth is wrenched off, leaving the root to sprout again. When times were good Woad fetched £20 or more per ton. It is not considered to be a native of Britain, although the natives seem to have possessed the plant before the advent of Caesar. It may still be found in a few places in the wild, but is regarded as an escape from cultivation. The discovery of a new route to India in the sixteenth century made the importation of Indigo easier and cheaper, and from that day the importance of woad declined.

In the Middle Ages this was a medicinal herb, and it will be found mentioned in old herbals. One of these tells us that 'Woad is drying and binding, not fit to be given inwardly, but good for cooling inflammations, quenching St Anthony's Fire, and staying defluxions of blood to any part of the body', when applied as an ointment.

WOODRUFF *Asperula odorata*

This sweet woodland plant contains coumarin, which imparts to the foliage, when dried, a scent resembling new-mown hay, similar to that

WOODRUFF

of Melilot, lasting for years. It was of old popular as a strewing-herb, used for the floor of a bedchamber, for stuffing the bed, and for storage among clothing and linen. In the Middle Ages bunches of Woodruff were hung in churches, together with Lavender, Box and Roses.

Medicinally, fresh leaves of the herb were bruised and applied as a vulnerary, and a strong decoction was employed as a cordial and stomachic. In Germany a hock cup is made by steeping fresh sprigs of Woodruff in Rhine wine; this is known as Maibowle and is traditionally drunk on May 1st. A delicious *tisane* may be made by infusing a handful of flowering tops in a pint of boiling water.

In the thirteenth century the name of this plant was written as Wuderove, later spelt Wood-rove. The *rove* was said to derive from the French *roselle*, a wheel, because the leaves are arranged in whorls with a spoke-like effect. In Old French the herb was called *Muge-de-boys*, Musk-of-the-Woods, because of its perfume.

The plant is small, about nine inches high, erect, fine-stalked, with bright green leaves and starry white flowers in May and June. It frequents woods and shady banks. Herbalists gathered their supplies from the wild, but in recent times it has been cultivated in gardens as ground cover. It is easily propagated from seed or by root division. There is also a pink Woodruff (*A. taurina*), whose flowers are flushed with a peach-pink hue.

WORMWOOD, COMMON   *Artemisia absinthium* [p. 135

The genus Artemisia contains about a hundred and eighty species; of these, only five are natives of Britain, namely Mugwort, Breckland Mugwort, Common Wormwood, Sea Wormwood and Scottish Wormwood. Many other species of Artemisia, including Tarragon and Southernwood, have been introduced and have found such favour with herb and flower gardeners that they now seem to be indigenous, although in fact they are aliens. Some authorities think that these plants took their name from Artemisia, the Carian queen who built the famous mausoleum for her dead husband, King Mausolus. Others suggest that the herb was named after Artemis, the Greek word for the goddess Diana. Apuleius must have thought so, for he wrote; 'Of these worts that we name Artemisia, it is said that Diana did find them and delivered their powers and leechdom to Chiron the Centaur, who first from these worts set forth a leechdom, and he named these worts from the name of Diana, Artemis, that is, Artemisias.'

An English country name for Common Wormwood, Green Ginger, is said to spring from the fact that its root has a gingery flavour; but so far I have not been able to trace any reference to the root of Wormwood having been used in the manner of ginger. Another name, St John's Girdle, comes from the old custom of throwing a wreath of the herb on the Midsummer Eve fire as a sacrifice, which supposedly kept the thrower safe from ill-fortune for the ensuing twelve months. Wormwood has also been known as Old Woman (although some say that this name belongs properly to Sea Wormwood), and Crusader's Herb.

This is one of the most bitter herbs we have, the other being Rue, and it is no doubt for this reason that tradition tells us the plant sprang up in the track of the serpent as this accursed creature writhed away along the ground after being driven out of paradise. It is heartening to know that even serpent-worts can be turned to good account. Wormwood took a high place in the list of healing herbs of benefit to mankind at a very early date, and in later years was esteemed as a strewing herb, powerful as a deterrent to lice, bugs, fleas, moths and other undesirable insects.

Thomas Tusser, in his *Five Hundred Points of Good Husbandry* (1557), wrote:

> While Wormwood hath seed get a handful or twaine
> To save against March, to make flea to refrain:
> Where chamber is sweeped and Wormwood is strowne,
> What saver is better (if physic be true)
> For places infected than Wormwood and Rue?

Wormwood was anciently held to be a potent antidote to poisoning 'by hemlock, toadstools, and the biting of the sea-dragon'. An old love charm consisted of marigolds, marjoram, thyme and wormwood, dried and rubbed to powder on St Luke's Day. The powdered herbs were stirred into a paste of honey and vinegar, and the mixture used to anoint the seeker, who must repeat these lines meanwhile:

> St Luke, St Luke, be kind to me,
> In dreams let me my true love see.

Unfortunately the results, if any, of such incantations are never divulged.

The root of Common Wormwood is perennial, and from it rise strong, erect and many-branched flowering stems, somewhat woody at the base, two or more feet high and of a whitish appearance, being covered with silky hairs. The leaves are also hairy and silver, and are deeply cut, with a ragged look.

The flowers are small, globular, greenish-yellow, and borne in panicles in July and August. The leaves and flowers are very bitter, and more powerfully aromatic than those of Mugwort. The leaves and flowering tops, gathered in late summer, were of old dried for medicinal use, their properties being listed as tonic, stomachic, febrifuge and anthelmintic.

Wormwood tea, made by infusing one ounce of the herb for ten minutes in a pint of boiling water, was administered in doses of a wine-glassful 'to relieve melancholia and help dispel the yellow hue of jaundice'. It was also supposed to prevent sea-sickness. The dried and powdered flowers were employed as a vermifuge. The bitter, tonic and stimulant qualities of the herb led to its use in liqueurs, of which absinthe is the chief—hence the specific name of this Artemisia.

Cultivation is easy, propagation being by means of root division in autumn, or by cuttings, or by seed sown as soon as it is ripe. Like most silvery plants, Wormwood is at its best on rather poor soil and a warm, sunny site. The pale, silky and aromatic foliage is pleasing in a garden as foil to brightly coloured blossoms, and invaluable to flower-arrangers.

> O mickle is the powerful grace that lies
> In herbs, plants, stones and their true qualities.
>
> *Romeo and Juliet*, Act II, Scene 3

III. Pomanders and Clove Oranges

In earlier centuries, especially when Plague and Gaol Fever (Typhus) were rife, the scents of spice herbs and essential oils were thought to possess prophylactic virtues. Queen Elizabeth I had her palaces fumigated with fragrant herbs, and wore a pomander or 'pomme d'ambre'.* Samuel Pepys was given a 'franchipan ball'—a type of pomander—by his nephew. At the Wellcome Historical Medical Museum in Euston Road, London N.W.1, fine examples of chased and pierced pomander balls may be seen. These were hung upon the person from waist or neck. Today containers made of pottery are obtainable from herb specialists, and clove oranges too. The latter are easy to prepare at home.

CLOVE ORANGE

Choose a thin-skinned orange and stick cloves into it as thickly as possible, leaving a strip free round the 'equator' and from the 'north to south pole'. (These spaces are to take a ribbon binding.) If the skin is tough, use a bodkin or nail to prick holes for the cloves, which are pushed in up to the heads. Then roll the orange in a powder consisting of equal parts of orris root powder and cinnamon. Orris is becoming scarce in shops, but the home-grown white Florentine Iris root, dried and pulverized, will be satisfactory. Leave the orange wrapped up with the powder in paper for two weeks, then remove, shake off surplus powder, tie a ribbon round in both directions and hang from a coat-hanger to perfume the wardrobe. Some people like to dry the orange on a rack above the kitchen stove before using it.

A SWEET AND DELICATE POMANDER

Take two ounces of Labdanum, of Benjamin and Storax, one ounce; Musk, six graines; Civet, six graines; Amber-grease, six graines; of

---

* She had also a favourite fumigant, composed of Ginger, Cinnamon, Aniseed, Caraway and Fennel seeds.

Calamus Aromaticus and Lignum Aloes, of each the weight of a groat; beat all these in a hot mortar, and with a hot pestall till they come to a paste; then wet your hand with Rose-water and rowle up the paste suddenly.

SIR HUGH PLATT: *Delights for Ladies* (1594)

TO PRESERVE FLOWERS WHOLE

Taken from a book of recipes used at the court of Queen Elizabeth I of England:

Gather dark red Roses, Clove Carnations, and Marigolds on a fair day after the dew has gone, and put the whole into a shallow box on a layer of dry sand. Pour sand over and around them until they are covered, keeping the flowers in their natural shape, and when done leave the open box in a warm, dark closet for two weeks. These should remain of good colour and fragrance through the winter, if set in a warm place (but not in the sun) after being taken from the sand.

SWEET-BAGS

Some recipes from America for herbal sweet-bags to repel moths:

(*a*) Four tablespoonfuls each of crushed Thyme, Tansy and Southernwood, mixed with one tablespoonful of ground Cloves.

(*b*) Four tablespoonfuls each of dried and crushed Mint, Santolina, Tansy and Wormwood, with one tablespoonful of powdered Cinnamon.

(*c*) Four tablespoonfuls each of Wormwood, Rue, Rosemary and Southernwood, sprinkled with mixed spices.

These mixtures are put into small muslin bags and laid among linen and clothing.

IV. Pot-Pourri

There are two varieties of pot-pourri, the 'wet' and the 'dry'. (Although some recipes contain brandy, these terms do not here relate to liquor.) For the dry kind, petals of Rose, flowers of Lavender, Rosemary and Jasmine, and leaves of Lemon Verbena, Woodruff, Melilot and of the scented 'Geraniums'—properly called Pelargoniums—such as *P. quercifolium* (with a musky scent), *P. crispum* (lemon scent), *P. tomentosum* (peppermint scent), *P. fragrans* (nutmeg scent) and P. Attar of Roses (Rose scent), must all be gathered in really dry weather conditions, and spread out thinly on trays or clean papers to dry thoroughly. For wet pot-pourri the drying is less complete, and Rose petals may be of a leathery consistency when used.

Scentless blossoms of good colour are often dried and added to the mixture for their gaiety. Most flowers and leaves tend to lose fragrance after drying, but those containing coumarin—Woodruff and Melilot—develop the scent of new-mown hay when dried.

A good mixture of spices for a wet pot-pourri:

Half a pound each of powdered Gum Benjamin, brown sugar, Allspice, ground Cloves and Cinnamon; two ounces each of Orris Root and Calamus Acorus; all mixed together well and moistened with half a pint of Brandy.

A wet pot-pourri will stand being uncovered better than a dry one.

For a dry pot-pourri, take half a pound each of Orris Root, Calamus Acorus (Sweet Sedge), Cypress Root, dried Orange peel, dried Lemon peel; well mix these, and add to the mixture four ounces of Coriander seed and two ounces each of ground Nutmeg and ground Cloves, with fifteen grains of Ambergris and Musk mixed, if you can get them.

Mix half a peck of dried Rose petals with four large handfuls of Lavender flowers, stripped from stems, one handful each of Sweet Marjoram and young Walnut leaves, and a small handful of Lemon Verbena leaves—also Woodruff and Melilot if obtainable—add the spices enumerated above, and store the well-stirred pot-pourri in a covered jar. This should retain its fragrance for years provided that it is not left uncovered for long at a time.

Recipe for Pot-Pourri used by Lady Betty Germain at Knole in Kent (1750)—from *Knole and the Sackvilles*, V. Sackville-West:

Gather dry, Double Violets, Rose Leaves, Lavender, Myrtle Flowers, Verbena, Bay Leaves, Rosemary, Balm, Musk, Geranium. Pick these from the stalks and dry on paper in the sun for a day or two before putting them in a jar. This should be a large white one, well glazed, with a close-fitting cover, also a piece of card the exact size of the jar, which you must keep pressed down on the flowers. Keep a new wooden spoon to stir the salt and flowers from the bottom, before you put in a fresh layer of bay salt above and below every layer of flowers. Have ready spices, plenty of Cinnamon, Mace, Nutmeg, and Pepper and Lemon-peel pounded. For a large jar half a pound of Orris root, one ounce of Storax, one ounce of Gum Benjamin, two ounces of Calamino Aromatico (Sweet Sedge), two grains of Musk and a small quantity of oil of Rhodium. The spice and gums to be added when you have collected all the flowers you intend to put in. Mix all well together, press it down well, and spread bay salt on the top to exclude air until the January or February following. Keep the jar in a cool place.

Recipe for Pot-pourri dated 1890:

Gather the roses on a dry day only, and lay them on sheets of paper to dry in the sun, and sprinkle them freely with powdered bay-salt. Pound smoothly together a small quantity of musk, storax, gum benjamin, dried Seville orange peel, angelica root, cloves, Jamaica pepper, coriander seed, and spirits of wine. Now take sun-dried rose-leaves, clove carnations, lavender, woodruff, rosemary, and any fragrant flowers, such as orange blossom, violets, etc., and place them in layers in a china or earthenware jar, alternately with salt and the pounded spices mentioned above. Or, pound very fine one pound bay-salt, two ounces of saltpetre, and half an ounce each of cloves and allspice, and mix these thoroughly with a grated nutmeg, the very finely pared rind of four lemons (being careful to omit all white pith), one drachm of musk and the same of spirits of lavender, essence of lemon and storax, six drachms of orris root and one ounce of bergamot. Have ready minced a handful each of bay leaves, rosemary, myrtle, lemon thyme, and sweet verbena. Place these all, when well hand-mixed, into a jar with a close-fitting lid, adding to them, as you can get them, six handfuls of sweet-smelling and dried rose leaves, three of orange blossom, three of clove pinks, and two each of rosemary flowers, lavender flowers, jasmine flowers, and violets. The roses must be gathered on a perfectly dry day, and may then, if liked, be placed in the jar at once—and the same applies to the other blossoms, for all sweet-scented flowers (as long as they are not succulent) can be used for pot-pourri—stirring them well into the mixture, for pot-pourri cannot be too much stirred, especially at first. But remember, no flowers must be added while in the least damp, either from rain or dew.

If the pot-pourri appears to become too dry, add more bay-salt and saltpetre; if too moist, add more spice and orris root; but always start your *beau-pot* (as our grandmothers called it) with the quantities given above, adding more flowers from time to time, as the spice retains its strength for years. As to the best flowers for the purpose, the old cabbage roses are really the most fragrant, but any kinds will do as long as they are dry; still, to have the scent perfect, there should be a strong proportion of the old-fashioned blooms; the more modern tea-roses are almost too faint to be entirely relied on. The question of drying simply depends on how long it takes to remove any moisture from the rose leaves. If gathered on a hot, sunny day, when absolutely dry, they need little, if any, exposure to the sun.

A quicker sort of Sweet-Pot, from *The Scented Garden*, by Eleanour Sinclair Rohde:

Take three handfuls of orange-flowers, three of clove-gilliflowers, three of damask roses, one of knotted marjoram, one of lemon-thyme, six bay-leaves, a handful of rosemary, one of myrtle, half one of mint, one of lavender, the rind of a lemon, and a quarter of an ounce of cloves. Chop all; and put them in layers, with pounded bay-salt between, up to the top of the jar.

If all the ingredients cannot be got at once, put them in as you get them; always throwing in salt with every new article. (*Domestic Cookery*, 1834.)

TWENTIETH-CENTURY POT-POURRI

The late Horace Annesley Vachell, who lived at Widcombe Manor at Bath, used this recipe:

One peck of dry rose petals, dried rose-geranium and lemon verbena leaves as they become available.

In a large jar put a handful of bay salt, then a handful of rose petals, then salt, alternating the layers and making the top layer of salt. Stand for four days, stirring up the mixture twice a day. After that, add three ounces of Allspice, and one ounce of stick Cinnamon. Leave for a week, stirring daily. Mix together one ounce each of ground Cloves, Cinnamon, Ginger and Aniseed, two ounces each of Orris root and grated Nutmeg, and half a pound of dried Lavender flowers. Take the jar in which the pot-pourri is to remain, and put in an ounce of the spice mixture, then a layer of Rose stock, then spice, adding dried Geranium and Lemon Verbena as you fill up the jar.

SWEET-BAGS FOR ARMCHAIRS

'On the backs of my armchairs are thin Liberty silk oblong bags, like miniature saddle-bags, filled with dried Lavender, Sweet Verbena, and Sweet Geranium leaves. The visitor who leans back in his chair wonders from where the sweet scent comes.' (From *Pot-pourri from a Surrey Garden*, by Mrs C. W. Earle.)

V. Cooking with Herbs

ANGELICA—candied. Cut young stalks into short lengths, spread them out in a shallow pan and pour over enough boiling sugar syrup to cover them completely. Let the pot, covered, stand until next day. Drain off the syrup, boil it up, strain it, and pour over the Angelica again in the pan. This should be done a third time, when the stems will be quite green. They should then be bottled, care being taken not to break them.

Another method. Gather the stems of Angelica in April or May and boil in salted water until tender. Remove and drain them. Scrape the outside of the stalks and dry them in a clean cloth. Weigh them, and make a syrup from the same weight of sugar, allowing half a pint of water to each pound of sugar. Pour this, boiling, over the Angelica. Repeat the process until nearly all the syrup has been absorbed by the stems, then leave them to dry off near the fire. This sometimes takes about ten days from start to finish.

Tisane of Angelica. A handful of leaves or half an ounce of seed, infused in a pint of boiling water, taken with lemon and honey; this is a good drink for sufferers from colds.

AROMATIC HERB SEASONING—for use with vegetables or meat. Take of nutmegs, mace and bay leaves one ounce each; of cloves and winter savory, two ounces each; of basil and thyme, three ounces each; of cayenne pepper and grated lemon peel half an ounce each; two cloves of garlic. All to be well pulverized in a mortar, sifted through a fine sieve, and stored in corked jar. (From *More Por-pourri from a Surrey Garden*, by Mrs C. W. Earle.)

BASIL. This herb is an ingredient of the *bouquet aromatique* (Basil, Chervil, Tarragon, Rosemary, Savory, and Celery or Lovage), also of *herbes à la tortue*—Basil, Marjoram, Common and Lemon Thyme —used in turtle soup. Herb vinegars are flavoured with it (see Vinegar) and a French salad dressing *aux fines herbes* (see Salad Dressing).

Vegetable Soup with Basil. One pound potatoes, half pound French beans, one pound tomatoes, one turnip, sticks of celery. Simmer all the chopped-up vegetables for half an hour. Add salt and pepper to taste. Chop up a clove of garlic and a sprig of Sweet Basil, mix with a little olive oil to a paste and add to the soup, with sphagetti or vermicelli to make as thick as desired. This may be served with parmesan cheese.

CARNATIONS, CLOVE—*Syrup.* Pour five pints of boiling water upon three pounds of the flowers, picked from the husks and with the heels cut off. After they have stood twelve hours, strain off the clear liquor without pressing, and dissolve in it two pounds of the finest sugar to every pint. This makes the most beautiful and pleasant of all syrups. ('Sir' John Hill's eighteenth-century recipe.)

CHIVES. The tender tops of Chives are used in green salads, omelettes, soups, meat loaf, cheeses, and to flavour potato salad and egg sauce. Many people like to rub beefsteak with chives before cooking it. Chives Butter is good with potatoes—see Herb Butters.

CORIANDER—*Curry Powder.* One ounce each of Coriander seed, Ginger, and Cardamom seed; three ounces of Turmeric and a quarter ounce of best Cayenne pepper. Have the ingredients finely powdered, and mix together before a warm fire. Store in tightly stoppered jars in a dry place.

ELDER—*Tea.* A pint of boiling water poured on an ounce of the flowers.
Elderflower Milk. Strip the blossom from two heads of flowers which must be just opened and fresh. Simmer these for ten minutes in a pint of milk. Add one level tablespoonful semolina, beat up with sugar to taste and a pinch of salt, and the yolk of one egg. Pour into a bowl, and when cold top with whipped white of egg and caster sugar. Sprinkle a little cinnamon over all.
Elderflower Pancakes. Pick fresh heads of blossom, leave the stalks on, dip the flowers in batter, fry, sprinkle with caster sugar and eat from the stalk.
Elderberry Chutney. Two pounds of Elderberries, one large onion, one pint vinegar, two tablespoons sugar, one teaspoon each of salt and

ground ginger, one saltspoon each Cayenne pepper and mixed spice, one teaspoon mustard seed (optional).

Wash, stalk and weigh the berries, put them into a pan and bruise with a wooden spoon. Chop onion and add to fruit with the other ingredients, including the vinegar. Bring to the boil and simmer until it thickens. Stir frequently, and take care not to let it burn. Put into jars and cover.

Elderberry and Apple Jam. Six pounds Elderberries, six pounds sliced apples, twelve pounds sugar. Boil apples to pulp and sieve to eliminate cores. Stew Elderberries for half an hour, then mix with apple pulp. Add sugar, and return to stove to boil until it sets on a saucer.

Elderberry Jam (without Apple). One pound Elderberries, one pound sugar, juice of two lemons, a quarter of a pint of water. Boil for twenty minutes or more, until set. (This may also be put through a jelly bag, with a little more water, to make Jelly.)

Elderberry Ketchup. One pint of Elderberries, one pint vinegar, one ounce shallots, one and a half ounces of whole ginger, half an ounce of peppercorns, a blade of mace.

Pick ripe berries and remove stalks, weigh and wash them. Put fruit into a crock or jar, pour over the boiling vinegar, and leave all night in a cool oven. Next day strain off the liquor (a cloth tied over the legs of an upturned chair serves well) and put it into a pan with the peeled and minced shallots, peeled and chopped ginger, peppercorns and mace. Boil for ten minutes, then put into jars or bottles and cork well, when cool.

Elderberry Pie. Blend berries with mixed spices and stew with sugar to taste, use as flan filling or in a pie. Elderberries were formerly preserved with spices for winter use when fruit was scarce.

Elderberry Rob. Five pounds fresh, ripe berries, crushed and simmered with one pound of sugar until the juice has evaporated and brought the Rob to a honey consistency. Can be bottled and stored for winter use, and taken at night for colds etc. (One or two tablespoonfuls mixed with hot water.)

Elderberry Syrup. Pick ripe berries only. Stew in a little water, strain, add half an ounce of whole ginger and eighteen cloves to each gallon. Boil for one hour, strain again, and bottle. Excellent for a cold, taken with hot water, and sugar if liked. Elderberries contain viburnic acid, which induces perspiration and is useful in bronchial troubles.

Elderflower Vinegar. Two pounds of dried Elder flowers, plucked from their stalks and carefully dried. Place them in a large vessel and pour over them two pints of best vinegar. Seal the vessel and put it in a very warm place. Shake it up from time to time. After eight days strain through a paper filter, and store the vinegar in well-stoppered bottles.

Elderberry Wine. Boil together one gallon of Elderberries and one quart of Damsons or Sloes in six quarts of water for thirty minutes, breaking up the fruit with a wooden spoon. Run off the liquor and squeeze the pulp through a sieve or cloth. Boil it up again with six pounds of sugar and one ounce of hops, and (in a muslin bag) two ounces of ginger and the same of bruised allspice. Let it boil about half an hour, then pour it off. When quite cool stir in a teacupful of yeast, and cover it up to work. After two days, skim off yeast and put wine into a barrel. When it ceases to hiss, in about a fortnight, paste stiff brown paper over the bunghole. After this it will be fit for use in about eight weeks. The bag of spices may be dropped in at the bunghole, suspended on a string so that it does not rest on the bottom.

Another Recipe. Strip the berries, which must be quite ripe, and to three gallons of fruit pour over two gallons of boiling water. Leave the pan, covered, in a warm place for twenty-four hours. Then strain all the juice out, under pressure; measure it, and allow to each gallon one ounce of mixed ginger and cloves, and three pounds sugar. Boil gently for about twenty minutes. Strain it into your cask, and add yeast when cool. Leave until still, then put in the bung, and bottle in six months. Large stone jars may be used instead of a cask, and there is then no need for bottling.

FENNEL. The foliage of both the green and the bronze may be used, fresh or dried, for culinary purposes. In Britain the leaves are used when cooking salmon, mackerel and other fish, and in fish soup. A small amount may be added to the milk and butter in which white fish is cooked, or a white sauce made in the same way as Parsley sauce but substituting leaves of Fennel. Fennel seed is an ingredient of *fines herbes* blends used in fish cookery, such as this: equal parts of Thyme, Basil, Sage, Sweet Marjoram and crushed Fennel seed. In America the foliage of Fennel is used in fish cookery and sauces, but it is also liked in salads; the seeds are put into cakes and confectionery, cheeses and egg dishes.

An old recipe (from *The Queen's Closet Opened*, 1662) *To Encrease Woman's Milk*: bruise Fennel seed and boil it in Barley Water and let the woman drink thereof often.

HERB BUTTERS. Summer Savory, Lemon Thyme, Chives, Parsley, Marjoram and Chervil, gathered fresh, may be chopped very fine and blended with creamed butter in quantities to taste, usually about three tablespoonfuls of the herb to half a pound of salted butter. These butters are good on small biscuits, and with jacket potatoes. Summer Savory butter is delicious with broad beans, and Marjoram with carrots.

HERBS, CULINARY. Seventeen basic herbs that every garden should grow: Basil, Balm (Lemon), Bay, Chervil, Chives, Fennel, Lovage, Marjoram, Mint, Parsley, Rosemary, Sage, Savory (Summer and Winter), Thyme (Garden and Lemon), Tarragon.

The most powerful are Bay, Mint, Rosemary, Lovage, Winter Savory, Sage; of medium strength, Basil, Fennel, Marjoram, Tarragon, Thyme (Garden); of subtler flavour, Balm (Lemon), Chervil, Chives, Parsley, Summer Savory, Thyme (Lemon).

Grown in full sun on light soil, they attain their maximum flavour; but on heavy soil and in semi-shade they will be milder. One tablespoonful of fresh-cut herb about equals half a teaspoonful of dried and finely rubbed product.

Bouquet garni, removed from a dish before it is served, consists of a sprig of Parsley, two sprigs of Thyme, and a Bay leaf, tied in a bunch or put in a muslin bag.

Bouquet aromatique: Basil, Chervil, Tarragon, Rosemary, Savory, and either Celery or Lovage. A sprig of each.

Fines herbes: mixture of one spoonful each of Parsley, Chives, Chervil and Tarragon; dried and rubbed herbs cooked in the food and eaten. For other blends, see Fennel, p. 175, Sage, and Salad Dressing, p. 178.

Herbes à la tortue: Basil, Marjoram, Common and Lemon Thyme.

MEADOWSWEET BEER. Take two ounces each of Meadowsweet, Betony, Agrimony and Raspberry leaves, and boil in two gallons of spring water for fifteen minutes. Strain, add two pounds of white sugar. Bottle when nearly cold. Does not require yeast.

MINTALE. Half a cup of equal parts Applemint and Spearmint. Half a pint of boiling water. Juice of half an orange. Juice of half a lemon. One tablespoon sugar. One small bottle of ginger ale. A sprig of Mint. *Method:* pour the water over Mints; when sufficiently infused strain out the herb, add sugar and juices, cool the liquid. Add ginger ale, ice if liked, garnish with sprig of Mint. Popular in the United States.

MINT-PASTY. Make with equal quantities of chopped spearmint, brown sugar and currants, beaten together and cooked between layers of thinly-rolled shortcrust pastry; popular in the north of England.

MINT TEA. Leaves of Spearmint, infused by themselves or in combination with Lemon Balm; one ounce of herb to a pint of boiling water, sweetened with honey.

ROSEMARY. *Conserve.* Pick the flowering heads when dry, rub them off the stems, sift them through a sieve, then weigh them, and to every pound add two and a half pounds of loaf sugar. Beat together in a stone mortar, adding the sugar by degrees. When thoroughly incorporated, press into jars without first boiling. Cover well, putting leather over the paper covers, and it will keep seven years. (Old Recipe.)

ROSE. *Butter.* Put into a stone jar a quarter of a pound of unsalted butter, and cover it entirely with Rose petals above and below and leave overnight in a cool place with the lid on. The butter can be used for spreading on very thin bread, and after a few Rose petals have been placed on the top, the bread should be delicately rolled, the petals being allowed to protrude at either end. (Old Recipe.)

Syllabub. Take the white of a new-laid egg, beat well, and beat into it a conserve of red Roses till the whole is the consistency of thick cream. This is excellent for a sore throat. (Old Recipe.)

Conserve. Take rosebuds and cut off the white part from the red, and part the red flowers and sift them through a sieve to take out the seeds, then weigh them, and to every pound of flowers take two and a half pounds of loaf sugar; beat the flowers pretty fine in a stone mortar, then by degrees put the sugar to them and beat it very well, till it is well incorporated together; then put it into gallipots, tie it over with paper, over that leather, and it will keep seven years. (Old Recipe.)

Honey of Roses. Infuse four ounces of dried rosebuds (red) in a little distilled boiling water for six hours; mix five pounds of clarified honey into the strained liquor, and boil to a syrup. (Old Recipe.)

SAGE. In British kitchens this herb is associated by tradition with Sage-and-onion stuffing for roast goose, duck and pork. It reduces the richness of these meats and assists digestion. It is best used with onion or chives only, and not in herb mixtures. American cooks use Sage with Thanksgiving turkey and often in chicken dishes; a *fines herbes* mixture of dried, rubbed, Sage, Basil and Summer Savory is liked in pork cookery, and Sage cheese, a delicately coloured layered cheese, is still popular.

Sage Pastry. Powdered Sage is added to the usual pastry mixture, rubbed in, and little cases of this pastry are filled with a cheese-and-onion savory for serving at the close of a meal or with cocktails.

Sage Tea. One ounce of the herb infused in one pint of boiling water. Some leaves of Lemon Balm improve the flavour. Laced with lemon juice and honey, this will help to stave off (or cure) a cold.

Deodorant. To dispel kitchen, sick-room or tobacco odours, the dried and powdered tops of Sage may be burnt on a shovel. This gives off a pleasing fragrance, which lasts for a considerable time.

Sage Sauce. Take two onions, a teaspoon of flour, six good leaves of Sage, a walnut of butter, half a pint of brown gravy, a teaspoon of vinegar, and salt and pepper. Scald the Sage, chop it finely and the onion too. Put the butter into a saucepan, melt it, sprinkle in the flour, add sage and onion, cover close and cook for ten minutes. Then add the vinegar, gravy and seasoning, and simmer for half an hour.

SALAD DRESSING, FRENCH, *aux fines herbes.* Six tablespoons salad oil, two tablespoons herb vinegar, four teaspoons of mixed Basil, Marjoram, Summer Savory, finely chopped. Salt and pepper to taste. Shake all ingredients up well together, and, if liked, add a small piece of Danish Blue or Roquefort cheese, mashed with a fork. (It will be noticed on page 176 that the proportion required of dried, rubbed herbs is roughly one-eighth that of fresh-picked herbs; for this recipe about half a teaspoonful of finely rubbed herbs should serve, or four of fresh.)

SORREL. Unless carefully treated, Sorrel may not agree with people who have gouty tendencies. The acid may be removed by a preliminary plunge into boiling water for two or three minutes, after which the water is thrown away and the Sorrel cooked in a very little water, then mashed with butter.

Sorrel Sauce. Country people used to mash the herb, mix with vinegar and sugar, and take it as a green sauce with cold meats.

Sorrel Soup. Take a good handful of Sorrel, a lettuce and some Chervil, and chop them roughly. Cook in four ounces of butter until tender, then add gradually a quart of stock, seasoning to taste, and simmer very gently for an hour. Rub through a sieve, and thicken with a yolk of egg just before serving. Serve with croutons of fried bread and sprinkle Parsley on top.

STUFFING, AMERICAN HERB. Four or five teacups of toasted breadcrumbs, one egg, a quarter cup milk or water, some grated orange or lemon peel, half teaspoon each of chopped fresh Lovage, Marjoram, Thyme, Summer Savory and Parsley. One onion, minced. Seasoning. Fry onion in butter to a golden brown, blend with crumbs, herbs and seasoning. Add beaten egg and milk. Poultry should be stuffed the night before roasting. Suitable also for pork and veal.

TANSY PUDDING, known as 'A Tansy'. Mix the crumbs of a French roll with a quarter of a pound Jordan almonds, blanched and pounded, one gill syrup of Roses, some grated Nutmeg, two table-spoons Tansy juice, three ounces fresh butter, some grated Lemon, half a glass of Brandy. Pour over the mixture one and a half pints of boiling cream or milk, sweetened, and when cold mix it up. Add the juice of a Lemon and eight beaten eggs. May be baked or boiled.

TARRAGON SAUCE. One and a half cups of milk, four teaspoon-fuls lemon juice, five teaspoonfuls flour, one teaspoonful Tarragon (dried), two teaspoonfuls capers, one hard-boiled egg, salt and pepper. Blend flour smoothly with a little cold milk until creamy, add the rest of the milk, then the seasoning, Tarragon, lemon juice and capers. Over a low flame heat slowly, stirring all the time until it thickens. Chop up the egg and add to the sauce before serving. Excellent with white fish.

VINEGARS, HERB

Tarragon. Use leaves picked on a dry day just before the herb comes into flower, remove leaves from stalks and dry slightly beside a fire. Place in a wide-necked bottle, cover with the best white wine vinegar, stand for three days, strain through flannel, bottle, cork down tightly. Tarragon vinegar is the correct vinegar for Tartare sauce. The Tarragon leaves, soaked as they are in vinegar, are usefully retained for use in salads or with fish. Some people bottle and store these.

Mint, Basil, Marjoram vinegars. Pack leafy tips of chosen herb into a wide-necked bottle, bruise with wooden spoon, cover with white wine or cider vinegar, leave to infuse for about a fortnight. Taste, and if not sufficiently flavoured replace herb with fresh supply and infuse again. Shake or stir the brew every other day. Period of infusion is halved if boiling vinegar used. Strain through muslin, flannel or filter-paper and store in tightly stoppered bottles.

Vinegar, Lemint. Made as above, with two parts of Spearmint to one part Lemon Balm, using cider vinegar. Excellent for making Mint sauce.

VI. Dyeing with Plants

Compared with chemical dyestuffs, it is generally true that the preparation of vegetable dyes takes longer, and the results may be less fast; but against these drawbacks must be set the richness, subtlety and 'life' of the colours produced by plants, and the fact that when deterioration does set in it usually comes about evenly, so that the effect is still pleasant. This is not commonly the case with aniline dyes, which tend to fade patchily. Also, the whole business of collecting and using vegetable dyestuffs is enjoyable, and there is endless scope for experiment.

Wool is the best material for amateurs to use, and if machine-spun hanks are bought it is better to obtain the unbleached, as chemical bleaches sometimes affect dyeing. Best of all is raw fleece, which is dyed and then handspun, or handspun yarn loosely tied in hanks and then dyed. Children gather sufficient fleece from hedges and fences to experiment with plant dyes, and make little spectra of woollen tufts to show their friends or put into school exhibitions.

Nearly all vegetable dyes, except the lichens, require that the wool should first be treated with a mordant (Latin *mordere*, to bite) before the colour will 'take' properly. By varying and combining mordants, the same dyestuff may be persuaded to produce several colours, sometimes surprisingly different and not merely shades of the same hue. Alum (Potassium Aluminium Sulphate) and chrome (Bichromate of Potash) are the most easily obtained and useful mordants for the beginner. If the local chemist does not supply the material, try that very old-established firm for all vegetable dyeing requisites: Messrs Skilbeck Bros Ltd, 55 Glengall Road, London S.E.15.

Plants that have a long history and are interesting subjects for the gardener to grow do not always make the best dyestuffs for home use. Woad in particular is easy to cultivate and its black, pendant seeds are decorative, but this material needs long and complicated processing before a good blue dye results. In fact, blue is the most difficult colour to obtain from plants, while yellow, green, brown and a fairly good black are comparatively simple.

Owing to the time required to gather and prepare enough of our native plants to dye the quantity of wool used in the professional hand-weaving business, most weavers today employ imported barks and other dyestuffs, which may be bought by the pound in ready-to-use preparations, either dry or in the form of paste. For this reason the textbooks usually provide many more directions for dyeing with foreign material than with indigenous plants.

Common British plants which give good results include: Agrimony (*Agrimonia eupatoria*), flowers of *Iris pseudacorus*, Cow Parsley (*Anthriscus sylvestris*), Heather tips and Dyer's Greenweed (*Genista tinctoria*), all producing yellows; Lady's Bedstraw (*Galium verum*) and Hedge Bedstraw (*G. mollugo*), whose roots produce rusty-red; Tansy tops (*Tanacetum vulgare*) picked in flower produce golden yellow on wool mordanted with alum, and the same dye-bath yields a deeper orange on wool mordanted with chrome and cream of tartar mixed. Onion skins also produce a variety of yellows and golds. Dandelion (*Taraxacum officinale*) gives a magenta from the root, Elder (*Sambucus nigra*) a purple from ripe berries, on wool mordanted with alum and salt. Browns come easily from Tansy on wool mordanted with chrome and cream of tartar, and from Crotal. (In each case the golden hue is obtained from short immersion, and browns come after longer time in the dye-bath.)

The foliage of Lily-of-the-Valley, Elder and Nettle all yield good greens, and Tansy root is said to do so also. The roots of Meadowsweet (*Filipendula ulmaria*) and of the yellow flag Iris (*I. pseudacorus*) produce black, with iron mordant. Blues, admittedly rather sad ones, are obtainable from the berries of Ivy, Privet and Elder, with alum mordant.

Wool should be carefully cleansed before mordanting, using (if possible) rain or spring water, and soap, not detergents. Lather prepared from Soapwort (*Saponaria officinalis*) is best of all. To make an alum mordant, heat the water in a bath or pan large enough to take the wool without cramping it: four gallons to one pound is usually correct. When at hand-warmth, dissolve three ounces alum and one ounce cream of tartar in a cupful of water, then add to the bath and stir well. Put the wetted wool into this, spreading it out and moving it frequently, gradually raise the temperature to boiling-point, but not above, which should take about one hour. Keep the wool in the liquid at this temperature for another hour, then remove and cool, take wool and gently squeeze out, place in a towel or cloth and dry slowly in a dark place. If the wool feels at all sticky it may be rinsed in clean water before drying.

Chrome is prepared in the same way, but only half an ounce, with one ounce cream of tartar, dissolved in half a cup of boiling water, is needed for four gallons. When cool enough to handle the wool should be rinsed in water of similar temperature, squeezed gently and put immediately into the dye-bath without being dried first. This mordant is sensitive to light, and the wool should be kept completely submerged. (A plate on top will ensure this.)

Iron mordant (ferrous sulphate) requires different treatment. The wool, after being washed, is lowered into the dye-bath and simmered gently until the colour has reached a fairly dark tone, then the wool is taken out and half an ounce of ferrous sulphate with one ounce of cream of tartar is mixed into the dye-bath, after which the wool is returned and simmered gently for about half an hour. It must be rinsed very well after using iron. The process is not strictly speaking regarded as mordanting; dyers call it 'saddening'.

The dye-bath usually needs about the same amount of soft water, four gallons to a pound of wool, and it is usual to break up the plant material, put it loosely in a muslin bag, and leave it in the bath overnight. It is then boiled up until the dye seems adequate; a little ammonia is useful to release the colour. The liquid must be made up to four gallons before entering the wetted wool. In general, barks and roots require longer boiling than leafy tops. Roots should be cleaned carefully and chopped up, lichens crushed, and barks chopped and soaked in water for twenty-four hours before being used. Alder bark, with alum, yields a good brown and birch produces yellow. The rinsing out of loose dye is important after all these operations, before the wool is hung up to dry.

Enamel pots are best for dyeing, and will easily be cleaned between dyes. Wooden rods will serve for stirring, but as they stain it is advisable to have one for each colour. Plastic buckets serve for rinsing, and rubber gloves are a useful preventive of green fingers or of being caught red-handed.

VII. Indian Herbs

The following list of herbs known to have been used by the 'Red' Indians of North America is derived from material compiled by the New York unit of the Herb Society of America at its Kitchawan Field Station.

BEDSTRAW. *Galium trifolium*. Medicine and dyestuff.

BLOOD ROOT. *Sanguinaria canadensis*. Acrid, astringent; root sap an expectorant for coughs. Orange sap used as war-paint.

BLUE LOBELIA. *Lobelia syphilitica*. Medicine.

BONESET, THOROUGHWORT. *Eupatorium perfoliatum*. Tonic, astringent, used to reduce fevers.

BOUNCING BET, SOAPWORT. *Saponaria officinalis*. Foliage produces a lather in water for washing.

BRISTLY SARSAPARILLA. *Aralia hispida*. Root used as a flavouring, and for tonic tea. Also WILD SARSAPARILLA. *A. nudicaulis*.

CALAMUS ROOT. *Acorus calamus*. Aromatic root, dried and used as a digestive.

CARDINAL FLOWER. *Lobelia cardinalis*. Used as a love charm, with Ginseng and Angelica.

CHICKWEED. *Stellaria media*. An eye lotion, fed also to hunting dogs to improve their eyesight.

CHICORY. *Cichorum intybus*. Root dried to make a tonic drink.

COLUMBINE. *Acquilegia canadensis*. An infusion was used for dropped palate.

DANDELION. *Taraxacum officinale*. Used to prevent the formation of calcium deposits in the joints. Dried roots used in a beverage, and fresh leaves as 'greens' and in salad.

DOCK. *Rumex crispus*. Seeds dried to make flour. Young foliage used as a potherb.

ELDER. *Sambucus canadensis*. Dried blossoms used for breadstuff. Berries and blossoms made into wine. Blossoms, with fat, as skin softener.

FALSE HELLEBORE. *Veratrum viride.* Reduces blood pressure, but can be very poisonous.

GINSENG. *Panax quinquefolium.* Tea made from the root was believed to prolong life. A nerve and digestive medicine, increasing capillary circulation.

HERB ROBERT. *Geranium robertianum.* Medicinal.

HORSE GENTIAN, FEVERWORT. *Triosteum perfoliatum.* Used to reduce fevers.

INDIAN TOBACCO. *Lobelia inflata.* Leaves were dried and smoked for easing lung congestion. Narcotic.

JEWEL-WEED. *Impatiens biflora.* Juice of the stems, soothing, used to allay ivy poisoning discomfort.

JOE-PYE WEED. *Eupatorium purpureum.* Named for a king of Pontus —who used it medicinally—and an Indian Medicine-man.

MAIDENHAIR FERN. *Adiantum pedatum.* Refrigerant and tonic, used also in a lotion to keep the hair sleek and in place.

MOUNTAIN LAUREL, CALICO BUSH. *Kalmia latifolia.* Wood used to make spoons, leaves in a skin ointment. A poison if taken internally.

PINK KNOTWEED. *Polyganum pennsylvaticum.* Medicinal.

PLANTAIN, LARGE-LEAF. *Plantago major.* Called The White Man's Footstep. Introduced by early settlers, leaves used as a poultice.

POKE. *Phytolacca decandra.* Berries used for dyes and ink. Young shoots eaten as 'greens'—old ones are poisonous.

RED CLOVER. *Trifolium pratense.* Used in poultices for skin troubles and growths.

SELF-HEAL. *Prunella vulgaris.* Astringent. A famous wound herb.

SHINLEAF. *Pyrola elliptica.* Leaves used to poultice bruises.

SNAKE ROOT. *Cimicifuga racemosa.* Leaves drive away bugs. Root an antidote for snake bite. A sedative if taken in large quantities.

SOLOMON'S SEAL. *Polygonum biflora.* Crushed root used to take discoloration from bruises. Young shoots eaten as a vegetable.

SPHAGNUM MOSS. *Sphagnum cymbidium.* Antiseptic, absorbent. Used to line papoose's cradle.

STAGHORN SUMACH. *Rhus typhina.* The seeds make a cooling drink tasting of lemon.

SWEET CICELY. *Osmorrhiza longistylis.* Roots employed to poultice boils. Seeds and roots pungent, used to flavour food.

TURTLE HEAD. *Chelone glabra.* Tonic. Used in liver disorders.

VERVAIN. *Verbena hastata.* A famous healing herb, a cure-all.

VIOLET. *Viola papilionacea.* Used in poultices, for skin troubles and growths.

WAKE ROBIN. *Trillium erectum.* Beth or Birth Root—used in child birth.

WILD GERANIUM, CRANE'S BILL. *Geranium maculatum.* Root used to make an astringent gargle, as a tonic, and in the treatment of dysentery.

WILD GINGER. *Asarum canadense.* Medicinal, and spicy root used as flavouring.

WILD LEEK. *Allium tricoccum.* Crushed bulb used to massage chilblains. Bulb also roasted with honey to relieve hoarseness.

WILD STRAWBERRY. *Fragaria virginiana.* Tea made from leaves. Crushed fruit used to clean teeth and to clear skin blemishes.

WILLOW. *Salix longifolia.* Cathartic. Leaves smoked to induce visions, as were those of the native Holly, *Ilex verticillata.*

WINTERGREEN. *Gaultheria procumbens.* Oil extracted to make a liniment to relieve muscular pains.

YARROW. *Achillea millefolium.* A wound herb. Dried leaves used for earache.

NOTE: *Hamamelis virginiana,* supposedly a 'Red' Indian herb, does not appear in the Kitchawan List. It is known to us as Witch Hazel.

According to Gertrude Foster (Editor, *The Herb Grower Magazine*), the Indians used a Gromwell (*Lithospermum ruderale*) as a contraceptive.

VIII. Terms used by Herbalists

*(Those marked * are out of date)*

ALTERATIVE. Herb used to improve nutrition and change character of the blood.

ANODYNE. Painkilling, soothing.

ANTHELMINTIC. Expelling or destroying worms.

ANTI-SCORBUTIC. Preventive of scurvy.

ANTISEPTIC. Preventive of mortification.

ANTI-SPASMODIC. Relieving spasms.

APERIENT. Opening, laxative.

APHRODISIAC. Exciting desire between the sexes.

AROMATIC. Agreeably scented, spicy.

ASTRINGENT. Causing contraction, particularly of soft tissues.

*BOLUS. A large pill, often decorated with gold leaf.

CARMINATIVE. Expelling wind.

CATHARTIC. Purgative.

DEMULCENT. Softening, sheathing or lubricating.

DEOBSTRUENT. That removes obstructions by opening passages or pores.

DIAPHORETIC. Promoting perspiration.

DIURETIC. Exciting discharge of urine.

DYSMENORRHOEA. Difficult or painful menstruation.

*ELECTUARY. A stiff paste compounded of powdered herbs and honey.

EMETIC. Having power to cause vomiting.

EMMENAGOGIC. Promoting menstruation.

EMOLLIENT. Softening, causing warmth and moisture.

EXPECTORANT. Helping to expel phlegm.

FEBRIFUGAL. Dispelling fever, allaying fever heat.

HAEMOSTATIC. Having power to stop bleeding.

*HONEY. Vehicle for administering drugs, made of honey.

*JULEP. Thin medicinal syrup for immediate use, not keeping.

*LOHOCH. Thick syrup for storage.

NARCOTIC. Causing sleep, stupor, insensibility.

NERVINE. For strengthening nerves, a nerve tonic.

*OXYMEL. Vehicle for drugs, made of vinegar and honey.

PECTORAL. Useful in diseases of lungs or chest.

*PENETTE. Medicinal barley-sugar.

PROPHYLACTIC. Precautionary, preventive of disease.

PURGATIVE. Causing evacuation (of bowels).

REFRIGERANT. Cooling, mitigating heat.

RESOLVENT. Disperser of swellings.

*ROB. Fruit juice boiled to a thick syrup with sugar.

RUBEFACIENT. Producing redness of the skin—a counter-irritant.

SEDATIVE. Depressing the vital powers. That has the property of soothing.

*SIMPLE. A medicine composed of only one herb.

*SOPORIFIC SPONGE. The earliest form of anaesthetic.

STERNUTATORY. Causing sneezing.

STIMULANT. Temporary quickener of some vital process.

STOMACHIC. Good for the stomach.

STYPTIC. Having power to arrest haemorrhage.

*THERIAC. A heal-all, specific against Plague.

TISANE. Herb tea.

VERMIFUGAL. Expelling or destroying worms.

*VULNERARY. Used to heal wounds.

Book List

(1) *Pre-Victorian*

Bartholomew. *De Proprietatibus Rerum.*
Coles, William. *The Art of Simpling.*
Culpeper, Nicholas. *The English Physician* and *Complete Herbal.*
Evelyn, John. *Acetaria, a book about sallets.*
Gerard, John. *Herbal.*
Hill, John. *Family Herbal.*
Parkinson. *Theatrum Botanicum.*
 Paradisi in Sole.
Pliny. *Natural History.*
Pratt, Ann. *Flowers and their Associations.*
Tusser, Thomas. *Five Hundred Points of Good Husbandry.*

(2) *Victorian and Modern*

Brooklyn Botanic Garden. *Dye-Plants and Dyeing.*
Brownlow, Margaret. *Herbs and the Fragrant Garden.*
 The Delights of Herb Growing.
Clarkson, Rosetta. *Herbs, their culture and uses.*
Earle, Mrs C. W. *Pot-pourri from a Surrey Garden.*
Fish, Margery. *Cottage Garden Flowers.*
Grieve, Mrs M. *A Modern Herbal.*
Grigson, Geoffrey. *A Herbal of All Sorts.*
Hewer, Dorothy. *Practical Herb Growing.*
Hunter, Kathleen. *Health Foods and Herbs.*
Jekyll, Gertrude. *Home and Garden.*
 Flower Decoration in the House.
Levy, Juliette de Bairacli. *Herbal Handbook for Everyone.*
 Herbal Handbook for Farm and Stable.
Leyel, Mrs C. F. *The Truth about Herbs.*
 The Culpeper Herbals: Herbal Delights—Compassionate Herbs—
  Hearts-Ease—Green Medicine—Cinquefoil—Elixirs of Life.
Mairet, Ethel. *Vegetable Dyes.*

Quelch, Mary Thorne. *Herbs for Daily Use.*
  Herbal Remedies.
Rohde, Eleanour Sinclair. *A Garden of Herbs.*
  The Old English Herbals.
  The Scented Garden.
  The Story of the Garden.
  Herbs and Herb Gardening.
Ryder, Joan. *Herbs for To-day and To-morrow.*
Sackville-West, V. *Knole and the Sackvilles.*
Thurstan, Violetta. *The Use of Vegetable Dyes.*
Young, Andrew. *A Retrospect of Flowers.*
  A Prospect of Flowers.

Suppliers of Herb Plants, Seeds and Prepared Herbs

Herb Plants and Seeds

The Herb Farm Ltd, Seal, Sevenoaks, Kent.
E. and A. Evetts, Ashfields Herb Nursery, Hinstock, Market Drayton, Shropshire.

Seeds

Kathleen Hunter, Barcaldine House, Connel, Argyll, Scotland.
Thompson and Morgan, Ipswich, Suffolk.

Herb and Foliage Plants

Margery Fish, East Lambrook Manor, South Petherton, Somerset.

Pinks, and Silver Foliage Plants

Mrs Desmond Underwood, Colchester, Essex.

Shrubs and Plants

John Scott & Co., The Royal Nurseries, Merriott, Somerset.
The Sunningdale Nurseries, Windlesham, Surrey (also Old Roses).

Old Roses

Miss Hilda Murrell, Portland Nurseries, Shrewsbury, Salop.

Junipers and other small conifers

The Wansdyke Nursery, Hillworth, Devizes, Wiltshire.

Prepared Herbs

Heath & Heather Ltd, St Albans, Herts.
Culpepper House, 21 Bruton St, Berkeley Square, London W.1.

Prepared Culinary Herbs and Spices

D. Napier & Sons, Bristo Place and Teviot Place, Edinburgh, Scotland.